Europe of the Dictators
1919–1945

Elizabeth Wiskemann was the child of a German father, settled in England but not naturalized, and an English mother. As a schoolgirl in London in the First World War she began, as she subsequently said, to live with the German problem that was to dominate her existence. After graduating from Cambridge in the early twenties research for her thesis took her to Vienna and a chance invitation led her to Berlin in the closing years of the Weimar republic. For many years she combined teaching at Cambridge with freelancing as a foreign correspondent for a number of papers and journals such as the *Guardian* and the *New Statesman*. After Hitler's accession to power the courage and honesty of her reporting resulted in her arrest by the Gestapo. Blacklisted by the Nazis, she travelled widely in Eastern and Central Europe, laying the foundations for such books as *Czechs and Germans* (1938) and *Germany's Eastern Neighbours* (1956).

During the war she worked in Switzerland for political intelligence and moved in 1945 to Rome as *Economist* correspondent. She then became Professor of International Relations at Edinburgh, moving to the University of Sussex on its foundation.  life she lived in London. Am the Rome–Berlin Axis (1949, r Dictators (1966) and The Eur

E. O. D.—I

Fontana History of Europe
General Editor: J. H. Plumb

Elizabeth Wiskemann

Europe of the Dictators 1919–1945

Fontana Press

First published in 1966 by Fontana Paperbacks,
8 Grafton Street, London W1X 3LA
Thirteenth impression August 1982
Fourteenth impression, in Fontana Press, March 1985

Reproduced, printed and bound in Great Britain by
Hazell Watson & Viney Limited,
Member of the BPCC Group,
Aylesbury, Bucks

Gift, Dec.'92
940.51
WIS
5438

FOREWORD

I wish to state at the outset that I make no claim to detachment about the history of Europe between 1919 and 1945, but I do not believe that to be involved with it obliges one to be inaccurate or dishonest. My volume in this series is bound to differ from the others because so many people still alive have lived through the period. Further, unique evidence for it exists in the German documents captured in 1945; I have thought it desirable to give frequent references to these.

I have deliberately dealt with the British Isles only peripherally. With regard to place-names I have probably been inconsistent, but, when the German name is simpler than the Slav, Magyar or Roumanian one, I have used it as a matter of convenience, Teschen, for instance. It is perhaps worth pointing out that the word revisionist is used in two distinct senses, the advocacy of (1) revision of Marxism as by Bernstein (2) revision of the frontiers drawn in the Peace Treaties.

I owe a tremendous debt of gratitude to the Library and Press Cuttings Library at Chatham House, that is to Miss Hamerton and Miss Campbell and their staffs; they seem to me to have taken endless trouble to be helpful. And of course I deeply appreciate the help and encouragement I have had from Mr. Richard Ollard.

ELIZABETH WISKEMANN

TO ALAN BULLOCK

CONTENTS

CONTENTS

Chapter I

GENERAL CHARACTER OF THE
PERIOD
1919-45

The period of European history between the signing of the peace treaties in 1919 and the final defeat of Nazi Germany in 1945 was one of much bitter discontent and disturbance. Contentment and satisfaction were also experienced, but it was the great age of the critical journalist, who had little time to record them. Nostalgia for the good old days before 1914 was a strong element in the atmosphere because the war from 1914 to 1918 had made people more, if unwillingly, aware of the fact that their society was an increasingly dynamic one. The unhappy ferment between the two world wars has often been attributed to the faults of the peace treaties. It will be seen that economically these faults were grave, but politically they were not. It will also be seen that many propagandists were interested in condemning the whole settlement, while idealistic young liberals like Maynard Keynes and Harold Nicolson at the time judged them by intellectualistic standards which were not entirely applicable. In order to make the period intelligible, it seems necessary to refer briefly back to the first industrial revolution which began in Britain at much the same time as the great political revolution in France at the end of the eighteenth century. The industrial revolution made familiar the concentration of industry in large-scale factories, and the French revolution propagated the ideas of liberty, equality and national self-determination. Coming together, the two formed a curious paradox. Europe east of the Elbe had persistently fallen behind Western Europe since the discovery of America. It had remained essentially a peasant Europe, while Western Europe, except for Spain, Portugal, Southern Italy and

Southern Ireland, was industrially developed. Western Europe had for centuries been more urban than the east, except for certain towns built by German colonists in Eastern Europe; thus Western Europe was readier to absorb the new industrialists. Since 1848, however, Eastern Europe had been plagued by the Western paradox, and the pressure of slowly advancing industrialisation had brought the slow extension of elementary education, though scarcely at all in European Russia and Turkey. New schools stimulated national consciousness because elementary education raised the question of the language spoken by the peasants. Increasingly, if they were Slavs or Roumanians, they came to resent the German and Magyar ascendancy under which they lived; increasingly their linguistic or national or racial consciousness tended to merge with awareness of being economically inferior, an employed class without rights. Their national awareness, however, remained dominant. These tensions, combined with the land-hunger of the peasants employed to work on estates often belonging to alien landowners, had shaken Austria-Hungary and Russia to their foundations, and probably made an explosion inevitable in 1914 or about then. By then, much of Germany, like Austria proper, was economically advanced, but politically she had retained the artistocratic, pre-industrial forms of government of Eastern Europe which seemed stable until 1914, but were being corroded. Thus Germany deliberately identified her fate with that of Austria-Hungary; in a sense the rigid conservatism of the Magyars dragged both Germans and German-Austrians into the vortex.

After the First World War everyone wanted to start afresh with frontiers which would express national self-determination and with constitutions which would provide perfect liberty and equality through universal suffrage for both sexes and proportional representation. This was strikingly revolutionary because before 1914 to be politically enfranchised was rather a privilege than a right. Social legislation in 1919 insisted upon a maximum eight-hour day and, very widely, upon the abolition of the death penalty. Eastern Europe, where agrarian reform was the burning question, lent itself ill to such programmes. There the various nationalities were almost inextricably entangled on the map: the newly enfranchised voters were mostly half-educated and quite inexperienced politically: they were also too poor not to work longer than eight hours if they had the chance. To have restored the old frontiers and suppressed the Poles again was no longer possible as it had been in the static days of the Congress of Vienna. The new frontiers were often inaccurate racially, and already in 1919 obsolete strategically, but the Covenant of the League of Nations provided for revision. Certainly far more individuals after 1919 were ruled by their ' own people ' than in 1914.

The new governments were faced with fearful tasks in Eastern Europe. Above all they were faced, like the new Asian and African governments of to-day, with under-development, lack of capital and inability to "take off" economically; they were faced, too, with the danger of slipping further behind, once the West recovered and moved forward again as it did in 1924. From this time onwards, it became evident that a further industrial phase of accelerating change had begun, with greater use of electricity and the production of more delicate machines involving more highly skilled labour which was more difficult to train.

After 1929, fresh troubles arose because the advanced West succumbed to an unprecedented depression; this meant that it ceased to buy up the food-stuffs supplied by Eastern Europe which in consequence appeared to be ruined. The last fatality in this story is the fact that Maynard Keynes did not make fully public to the world until 1935 his justified criticism of the deflationary methods used to combat the depression; by 1935 it was over. Meanwhile its repercussions in Germany and Eastern Europe had given precious opportunities to Adolf Hitler.

This, then, was the basic problem of Europe between the

wars, the under-development of her eastern half, and, for different reasons that of Spain, Portugal, and Southern Italy. New frontiers only contributed to the trouble insofar as they multiplied tariff barriers. The problem was greatly intensified by the fact that Soviet Russia was sharply cut off from the rest of Europe by her rejection of Western political and economic notions. This obliged the smaller east European states to look exclusively to the West, and later to Germany, for markets and capital, while Russia after 1928 went through the fearful convulsions of industrialising herself according to the Communist plans at top speed. At the end of the period when Russia had " taken off " and survived the German attack, it was her new political and economic system which she imposed upon the backward countries east of the Elbe. In the European structure, Germany was the hinge between West and East.

Chapter II

THE POST-WAR CRISIS
1919-24

Woodrow Wilson, the heaven-sent messenger from the other side of the world, the President of the United States, insisted that the Treaty of Versailles should begin with the Covenant of the League of Nations. Immediately after the treaty had been signed, on 28th June, 1919, Wilson left for Washington. Yet in November Congress refused to ratify this Covenant, and the refusal was confirmed on 19th March, 1920, two months after the Treaty of Versailles had come into operation. This American withdrawal from the new European scene as conceived by Wilson helped to distort European history until 1941. The primacy of Europe in the world continued unchallenged, although it no longer represented the facts of the case. The invalidation of the Anglo-American guarantee to France, without which the French felt that they had been cheated of their security, was the worst immediate outcome in 1920.

The signature of the major peace treaty of Versailles led to Clemenceau's withdrawal from French politics. The period of the French *après-guerre* until 1924 was dominated by the figure of the Lorrainer, Raymond Poincaré, although in this first period he was only Prime Minister from January 1922 to June 1924; he was to return for a longer and more crucial term later in the 'twenties. As in Britain, there were what might well be termed khaki elections in France in November 1919, followed by a period of the fairly harsh repression of a series of strikes. Bitter social feeling led the majority of French Socialists at a congress at Tours in December 1920 to vote in favour of joining the new Communist Third International or *Comintern* set up by Soviet Russia in March 1919: the Socialist or Second Interna-

tional had not yet been revived. It was at this point that
l'Humanité, which had been the organ of so moderate a
Socialist as Jaurès, became the voice of the French Communists.
At this stage the new Russia under Lenin still fervently
believed that Communism was bound to spread over Europe :
the French Socialists were prepared to welcome this
development, while the French Centre and Right denounced
the Socialists as traitors. The spirit of the times, nationalistic
at one moment and socialistic at the next, dictated legislation
in favour of a maximum eight-hour working day, but the
organisation of labour in only partially industrialised France
was not sufficiently strong for this to be systematically
enforced. In reply to exasperated Leftism, rightist groups
were extremely active. Léon Daudet, son of the famous
writer, was the only representative of the anti-republican
Action Française elected in Paris in November 1919 to the
Chamber; he became "the most forceful spokesman of
extreme nationalism at a time when extreme nationalism was
much in fashion."[1]

The central problem for France after the ravages of the
war was to reconstruct her economic life. The basic mis-
calculation made by her governments was the presumption
that vast reparations from Germany to cancel out all war
damage would pay for all reconstruction; hence they budgeted
only for normal expenditure. The misreading of the German
situation together with a misreading of the Russian one
as transitory, combined to shape the life of France in this
period. Towards the end of it the Radical Herriot and
others on the Left protested more and more insistently
against this misrepresentation.

France, like Belgium, and to a lesser extent Britain, had
been profoundly shaken by the war. These West European
countries, however, had not had the framework of their
political life destroyed. Still less had the neutrals of
Scandinavia and Holland. Indeed in those countries euphoric
hopes of progress were at their height. All the democratic

[1] E. Weber. *Action française,* 1962.

reforms were rushed through, universal suffrage and proportional representation together with advanced social reforms
which, while scarcely affecting private enterprise, made the
trade unions powerful. In Norway women had been enfranchised since 1913, in Holland since December 1917. Oddly,
in France and Switzerland, where universal suffrage for men
had been born, women remained without a vote throughout
the inter-war period, as they did in Portugal, Yugoslavia and
Greece. In Belgium, Hungary and Bulgaria, as at first in
Britain—the scene before 1914 of the most passionate suffra-
gist struggles—only selected women were enfranchised.

At the end of the war there was much talk of disarmament.
The League of Nations, it was hoped, would bring about
the disarmament of the victors as well of the vanquished.
Immediately only the Danish Government took the matter
seriously. At this point the Danes also paid tribute to the
principle of self-determination by making Iceland independent,
though still under the authority of the King of Denmark.
Sweden and Norway tended in any case to be cut off
linguistically and geographically; the revolution in Russia was
relatively near to them, and the emergence of an independent
Finland somehow stabilised their relations with the U.S.S.R.

Switzerland owing to its German, French, and Italian-
speaking areas was, on the contrary, to mirror the life of its
neighbours in spite of its relative affluence. Thanks to
Lenin's exile in Zürich before his final return to Russia,
Swiss socialism in the person of the Socialist leader,
Robert Grimm, felt his influence directly; indeed a general
strike aiming at social revolution was attempted in November
1918 and embittered class relationships in Switzerland for
many years.

In spite of their colonial empires, Spain and Portugal had
long seemed in a condition of chronic decay which was
perhaps slightly accentuated by the war and its by-products.
North of the peninsula, an Atlantic island was in 1919 in
the middle of a revolution which culminated in 1922 in

the establishment of the Irish Free State, Catholic Eire.
In a sense this was a revolutionary inroad upon the framework of British political life. The British Government
without alacrity recognised the necessity to make this concession to national self-determination, while preserving the
Protestant north as part of the United Kingdom.

It was in Eastern Europe where the war had begun as
a clash between Slavs and Germans that its effects were in
many senses revolutionary. Three great empires, first the
Russian, then Austria-Hungary, then Germany, had collapsed
(the Ottoman empire had collapsed, too, but that affected
mainly the non-European shores of the Mediterranean). The
three had been essentially dynastic and multi-racial, though
in Germany only the Poles had constituted a big non-
German minority. The three had also been essentially
aristocratic, their bureaucracies dominated by their aristocrats
who often owned huge landed estates and exerted great
power or at least strong influence over the rural population,
many of them still almost servile; in Germany this had on
the whole been true east of the river Elbe. The Hohen-
zollern-Habsburg alliance had postulated a Germanic social
superstructure—with a Magyar outpost in Hungary—throughout Central Europe: even the Russia of the Romanovs had
had its German minorities and its German-speaking bureau-
crats and diplomats in the Baltic barons.

In 1918 the German tide had gone out, leaving isolated
German groupings dotted about the map of Eastern Europe
as far east as the Volga. The tide which came in was
that of the new or extended or revived Slavonic states,
plus Roumania, all trying to be or to look Wilsonian. Only
the Russian, Ukrainian and Macedonian Slavs were missing,
the Russians because Moscow had become the capital of
a Bolshevik régime at that time still sincerely internationalist,
and the Ukrainians because after a preliminary flourish they
were redivided between the Poles, the Czechs, the Roumanians
and Soviet Russia itself. As for the Macedonians, they
remained submerged beneath Balkan rivalries.

The most obstinate nationalistic problem was, as it had been earlier, that of the Germans. If they were to be territorially united, as they had planned in their war programme of a German *Mitteleuropa*, they were bound to subject many non-Germans. The opposite extreme would be what Hitler brought about in the end, that they should be re-deployed and concentrated mainly to the west of the Elbe.

Perhaps the most unWilsonian article of the Treaty of Versailles was article 80 which forbade the union of the Austrian Germans with Germany: this was not merely unWilsonian, it was Bismarckian. Indeed of all the experiments attempted by the peace settlement in 1919, Austrian independence, the conception of an Austrian nation, seemed the most unlikely to be realised. Thanks to Hitler's oppression, however, it seems that a new patriotism based upon a fragment of the Habsburg empire without a Habsburg has to-day become reality.

From 1919 to 1938 the humiliations and frustrations which the post-imperial age inevitably imposed upon the Austrians made their republic appear more chaotic than its economic circumstances dictated. Now that the Habsburgs were gone the dreams dreamt in 1848, and by the Pan-Germans since 1866, of union with the rest of Germany seemed at first, if briefly enough, more tangible. The Austrian Socialists, particularly in the person of the moderate, Karl Renner, had for long been at pains to transform Habsburg Austria into a federation of nationalities; it is worth noting, too, that the Austrian Socialists had for long been more nationalistic than their German colleagues, partly in order to keep the allegiance of German Austrian workers who resented cheaper Slav labour. It was a bitter disappointment, in the leftist mood of 1919, not to be allowed to unite with the new, apparently socialist, German republic. In May 1919 the Vorarlberg, the Austrian province adjacent to Switzerland, voted by a huge majority in favour of union with the Swiss. At about the same time the fiercely Germanic Tyrol, the southern part of which had been allotted by the peace settlement to Italy, declared itself independent. But both these provinces were persuaded by Vienna to accept federal status in the new decentralised Austrian republic to which they were bound by their economic, as well as their political, traditions.

Austria-Hungary had constituted a customs-free area in the Danube basin within which over fifty million people had lived. Now the new Republic of Austria was inhabited by less than seven million Germans, nearly a third of whom were concentrated in the old imperial capital. Vienna seemed indeed banished to the country's eastern marches, flanked though it soon was to be by the acquisition from Hungary of the backward province of Burgenland. It was easy to jump to the unsound conclusion that the new Austria could never be economically viable. Certainly with war debts and reparations to be paid off, a currency collapsing for these and other reasons, and with tariff barriers being thrown up by the new successor states, the immediate outlook was dismal.

The victorious powers and the League of Nations did nevertheless display some sense of responsibility towards the Austria they had determined to establish. This Austria became a member of the League in December 1920 and the League thereafter frequently provided Austria with economic assistance on conditions. In August 1922, the Republic seemed to be collapsing under inflation. By October the League of Nations, in the form of a committee which was presided over by Balfour and included Seipel, the Austrian Chancellor, had imposed a reconstruction scheme. With well organised foreign assistance new Austria survived the early twenties and was steered into the period of stability.

For many Austrians the most bitter thing of all in 1919 was the loss of three million of their former German-speaking fellow-citizens in Bohemia, Moravia and formerly Austrian Silesia to the new republic of Czechoslovakia. Many of these three million were fervent Pan-German patriots who had traditionally despised the Czechs. Most of them lived scattered along the ancient historic frontiers of Bohemia and Moravia which it was a *point d'honneur* for the Czechs to preserve. At first these Germans had tried to resist the new Czech forces and they had sent their representatives to the constituent assembly in Vienna, casting longing glances, as they went, towards Berlin. By the autumn of 1919 when the peace treaties, including those with Austria and Bulgaria, were signed, many of the Bohemian and Moravian Germans were opposed to possible frontier rectification, such as the cession of South Moravia to Austria: it was felt that, if there was to be a German minority in Czechoslovakia, then the bigger the better. It was only later that these Germans were persistently named Sudeten Germans: to speak of their homes as the Sudetenland was originally a deliberate misrepresentation since these homes were scattered—in no sense a compact territory. The Sudeten mountain range after which they were named was far away to the east near Troppau.

The new Czechoslovakia was in many ways the most satisfactory and the most successful of the successor states: unlike its neighbours it never succumbed to any form of dictatorship, even when bad times arrived. The western Czech half, Bohemia and Moravia, was economically advanced, with important lignite mines and textile and other industries Although the local Germans were often industrialists, there were plenty of Czechs with experience in industry and banking, and Prague, not long before superficially German, by now was a great Czech city. In pre-war Austria there had been many second-grade Czech officials so that Czechoslovakia had a ready-made civil service, naturally lacking senior officials at the beginning. In February 1920, the Czechoslovak constituent assembly drew up a constitution of the usual new kind with universal suffrage for women as well as men, proportional representation and so on: it was workable because the Czechs were a literate population. This constitution virtually incorporated the Minorities Treaty signed at Saint-Germain on 10th September, 1919, giving

the Germans and Magyars in Czechoslovakia protection for
the use of their language. Agrarian reform was rapidly
introduced; it cleared away the archaic pattern of land-
tenure in Bohemia and Moravia, as in formerly Hungarian
Slovakia and Ruthenia—these latter two now formed the
eastern half of the Czechoslovak Republic. Although this
feudal structure was transformed so late, its fairly advanced
industrial character made the western part of Czechoslovakia
qualify for western status; this very fact drove a wedge
between the Czechs and the Slovaks. Slovakia remained part
of the under-developed stretch of peasant Europe between
the highly industrialised though temporarily paralysed area of
Germany with Austria and Bohemia on the one hand, and
on the other, backward Russia. It was one of the paradoxes
of history that this Russia, and not highly-developed Germany,
had taken the lead in political revolution. For Czechoslovakia, with its Pan-Slav traditions, this was to be poignantly
fateful by the end of the period.

The new Czechoslovak Republic was fortunate in its first
President and Foreign Minister. Both were outstanding
leaders typical of the new post-war age, for they were self-
made men. Thomas Masaryk was the son of a Slovak
coachman. He had worked himself up into the position of a
professor of philosophy in Vienna when in 1882—he was 32
at the time—he was invited to hold a chair of philosophy at
the new Czech university in Prague. Thus by 1920 when
he was elected President he was 70, but no one felt that
this was a disadvantage: he had a noble record of exposing
bogus patriotism wherever he found it, and he was essentially
forward-looking. Edvard Beneš was a Czech of the next
generation who had worked his way up rather more easily
and had come to Masaryk's notice. He was persistent rather
than great, but he certainly took pains. Because, caught in
the end between two giant millstones, he may have lost
his grasp, it would be mistaken to ignore his success in the
1920s. He was one of the leading figures at Geneva in the

decade when—this is often forgotten—the League of Nations was, for so new an organisation, astonishingly successful.

There was a more troublesome aspect of Czechoslovakia. In spite of the peacemakers' genuine attempts to equate states with nations the practical difficulties were often insuperable. Naturally the benefit of the doubt went to those on the winning side. Hence the Czechoslovak state inherited some of the problems of Habsburg Austria as a *Nationalitätenstaat* without a traditional dynasty to blunt the edges of racial controversy. In addition to three million Germans, there were Magyars in Slovakia and Ruthenians who were mostly western Ukrainians. Even the conception of a Czecho-slovak person was at first hypothetical, except in cases like that of the Masaryk family. For although the Czechs and Slovaks, living apart under Austria and Hungary, had miraculously preserved almost exactly the same language, the very Catholic Slovak peasants felt themselves to be different from the more sophisticated, sceptical, far more often urban Czechs. Further, there was increasingly bitter dispute as to the degree of autonomy which Masaryk had originally promised to the Slovaks. Yet, if common interests could be created and racial fanaticism diluted by them and by more modern notions, the circumstances at that time were fluid and the outlook for Czechoslovakia therefore promising.

At first the Slovaks were glad enough to be no longer subjected to Hungary, the eastern partner of the German Austrians in the former Dual Monarchy. In Habsburg Austria, the non-Germans had finally enjoyed considerable recognition, but in Hungary non-Magyars had been subjected to Magyarization: even in autonomous Croatia there had been increasing Magyar pressure. In June 1920, however, the Treaty of Trianon had chopped Hungary down in favour of the successor states so that only about seven and a half million Magyars were left in the mother-country, while some three millions formed minorities in Czechoslo-vakia, Roumania and Yugoslavia. After an abortive Communist revolution led by Bela Kun, the old Hungarian ruling classes, the magnates and the squires, re-established themselves fairly ruthlessly. A merely nominal land reform left the large estates deprived of little but the land lost to Hungary itself; it made no provision for some three million landless labourers who became the distinguishing mark of inter-war Hungary.

The Transylvanian magnate, Count Stephen Bethlen, appointed Minister-President in 1921, was the chief political influence in Hungary throughout the 'twenties—an opportunistically conservative one : since the Magyar ruling classes would not abandon their status as the pillars of St. Stephen's kingdom, they appointed a former Habsburg admiral called Horthy to be Regent of their land-locked state. Just as in August 1922 the League of Nations had come to the financial rescue of the Republic of Austria, so some eighteen months later it rescued the kingless Kingdom of Hungary from a similar predicament by two Protocols signed at Geneva on 14th March, 1924. Austria's reparations had been cancelled and now Hungary's were greatly reduced; she was obliged to subscribe afresh to the Treaty of Trianon although it was well-known that Hungary remained incurably irredentist. It was a great personality of the League of Nations, then Sir Arthur Salter, who was the architect of the financial rehabilitation of both Austria and Hungary.

The biggest territorial cession the Treaty of Trianon obliged Hungary to make was that of Transylvania to Roumania; altogether about one and a half million Magyars there became Roumanian citizens. Although many hardships were involved, this province certainly contained more Roumanians than Hungarians, yet like Bohemia it comprised an old historic territory difficult to partition; there were Magyar populations, the Székler, far to the east and isolated from Hungary proper. Hungarian indignation, like that of the Germans in the case of Poland, was increased by contempt for other east European races; in the Magyar case the contempt was particularly disdainful towards the

Roumanians. Consequently the latter, during the inter-war period, were usually on better terms with their substantial German minorities. The Roumanians were unique in combining their mainly Latin language and Latin script with the Greek Orthodox religion. Owing to the oil-wells in the Regat or Old Kingdom formed of the two Danubian principalities of former times, and owing to the control of the mouths of the Danube itself, Roumania's importance had been bound to grow. Now the peace settlement had doubled her territory, bringing in addition to Transylvania, formerly Russian Bessarabia with a population of Roumanians, Russians and Ukrainians, formerly Austrian Bukovina which was mostly Ukrainian, and the formerly Bulgarian Dobrogea which was partly Bulgarian. The Hohenzollern dynasty, looking rather out of place, survived in Roumania throughout the inter-war period; it survived in spite of the notorious love-life of King Carol who succeeded his father Ferdinand in 1927.

In some ways the most interesting child of the peace-makers was the new Yugo- or Southern-Slavia. The war of 1914 had arisen most conspicuously out of the South Slav question in Austria-Hungary. Now most of the Slovenes, formerly Austrian, and Croatia, formerly a nominally autonomous portion of the Kingdom of Hungary, were joined with Orthodox Serbia in the Triune Kingdom of the Serbs, Croats and Slovenes, under King Alexander Karageor-gević of Serbia. The prospect in Yugoslavia was clouded by the anxiety of the Catholic Slovenes and Croats in face of the so-called Pan-Serb attitude at court and in the capital, Belgrade, which was dominated by the Greek Orthodox Church. In eastern Europe religion was as much a tribal badge as language.

In the beginning, however, the rulers of Czechoslovakia, Roumania and Yugoslavia were above all afraid of Hungarian revisionism, which was almost morbidly vigorous; they were afraid, too, of the return of Charles of Habsburg who had succeeded the Emperor Francis Joseph in 1916. The anxiety

of the three successor states was increased in the spring of
1920 by friendly negotiations, for which the diplomatist,
Maurice Paléologue, seems to have been responsible, between
the Quai d'Orsay and Hungary after Kun's regime had
collapsed : the French armaments firm of Schneider-Creusot
appeared to be interested. This situation impelled Czechoslovakia, Roumania and Yugoslavia to sign a treaty guaranteeing the newly established *status quo*. The Little Entente,
as it came to be called, was soon fortified by the succession,
before the end of the year, of Berthelot to Paléologue as
Secretary-General at the French Foreign Office which reversed
its attitude. With keen French support, and after two
attempts made by Charles of Habsburg to re-establish himself
in Hungary had failed in 1921, the Little Entente felt
greater confidence : this was confirmed by the early death of
Charles in 1922 leaving an heir, Otto, who was only ten
and would not be heard of till the 'thirties.

Czechoslovakia, Roumania and Yugoslavia, then, were the
heirs to Austria-Hungary, and the two latter also in some
measure to the Ottoman Empire. The Greeks, however,
claimed the leading role here, as they had since the eighteenth
century. They hoped not only to drive the Turks out of
Europe, bag and baggage, but also to incorporate part of
Asia Minor where Greeks had lived from time immemorial.
The Treaty of Sèvres, creating this greater Greece associated
with the name of Venizelos and supported with interest by
Britain, was not signed until 10th August, 1920. Owing
to the emergence of the Turkish leader, Mustapha Kemal
Pasha, with his troops, the Treaty of Sèvres proved completely
abortive. Finally in the summer of 1922 the Greeks were
disastrously defeated in Asia Minor by the Turks. This led
to a conference at Lausanne. Here on 24th July, 1923, the
Greeks accepted a treaty which not only expelled them from
Asia Minor, but brought back the Turks into Europe up
to the line of the river Maritza, giving them eastern Thrace.
Thus well over a million Greeks were left under Turkish
rule with rather less than half a million Turks in Greece.

Thanks to the initiative of Nansen, the League of Nations High Commissioner for Refugees, the experiment was made of exchanging these populations. This interesting operation, at a heavy price for those who were uprooted, may nevertheless be regarded as having been successful. It did more than anything else to heal the breach between Greece and Turkey whose relations were not again seriously disturbed until, much later, the problem of Cyprus became acute. It was often asked in the following years why the precedent of exchanging populations was not followed elsewhere.

The abandonment of the most cherished Greek ambitions was inevitably accompanied by factious inter-Greek quarrels between monarchists and republicans, Right and Left. Then Greek catastrophe seemed to culminate in the murder by unknown persons on 27th August, 1923, of General Tellini and four of his suite on Greek territory. Tellini was the Italian President of the International Commission for the delimitation of the Greco-Albanian frontier on behalf of the Council of Ambassadors or Big Four representing Britain, France, Italy and Japan. The assassination brought a head-on clash with Italy ten months after Mussolini had become its Prime Minister. It will be seen below how the League of Nations barely helped to save the peace on this perilous occasion.

Another much larger nation politically united only since 1870, after liberation from Austrian domination, jostled Yugoslavia in the Adriatic, and interested itself in the Turkish heritage. Italy, whose language offered a favourite word for the after-war, the *dopo-guerra*, provided examples of all the problems facing both victors and vanquished. In 1914 much of the country had been poor and backward; the industrial triangle of Milan, Turin and Genoa in the north had, however, precociously matured, in spite of the necessity to import all coal and iron. In effect, northern Italy belonged to Western Europe, but the south was east-Elbian, Balkan, almost Arab in its poverty. Public opinion had been divided in 1914 and 1915 over intervention against Italy's former allies. In 1917 Italy had experienced desperate defeat. In 1918 there was victory after all, at the cost of profound and complicated economic dislocation.

The soldiers streamed home, many of them poor peasants who had left their homes for the first time and who had now learnt to hope for the millenium, above all for more land of their own. The returning soldiers, the *reduci*, were excited by the Socialists, themselves stimulated by the Russian revolution into shrill abuse of the ruling classes, and into the new demands for soviets or workers' councils to control industry. The *reduci* were excited, too, by the poet D'Annunzio and by the Nationalists into fury that Italy was faced with competition in the Adriatic from the Yugoslavs, so recently hailed as brothers in the anti-Habsburg struggle. Now the Brenner frontier, Trieste and Istria, bringing Austrian-German and Yugoslav minorities, were not enough. As elsewhere, but perhaps more flagrantly, the longing of many for an end to violence was rivalled by the longing of others for its continuance and glorification.

Fiume was a classic case of competing claims. It had been Hungary's port with a mainly Italian population and a Croat suburb at Sušak. It had not been promised to Italy by the Allies in the secret Treaty of London in 1915. After a preliminary Italian-Serb clash there, French, British and American troops had arrived, and in the summer of 1919 there were incidents between French and Italian soldiers. In September at the head of about a thousand demobilised Italian officers and exalted young volunteers called *Arditi* in symbolically black shirts, D'Annunzio marched into Fiume to establish his *Reggenza del Carnaro*. Here the poet created many precedents. He established a corporative state under his own dictatorship, hedged in with elaborate political ritual, uniforms, salutes, intoned responses from the crowd, and based upon intimidation. In the end Fiume was ruined by D'Annunzio but he kept up his farce for over fifteen months.

In the previous March a curiously disorientated excessively

leftist journalist named Mussolini, who had been a sudden convert to interventionism in 1914, had founded a Fascist Party as he called it; this was an innocuous name since *fasci* merely meant groups. When elections were held in Italy in November 1919 neither D'Annunzio nor Mussolini seemed to matter—no Fascists were elected—while the Socialists and Don Sturzo's Catholic leftist *Popolari* polled well. During 1920 there almost seemed to be a recovery. Towards the end of the year, Sforza, who was Foreign Minister under the veteran Liberal Statesman, Giolitti, negotiated the Treaty of Rapallo with Yugoslavia: official Italian forces expelled D'Annunzio from Fiume which became a Free City.

In 1921, however, things began to look very different in Italy. The left was weakened by Socialist divisions, in particular by the breaking away of the Communists who followed Moscow. Mussolini, who had offered D'Annunzio lukewarm support, had profited from his example; a number of industrialists were willing to pay blackshirt thugs to intimidate the Socialists and Communists who had over-played strike action. In May Giolitti went to the country in perverse alliance with the Fascists from whose violence he vainly hoped to profit. This brought thirty-five Fascist deputies into the Italian Parliament. Some of them were mainly interested in violently crushing the left, but Mussolini wanted positive political power though he scarcely knew for what purpose. During 1922 he edged round the political map so as to abandon his early republicanism and anti-clericalism. Succeeding governments were weak and Italy's economic condition precarious. Nationalistic talk and intimi-dating paramilitary squadrons, the *Squadre*, seemed to do the rest. The much-heralded Fascist March on Rome really followed the royal offer to Mussolini in October 1922 to become Prime Minister. He was appointed head of a coalition government, and still no one, not even Mussolini, knew what Fascism meant beyond anti-leftist thuggery. It seemed to spell a protest against the former Liberal State, but this protest had come from the left too. The Marxists

declared that Fascism was the last indirect fling of the
propertied classes to prevent a Socialist State, but an essential
part of Fascism was Mussolini's personal search for personal
power; he felt his way half-blindly into a dictatorship based
upon popular ovations, created and responded to by him;
these ovations represented widespread popular but not general
enthusiasm. The enthusiasm was stimulated by the annexation
of Fiume in July 1923 and the occupation of Corfu after
the murder of Tellini in August.[1] According to the Pact of
Rome made with Yugoslavia in January 1924 the town and
port of Fiume were recognised as Italian and the outskirts as
Yugoslav.

Elections were held in April 1924 with generous use of
intimidation. Yet over a third of the electorate voted against
the Fascists, although it required great courage to do so.
When in June 1924 Matteotti was murdered because of his
protests against the Fascists' terrorism during the election
campaign, indignation in Italy was so great that many
believed Mussolini's career at an end—he himself seemed
afraid and flinched before the pressure exerted by his own
extremists and before hostile public opinion. The parliamentary opposition, artificially diminished by the new electoral
law which gave the strongest party two-thirds of the seats,
in any case threw away its chances by withdrawing from
the Chamber. Finally Mussolini discarded conciliatory
thoughts, and taking advantage of the general renewal of
confidence in Europe thanks to the Dawes Plan, on 3rd
January, 1925, he made a speech in parliament which
committed him to an interpretation of Fascism as political
dictatorship in a one-party state. Fascism, however, was
capable of compromise with other institutions, such as the
Monarchy and the Catholic Church; it was not, like Hitler's
National Socialism, totalitarian.

The remaining successor states to emerge from the peace
settlement were Poland, the Baltic States and Finland. Poland
had disappeared from the map at the end of the eighteenth

[1] See below pp. 49-50.

century. At that time the Poles had been an aristocracy rather than a nation, but oppression and social change and the *Zeitgeist* of the nineteenth century had created out of indifferent serfs a peasant nation to back their aristocrats. In Prussian Poland and particularly Silesia, Polish industrial workers often became class and race conscious at the same time in the later nineteenth century, since their employers were mostly Germans. It became one of the Allies' war aims to restore Poland, and the thirteenth of Wilson's fourteen Points had guaranteed her access to the sea.

The resurrection of Poland was fraught with every imaginable difficulty. Although the three empires to which the Poles had been subjected had collapsed, which provided a unique opportunity, it would not be easy to create a national administration out of the three different experiences provided by Prussian, Russian and Austrian rule. The Poles were Western Slavs but oddly anti-Slav themselves. They were not merely anti-Russian which was comprehensible; thanks to social and political relationships within former Austria they were on bad terms with the Czechs. This embittered a squabble over the economically important territory of Teschen, rich in bituminous coal and iron which the Czechs lacked. In a settlement reached at Spa in July 1920 the major part of Teschen was allotted to the Czechoslovak Republic; the Poles never forgave this, although from the point of view of the mixed population the decision was not an unjust one.

Lithuania, too, had been part of Tsarist Russia before 1917 and it had a long historic connection with Poland; indeed their territories had been inextricably entangled, and it was characteristic that Poland's national hero, Pilsudski, should be of Lithuanian origin. In the past Poland had owned large areas of the Ukraine as well. And since many Poles believed that Poland had only re-emerged because Polish claims had always been intransigent, Polish policy between the wars was on principle uncompromising, above all in dealing with Russia and Germany.

For it was Poland's fate to stand or fall between these two

centres of gravity. To her east and north-east there lay the still vast expanse of Russia, since 1917 ruled precariously by Lenin in the name of doctrines abhorrent to the Catholic Poles. Almost until his death at the beginning of 1924 Lenin believed that the Communist revolution would quickly spread westwards across Poland into Germany and thence farther. Although he was wrong, the social repercussions of the revolution were considerable throughout Eastern Europe, except in Poland and Roumania.

To Poland's west lay Germany quivering in defeat, the country upon which interest was to be centred throughout the inter-war period, the country Marx had destined to lead the Communist Revolution. A crucial part of the Treaty of Versailles was concerned with Poland's frontiers with Germany; all Posen or Poznania and the major part of Pomorze were marked down for Poland. This approximately meant, as in much of Eastern Europe, that sovereignty went to the state which enjoyed the true allegiance of the rural population, while the partly German towns such as Posen or Poznan, Bromberg (Bydgoszcz), Thorn (or Torun), became Polish with some unwillingness. The most difficult case in this area was the port of Danzig at the mouth of the Vistula. This town, together with its immediate hinterland, was overwhelmingly German, but the Vistula was the new Poland's most important river, and without Danzig Poland's access to the sea would include no harbour of any value. Hence the Poles, supported by the French, claimed Danzig, while the British and other Allies felt this would be too harsh towards Germany. Eventually a compromise was reached according to which Danzig and the adjacent territory, which had only been part of Prussia for just over a century, became a Free City[1] within the Polish customs area, represented abroad by Poland: a High Commissioner appointed by the League of Nations was to mediate between Poland and the Free City and watch over the democratic constitution of Danzig which was guaranteed by the League. Even

[1] This followed a Napoleonic precedent.

with regard to the Polish frontiers with Germany, the Treaty of Versailles left several questions open. One was that of the Polish-speaking Masurians in the Allenstein area of East Prussia who voted overwhelmingly in favour of Germany in a plebiscite organised by the Powers in July 1920; this area therefore remained German. The same thing happened in Marienwerder. The most difficult German-Polish problem to solve was the immensely complicated one of Upper Silesia: here a plebiscite was not held until March 1921.

Upper Silesia adjoining Teschen was the main part of the only highly developed East European network of coal and iron mines: the territory where these were situated had belonged to the Bohemian crown until Frederick the Great detached it from Maria Theresa's inheritance. In the second half of the nineteenth century the rapid industrialisation of the area was also one of the germanisation of the Polish-speaking population which lived apart from the rest of the Poles and was glad enough to enjoy the then obvious advantages of being German. By 1903, however, a Silesian-Polish deputy called Korfanty had made his appearance in the German Reichstag as leader of a Polish nationalist movement in the Silesian industrial town of Katowice. Polish patriotism combined with Polish economic need in 1919 to claim Upper Silesia for Poland. The population seemed in all senses confused, many miners really not feeling sure whether they wished to be German or Polish.

French, British and Italian troops occupied Upper Silesia early in 1920. Korfanty and a troop of Polish volunteers had tried to seize it in August 1919, but German volunteers, former soldiers enrolled in the post-war *Freikorps*, had resisted them. In August 1920 the Allied troops were unable to prevent further fighting between Poles and Germans; indeed the Germans claimed that the French helped the Poles. In such circumstances it was felt to be impossible to hold a plebiscite until 20th March, 1921. In the area concerned there were on that day 707,393 votes for Germany, and 479,365 for Poland, the pro-German communes being particularly in evidence in the east close to indisputably Polish territory. A committee of the League of Nations decided that Upper Silesia must be divided, but on the condition that its economic unity be prolonged for fifteen years: the Poles and the Germans were induced to sign a convention to this effect on 15th May, 1922.

While the Poles had been the favourite Slavs of the pre-war Austrian authorities, the Germans of Germany felt a particular contempt for them; they had certainly been the backward part of the population in Pomorze and Poznania, and most of all in Silesia. Although the German-Polish frontiers according to the Treaty of Versailles were not grossly unjust, nationally or racially, the Germans almost to a man determined never to accept them. Socialists, Liberals and most moderately-minded people in Germany agreed to the cession of Alsace and Lorraine to France, but German revisionism towards Poland was as fierce as that of the Magyars towards their neighbours. It exploited every propagandistic device, most of all perhaps the outrage, as the Germans saw it, of the Polish 'Corridor'; the latter was said to isolate East Prussia and denationalise adjacent Danzig (East Prussia had been isolated before Poland was partitioned). Many influential Germans were, indeed, determined to destroy the new Poland utterly. This the twentieth century could still less accept in the last instance than the condition of the Germans who, it has been seen, were now scattered across Eastern Europe in greater political disunity than before 1914.

The problems of Poland's frontiers with Russia were beyond the reach of the Versailles peace-makers. At the beginning of 1920 Trotsky, who was the Soviet Commissar for the Army, had succeeded in defeating the Russian counter-revolutionaries. The Soviet régime was, however, still exceedingly vulnerable, and Pilsudski thought he saw his opportunity. He led Polish troops into the Ukraine and on

7th May occupied Kiev, aiming at a Polish-Ukrainian
" Federation," or in other words at an anachronistic revival
of the extended Poland of the eighteenth century. The
Russians riposted—a Polish war united them all—and in
August 1920 their soldiers led by Tukhachevsky were on the
threshold of Warsaw. It was a dramatic moment. French help
under Weygand reached the Poles to the anger of both German
and Czech Communists, then numerous : the Czechs in the
Polish view exploited the Russo-Polish war to dig themselves
in at Teschen. The Russians were defeated and were consequently induced to accept the Treaty of Riga in March 1921.
According to this the roughly ethnical Curzon line, which
had been put forward by the British Foreign Office, was
abandoned in favour of a Polish-Russian frontier far to
the east of it; thus about six million Orthodox or Uniate
Ukrainians and White Russians were brought unwillingly
into Poland. Although in the west much more was heard
of German grievances against the new Polish Republic, its
quasi-Russian minority was incomparably bigger than its
German one; it consisted almost entirely of poor peasants
and was therefore more helpless. Most Russians, whether
Communist or not, regarded Ukrainians as Russians. Hence
inter-war Poland, which was decried by Communist propaganda as a country of anti-proletarian " gentry "—although
most Poles were poor peasants too—was as inacceptable to
the U.S.S.R. as it would have been to Tsarist Russia. The
post-Versailles extension of Poland was ominous, though it
was widely disregarded or even welcomed as a contribution
towards the containment of the Soviets. Some Polish
intellectuals genuinely believed that Polish civilisation might
absorb and be absorbed by the populations of these Russo-
Polish borderlands although the confessional cleavage had
prevented this even in the much more illiterate and less
nationalistic past.

There was another tangled knot in North-Eastern Europe
which cannot be ignored. On 9th October, 1920, between
the battle of Warsaw and the Treaty of Riga, the Polish

General Zeligowski seized the city of Vilna, capital of the province of that name which Soviet Russia had ceded to Lithuania. Like so many East European towns, Vilna had a mixed population, and it was true that its more educated section was predominantly Polish. Now Lithuania imitated Polish intransigence; she refused to recognise Vilna as Polish for over seventeen years. Further, the Lithuanians began to show impatience in the matter of Memel (or in Lithuanian, Klaipeda) which port with the surrounding territory the Allies had separated from Germany, that is to say from East Prussia. Without Memel, Lithuania had no port, but Memel like Danzig was German in population, though the villages around it were Lithuanian. Thus it came as no surprise that in January 1923 the Lithuanians took possession of Memel—with the Poles at Vilna it was difficult to rebuke them with effect. In the following year the Council of Ambassadors representing Britain, France, Italy and Japan did, however, induce the Lithuanians to agree to a statute which provided Memel with autonomy—in this case, unlike that of Danzig, the League of Nations was not concerned. The whole complex Danzig-Vilna-Memel gave scope for much intrigue, Poles, Lithuanians and Germans all trying to exploit the situation at someone else's expense. The Memel statute was only finally accepted a few months before the Dawes Plan went into operation in Germany in 1924.

Unlike Catholic Lithuania, Latvia and Estonia were mainly Lutheran; their capital cities, Riga and Tallinn (formerly Reval), had been German colonies on the Baltic, and their land had been largely owned by German barons. Peter the Great had conquered these Baltic provinces from the Swedes, and now the three Baltic states became successor states to Tsarist Russia. The German landowners, who had planned in the heyday of the war for German rule to absorb the Baltic provinces, were now expropriated; they mostly went to Germany and added a particularly truculent element to the uprooted *Auslandsdeutsche* in the Weimar Republic One notorious Balt who turned up in Munich, the Nazi ideologist, Alfred Rosenberg, was, however, not a baron, but an urban refugee born in Reval. It should be added that the new Poland hoped to provide political leadership for the small Baltic states with their tiny populations of only between one and two millions each.

A last successor state of the Russia of the Romanovs was Finland which had been transferred from Sweden to Russia in the Napoleonic period. Although Finland looked large on the map, even she could only boast of rather more than three million inhabitants, of whom about 10% were Swedes. In December 1917 the new Bolshevik regime, in order to illustrate its enlightenment, sent Stalin to Helsinki to pronounce Finland independent; in 1918, however, German troops under von der Goltz conquered part of the country. For a time von der Goltz's German Army, with considerable numbers of German Balts among the *Freikorps* men who had volunteered to save *Deutschtum* in the north, was established in the Baltic states as well. By the end of 1918 the Finn, Mannerheim, who had been a Tsarist general, succeeded in driving out both German and Bolshevik troops from Finland. With some Allied help the native leaders in the Baltic states were equally successful. In all three Baltic states and Finland advanced democracies with votes for women were established. Thanks, possibly, to some training in farming co-operatives, these systems did not work badly in the earlier years.

After the defeat at Warsaw, the Soviet leaders felt oppressed by the results of war and civil war and by a sense of isolation which contrasted strangely with their belief in the brotherly solidarity of the "masses" almost everywhere. In fact the Russian peasants had begun to turn against their new régime. The Polish war, moreover, had shown a grave difference of opinion between Trotsky, the creator of the new Soviet Army who had wished to stop before invading ethnic Poland, and the Zinoviev group which had begun to work against him. In 1920 there was still considerable freedom of discussion in Russia. In March

1921 came the rising of all kinds of malcontents at Kronstadt. Although this was put down, Lenin decided that he had been too ambitious and he drew back to the compromise of the New Economic Policy, a partial return to individual ownership: the famine in the Volga region also constrained him to caution. In May 1922 Lenin suffered his first stroke, a month after the Georgian Stalin had become General-Secretary of the Central Committee of the Communist Party. Stalin was also Commissar for Nationalities and seemed indeed to have concentrated the most important administrative powers under his control. The substitution of Stalin, Trotsky's bitter enemy, for Lenin as the central influence in Russia transformed the situation; Lenin's invention of the One-Party State gave the Secretary of the Communist Party unprecedented power if he chose to use it. Although Lenin seemed to recover, late in the autumn he suffered a second stroke. Early in 1924 came his death.

It is almost impossible to find words for the disarray of Germany in 1919. A nation renowned for its rapid rise to every kind of power, and the conviction and arrogance with which this power was crowned, was deserted by its dynasts and by its chief military leader, Ludendorff, who fled to Sweden in disguise. All the assumptions of national life were denied by defeat, famine, disorder, the war-guilt accusation, the loss of the colonies; all the assumptions, that is to say, except some of those of the German Socialists. The Social Democrats, thanks to solid organisation and the revisionist principles of Bernstein rather than the ideas of Marx, had been the biggest single party in the Reichstag in 1914, but one which had never thought in terms other than those of opposition. In theory the German Marxists should have been ready for revolution but psychologically they were completely unprepared; the collapse of the old authorities seemed merely to create or accentuate Socialist Party divisions. Yet the Socialists' organisation had provided solid self-educated men who, in order to win concessions for the working-class, had adopted an essentially liberal attitude, objecting to arbitrary administration and the use of force, and insisting as far as possible on the rights of majorities. Now no one else would face the responsibility of government. These, then, were the men, Ebert, Scheidemann, Noske, who were obliged, with the support of a few Catholics and Liberal Democrats, to organise a new German Republic on the basis of the German trade unions. The last thing most of these people wanted was a Communist revolution to sweep away the framework of the society they knew.

A National Assembly was elected in January 1919 and met a little self-consciously in Goethe's Weimar on 6th February to work out a new constitution. The chief inspirer of this assembly was a Liberal lawyer called Hugo Preuss who would have preferred to transform the new Germany into a unitary state. As it was, particularist sentiment was too strong—it was, indeed, fortified by the collapse of the Bismarckian Reich and its army. The new constitution guaranteed the basic personal liberties and introduced universal suffrage for men and women over twenty at all levels : it also introduced proportional representation which in Germany as elsewhere led to a proliferation of parties. The anomaly of the Prussian three-class franchise was thus at last swept away, and the confusion created by Bismarck between Reich and Prussian government was attenuated by the creation of separate Reich and Prussian ministries and a Prussian premiership distinct from the office of Chancellor of the Reich. The Reich was now free to levy any tax, not only indirect ones, and large numbers of fiscal officials were therefore transferred from the service of the old states to that of the new Reich Ministry of Finance. The retention of Bismarck's Prussia, however, as one of the *Länder* and an administrative unit with its centre in Berlin, preserved potential confusion between Prussia and the Reich. With a population the size of France, and with the Ruhr and Silesian mines (even without Polish Upper Silesia) Prussia remained something quite different from, and much more powerful than, the largest of its rivals, Bavaria. For the Prussian Ministry of the Interior controlled the police in nearly two-thirds of Germany and the territory of Prussia was not compact. Thus the Reich Minister of the Interior could not compete with him in the preservation of order unless he appealed to the Army.

The other most critical decisions taken at Weimar concerned the office of President of the Republic which interestingly enough continued to be called the Reich. It was decided to follow the example of the United States rather than that of France, and arrange for the President to be elected directly by the people. He was to choose the Chancellor and be Commander-in-Chief of the Army; article 48 gave him absolute power with the Chancellor's assent in an emergency, although the Reichstag would be able to annul his special action when the emergency was over. Friedrich Ebert, the harness-maker's apprentice whose provisional election as President was confirmed, used article 48 but never abused it. Only after his death in 1925 did its dangers emerge.

These sections of the Weimar constitution were big with consequence. Significant too, though apparently trivial, was the quarrel in the Weimar Assembly about the country's flags. The black-red-gold colours of 1848 were adopted for the new Republic, which decided, however, to retain the old imperial flag (black, white and red) for the merchant marine, with the republican colours inserted in one corner.

Catastrophic developments in Germany continued to shake Europe. The Treaty of Versailles, much of it disputable and easy to exploit propagandistically, was perhaps most to be condemned for the Allies' demands for reparations from Germany. Basing themselves upon the principle of German war-guilt, the Allies did not in fact fix the sums or quantities of goods to be claimed; they appointed a Reparations Commission which was to present the bill for all war damage to Germany not later than 1st May, 1921; before this date twenty million gold marks were demanded in advance. The rest of the payment was to be made within thirty years in money or goods or restitution. The reparations question darkened the sky of Europe with uncertainty and bitterness for the five years until the Dawes Plan. The passions it aroused were vastly stimulated by the publication before the end of 1919 of *The Economic Consequences of the Peace*. This was a polemical book by the still young Maynard Keynes, a remarkable Cambridge don who was to leave the marks of his genius on later decades. As a Treasury official he had been at the Peace Conference in Paris. His outburst against French policy as personified by Clemenceau in his old age was natural enough for a young intellectual idealist brought up in the Arcadian groves of pre-war Cambridge. Above all Keynes objected to the idea of long-term payments which would visit the sins of their fathers upon German children. It was hard for the French to accept Keynes' furious criticism since Clemenceau had been more conciliatory over Western Germany than Foch had wished. And it was hard for any German not to take advantage of Keynes' formulation; German chauvinists played it up fantastically for years.

A mistake only tardily recognised was to be found in the clauses in the Treaty of Versailles which reduced the German Army to a professional force of only a hundred thousand men (Article 160) to be engaged however for twelve years at least (Article 170). In the last instance the governments of the Weimar Republic depended upon this *Reichswehr* which recruited its men only from among anti-Socialists, preferably East German peasants' sons. In imperial days German officers had had to remember that many of their conscripts were Socialists. Now the Republic depended upon a small professional army whose ranks were consistently anti-Republican. In this same connection an event which occurred on 18th November, 1919, was of sinister importance. The National Assembly had set up an inquiry into the causes of Germany's defeat. Ludendorff, now back from Sweden, engineered a statement from Hindenburg asserting that the German Army had, according to a British general, been stabbed in the back by the German people and its political parties. This invention (the British general was never identified) poisoned the air into which the Weimar Republic was born; it expressed and fortified the determination of most Germans never to face the fact of their defeat.

After a brief period of Wilsonian dreams, the Treaty of Versailles followed by the legend of the stab in the back brought bitter disillusionment in Germany and a political swing back to the Right. Some *Freikorps* officers attempted to destroy the Republic and make Wolfgang Kapp Chancellor in March 1920. The trade unions, however, organised a successful general strike to prevent this, and Kapp disappeared. Elections in June showed big socialist losses and gains on the Right as well as on the extreme communist Left. Germany still appeared highly unstable and various extremists made attempts to gain control of certain areas. The German Communist Party, which had grown out of Rosa Luxemburg's[1] Spartacus League, was strong in Hamburg and Saxony, but of all the *Länder* perhaps Bavaria was the most disturbed between 1919 and 1924.

This mysterious portion of Germany, so much influenced by France in the past, so close to Austria geographically and confessionally, had paradoxically long ago become a headquarters of the anti-clerical and racialist Pan-Germans. Thus in Munich clericals and anti-clericals jostled one another, while the intellectual world of Paul Klee and Ernst Toller mocked at both factions. Immediately after the war, the socialist journalist, Kurt Eisner, set up an extreme leftist Bavarian Government. After Eisner was murdered in February, 1919, although a Socialist Government under Hoffmann was elected, a Soviet régime which included Toller tried its hand in April 1919; Hoffmann fled to Bamberg. It was this situation which caused Captain Karl Mayr of the *Reichswehr* to pay a not yet demobilised soldier of Austrian birth called Hitler to look into the matter of counteracting Red influences with 'patriotic'

[1] Rosa Luxemburg was a brilliant Polish Jewess who became a leftist extremist in Germany and was murdered with the German Socialist leader, Liebknecht, in January 1919.

ones. The Communists soon collapsed and Hoffmann returned to Munich. Meanwhile all sorts of demobilised soldiers were organising themselves into *Wehrverbände* and clamouring for all kinds of things. (Hitler himself was demobilised in March 1920.) They all intended to 'save Germany'; Bavarian Pan-Germanism usually aimed at breaking away from Berlin in order to remake Germany in the image of Bavaria, not of Prussia. When the Kapp *putsch* came in Berlin, there was anger in Munich at having been forestalled. But when Kapp was defeated by the trade unions Munich struck out on its own course and called in the military under General Möhl. On 16th March, 1920, Hoffmann was obliged to resign and Ritter von Kahr was elected by the anti-Socialist Parties, in particular the Bavarian *Volkspartei*, to be Prime Minister of the Free State of Bavaria: the Bavarian monarchists hoped that he might bring back the Wittelsbach dynasty, and most Bavarians demanded that he should restore at least the special rights enjoyed by Bavaria in Bismarckian Germany. The quarrel between Munich and Berlin was exacerbated by the Allies' objections to the accumulation of armed *Wehrverbände* in Bavaria; since the German Government in Berlin had undertaken to 'fulfil' the Treaty of Versailles, it was bound to try to induce the Bavarian authorities to disarm the Bavarians; since Kahr would not attempt this, he resigned in September 1921. The jungle of rampant 'patriotic' societies had thickened when, in the summer of 1920, an admirer of Ludendorff's presented him with a villa near Munich which became another nationalistic headquarters, dedicated by Ludendorff's wife to the cult of Wotan.

During 1921 the relations of Germany with Soviet Russia became increasingly complicated. In February and March there was an abortive move of the German Communists in Saxony which was put down by the police. The likelihood of the extension of revolution from Russia to Germany was thereby diminished, though Lenin never abandoned the idea. Thus the authorities of Russia lived in hopes of destroying the German régime, a government which usually consisted of some kind of coalition of Catholics with Socialists or Conservatives, dependent upon the Reichswehr Command: the latter, politically a good deal further to the right, was scarcely willing to tolerate a Communist Party in Germany at all. At the same time both Russians and Germans felt isolated and outcast, and they felt a common interest against the Allies who stood behind the Versailles settlement and the new Poland. The creator of the Reichswehr, General Hans von Seeckt, was an intelligent die-hard who had emerged from Germany's military catastrophe as *Chef der Heeresleitung*. Casting about in his mind for ways and means of circumventing the disarmament of Germany and planning the destruction of Poland, he got into touch with the Russian military authorities, secretly and indirectly. It seems to have been about the spring of 1921 that Seeckt's *Sondergruppe R* sent three German officers to Moscow. The conversations which preceded a commercial treaty between Russia and Germany signed in May 1921 provided cover for military talks in Berlin. It was agreed that Germans should take part in tank and aviation training-schools in Russia, and that war material, including aeroplanes and poison gas, should be jointly manufactured on Russian territory. "The first and most important of the Russo-German training centres established by the military agreement in August 1923 was the air-base at Lipezk."[1] It is interesting that already on 3rd December, 1923, Mussolini wired to Moscow to confirm the address, provided by the Italian Naval attaché there, of a factory producing German poison gas. This military collaboration between Soviet Russia and Germany had been inaugurated before the Treaty of Rapallo; it may be regarded as a parallel development.

After a preliminary conference at Cannes, Lloyd George was the main instigator of an economic conference at Genoa which opened on 10th April, 1922. For the first time Soviet

[1] Gerald Freund. *Unholy Alliance*, p. 205.

Russia was invited, together with the delegates of thirty-three other states including Germany, to participate in an international meeting. The discussions proved abortive. The only important outcome was the signature at Rapallo on Easter Sunday, 16th April, of a Russo-German treaty already drafted in Berlin which normalised the diplomatic and commercial situation between the two countries.

The Treaty of Rapallo was big with short- and long-term consequences. Immediately the pro-Russian, anti-Polish tradition of the German Army leaders and the German Foreign Office was emphasised. Soon Germany was once again a power to be reckoned with diplomatically; soon, and particularly in 1925 and 1926, Stresemann's hand was to be visibly strengthened by the Rapallo Treaty. And yet Rapallo boded ill all round. The word became a symbol for German treachery towards the West. Above all, the treaty and the secret military understanding involved the Germans in a network of schizophrenic activity; to many an officer and diplomatist it became at the least a patriotic duty to look the other way, or to co-operate in order to snatch temporary advantages with that very communism which he condemned as pernicious. One can exonerate a Stresemann for saying to D'Abernon on 18th November, 1923, that "the talk about German arms factories in Russia is nonsense," but for less exalted persons the double-talk was demoralising and prepared the way for coming to terms with Hitler and his methods. As for the Russians, after the Communist rising in Germany in October 1923 had failed, in 1924 Stalin's "Socialism in one country" became their motto, and, while their doctrines sanctioned deception of the enemy class and its governments, from this time onwards they offered almost straightforward international co-operation. After 1935 Moscow was to carry its willingness to sacrifice leftist principles abroad to extreme lengths.

Meanwhile in 1920 and 1921, to the accompaniment of the Russo-Polish War and the plebiscites in particularly disputed regions, the controversy over reparations raged and the value of the mark declined. The inflation which was to culminate in 1923 had originated with large-scale German borrowing during the war when victory, it was presumed, would soon cover the cost. Defeat, followed by the Allies' demands and Germany's virulent reaction to them, was bound to have disastrous financial consequences; it was notorious, too, that some of Germany's major industrialists, Hugo Stinnes for example, saw advantages in aggravating the situation.

After a series of Allied consultations in which the British strove to modify the more rigid demands of the French, in July 1920 at the conference at Spa, three German ministers, Fehrenbach, Simons and Wirth, for the first time participated as accepted partners in negotiations on the reparations question. The German representatives, mindful of the election results in the preceding month, refused to make concessions. All that was achieved at Spa (apart from the Teschen settlement) was a decision as to the percentages of German reparations which each of the Allied and Associated Powers was to receive. Article 233 of the Treaty of Versailles had stated that Germany was to be informed of the magnitude of the reparations she was to make not later than 1st May, 1921, and at Paris in January 1921 the bill was drawn up. It amounted to a demand for two series of forty-two annuities, the fixed one rising to the value of six million gold marks in 1932 and remaining at this figure until 1963, and the other amounting to 12% of the annual value of German exports. When the Germans declared these requests impossible to fulfil, on 8th March Marshal Foch occupied Duisburg, Düsseldorf and Ruhrort with no result beyond further exacerbation. The mood of Germany was disagreeably expressed when Erzberger was murdered on 26th August, 1921, a scapegoat because he had been obliged by pressure from the defeated Ludendorff to sign the Armistice in November 1918. Ten months after Erzberger's death, in June 1922 it was the turn of Rathenau who as Foreign Minister had uneasily agreed to the Treaty of Rapallo that

April. His major offence was that he was Jewish: he was also condemned for the agreement he had made with a French representative, Loucheur, in October 1921 at Wiesbaden. There was little serious effort to punish the assassins in either case; already a considerable section of German public opinion condoned this type of crime, while throughout the period of the Weimar Republic the attitude of the judges, most of them left over from Hohenzollern Germany, was one of leniency towards criminals who could be excused as patriots.

On 1st August, 1922, in the Balfour Note to the Allied Governments the British Government took up the position that "in no circumstances do we propose to ask more from our debtors than is necessary to pay our creditors." For the time being this displayed the rift between Britain led by Lloyd George and France led by Senator Poincaré. By the end of 1922 the mark had deteriorated to such an extent that the German Government could claim with conviction that it was impossible for Germany to pay further reparations. In January 1923, with the British representative abstaining, the Reparations Commission declared that Germany was in default with regard to her payments to the Allies in coal. Thereupon French and Belgian troops occupied the Ruhr Basin.

Looking back to the year 1923 it appears as one of those periods of crisis which served the purpose of making clear to all sides that Europe could only be saved by some form of co-operation. The French reaped nothing but trouble and expense from the occupation. On the other side the outburst of patriotic emotion which united the Germans in their passive resistance to the French and Belgians led nowhere but to complete bankruptcy and national destruction. On 13th August, 1923, President Ebert of Germany named Gustav Stresemann of the *Deutsche Volkspartei* to be Chancellor. Stresemann, a man of forty-five at the time, had been a nationalist and a monarchist of the Right so recently as 1920. Between 1920 and 1923, although he remained both a nationalist and a monarchist, he learnt by experience

with remarkable speed to become a *Vernunftrepublikaner*,[1]
as someone said. He was genuinely shocked by the murders
of Erzberger and Rathenau, and he saw that the Republic
could supply machinery which would preserve what was
worthwhile from the past but also extend the social depth
of the new state in accordance with contemporary reality.
Indeed Stresemann was the first German Chancellor to form
a 'Great Coalition' Government with four Socialist, three
Centre, two Democratic Ministers and two from his own at
that time rather ambiguous party. At first Stresemann did
not appoint a Foreign Minister, but temporarily, as he
thought, took over the Wilhelmstrasse himself.

Stresemann had been an enthusiastic champion of passive
resistance at the beginning, but again he was willing to
look the facts in the face. Thus on 20th September he
and his colleagues called off the resistance to the occupation
forces. It required great courage to take this decision. It
had been said that after Bismarck only Poincaré had succeeded
in uniting the Germans: now Stresemann risked re-division.
At about this time it was decided in Moscow, without
sufficient backing in Germany—indeed it came as a rescue
operation for Stresemann—that the time had come for a
'German October' which should strike down the bankrupt
German 'bourgeoisie.' Incipient Communist revolution in
Thuringia and Saxony was forestalled by Reichswehr action
approved by Stresemann. The suppression of the Communists
in Central Germany reconciled the rightist Bavarian
Government which was threatening separation from Berlin.
In Munich Hitler on Captain Mayr's behalf had discovered
a party of 'patriots' which he then adopted and reconstructed as the *National Sozialistische Deutsche Arbeiter
Partei*. (N.S.D.A.P.) His wild followers, deceived by the
new year-old Italian myth, spoke excitedly of a "March on
Berlin." In fact on 9th November Hitler and Ludendorff
attempted to seize power in Munich as a beginning. At first
they thought the Bavarian Government would back them,

[1] A republican because common sense made him one.

but by Seeckt's orders they were resisted by the Bavarian
police based on Reichswehr support, and Hitler and several
of his friends were arrested. Thus the Reichswehr made
possible Stresemann's policy of fulfilment in the West.
Feeling in France was significantly rising against Poincaré,
although the elections in which he was defeated did not
occur until May 1924.

Meanwhile in October 1923 the British Government had
asked the United States whether Americans would be willing
to take part in a grand new inquiry into reparation potentialities. The answer was favourable and it was the name
of an American, General Dawes, which was given to the
plan for Germany's rehabilitation. Two committees of experts
were forthwith set up by the Reparations Commission in
November 1923 : " One will be charged with seeking methods
of balancing the (German) budget and the measures to be
taken to stabilise the currency. The other will have to seek the
methods of estimating the amount of exported capital and of
bringing it back into Germany."

Once the *Rentenmark* currency had been established as
proposed by the financier Schacht already in 1923, the
Dawes Plan laid down that Germany should meet reparations
charges from her customs, railways and industry, and it
organised their transfer to her creditors through the *Reichsbank*, half of whose board would represent foreign nationalities. After a final conference in London in August the Plan
went into operation on 1st September, 1924, with astonishing
speed and success; Germany, and, around her, Europe, was
about to enjoy five years of prosperity.

Delayed by the preceding five years, peace, it seemed, had
come at last. Following upon the victory of Communism
in Russia, the catastrophic inflation in Germany and Central
Europe had shaken society to its foundations. It called
everything in question. It robbed most of all the middle
classes, but also the better-off workers, of their savings,
while it enriched those who owned land and industrial
plant. In the short run the urban worker suffered most.

Conveniently the peace settlement could be held responsible for the inflation. Without the great depression which began to appear during 1929 the inflation might, however,—it is impossible to tell—have left relatively little impression.

The most interesting and the most encouraging development in the period of Europe's survival between 1919 and 1924 was that of the League of Nations with its headquarters at Geneva in neutral Switzerland; in spite of her neutrality, and a sharp division of Swiss opinion on this issue, Switzerland became a member. Beginning from scratch the League was regarded with suspicion, indeed with derision, by professional soldiers and many diplomatists. Although it had no physical power[1] nor traditional authority, the Covenant being an experiment, and although it was mocked at by the defeated Powers as a piece of hypocrisy aimed at preserving their spoils for the victors, the League made fairly steady progress. It seldom attempted more than it was equipped for. Thus, against Lloyd George's wish, the League avoided the major quarrel over reparations; this was said to show subservience to Paris but was merely sensible.

The League of Nations established a fair and competent administration of the Saar Basin, that German territory whose mines went as reparations to the French state but whose people were ruled by a mixed Governing Commission of the League (five members to include a Saarlander and a Frenchman) for fifteen years. The League of Nations also provided High Commissioners for Danzig who won respect.

Thanks to the Minorities Treaty accepted by the Successor States in 1919 and 1920 (but not by any state with Great Power status), the League of Nations sifted complaints from the mainly German, but also Magyar and Ukrainian, minorities in Eastern Europe, and exerted pressure upon governments to restrain their officials where they had erred. Indeed this became one of the League's major occupations, and, owing to the meetings of minority leaders in Geneva they were

[1] As in the case of the U.N. the attempt to create a standing international force failed.

able to attract much publicity. It has been seen that fewer individuals lived under alien government than before 1918 when those who did were regarded merely as subject peoples. Now the new conception of a minority, whose rights might not be infringed, created a more differentiated grievance of which much more was heard: the deposed German and Magyar ruling-classes knew how to put their case and that of the humbler members of their own race. It is interesting that one of the earliest decisions of the League of Nations was to preserve the Aaland Islands for the new Finland, although their population was predominantly Swedish and wished to join Sweden; in 1921 it was decided that these Swedes should be a protected minority in Finland.

Two of the greatest achievements of the League of Nations in this period were the settlement of Upper Silesia and the prevention of war after Mussolini bombarded Corfu in the summer of 1923. In Upper Silesia two League officials, originally a Swiss and a Belgian, respectively presided over the Mixed Commission and the Tribunal of Arbitration which supervised the German-Polish co-operation preserved here by the League for fifteen years in order to prevent economic dislocation. In spite of all the hatred between the two nations, to everyone's astonishment their representatives often worked well together until the end of the arrangement in 1937.

The murder of General Tellini on 27th August, 1923, has been referred to above: it was a mere nine years since the murder at Sarajevo and a shiver ran down Europe's spine. It was followed by an impossible Italian ultimatum to Greece and on 31st August the bombardment and occupation of Corfu. The Greek Politis was already in Geneva on account of the Greek refugees from Anatolia, and he appealed to the Council of the League. Strictly speaking it was for the Conference of Ambassadors, to whom Tellini had been responsible, to act. But in Geneva Cecil and Branting insisted upon the relevance of the Covenant of the League. Strictly speaking the quarrel was in fact settled by the Ambassadors, but there was no doubt it was settled in accordance with opinions held in Geneva rather than Paris. For Poincaré had at first been said to wish to buy Italian support in Germany by backing Mussolini, but in effect Mussolini was made to feel that the world was against him, and he evacuated Corfu without too greatly humiliating the Greeks. This spelt a certain success for the small Powers who had checked the arrogant behaviour of a great one.

The League of Nations did in fact give greater weight to the small powers whose representatives provided many of its most impressive figures, Beneš of Czechoslovakia and Titulescu of Roumania, for instance. It was at Geneva that Irish delegates first made Europe aware of the new Irish Free State. Sweden and Norway offered the great personalities of Branting and Nansen, the latter of whom was for many years the League of Nations High Commissioner for Refugees. Nansen, ten years junior to Masaryk and now in his sixties, was a great music-lover as well as a˙famous explorer and athlete; in many ways he was the hero of his age. He devoted the later years of his life to bringing home prisoners of war and fighting famine in Russia. His name is best remembered for his efforts to supply stateless persons with passports.

It might well be claimed, however, that the dominant figure at Geneva was Lord Robert Cecil who defied any slogan describing the new era as the age of the Common Man. This essentially aristocratic figure gave the League of Nations its ethos by his faith in its potentialities. Cecil shared with Woodrow Wilson the new belief in open diplomacy which was characteristic of the ideology and technology of the period: discussion was ever to be public and this would give ever more power to free journalism. The new techniques, however, fostered the publicity or propaganda increasingly developed by the one-party states and their rulers. Thus by the time of the Second World War it was generally agreed that the secret treaties were not the main cause of the war of 1914; it was now believed that secret negotiations had their use in one kind of circumstance just as open diplomacy has in another, and that both in their wrong context could be dangerous.

The League of Nations was spiritually as well as physically based on Europe, although the Canadians and Australians, the South Americans, the Japanese and Chinese, played a noticeable part. The least European activity of the League was its mandatory system. Thus Germany's former colonies lost by Article 119 of the Treaty of Versailles, and Turkey's former dependencies, were not annexed by the victors but placed under separate mandates controlled by them. In the period with which we are concerned this brought independence to a Middle Eastern country like Iraq in 1932: in the long run it has indirectly led to the independence of the African states after periods under United Nations' trusteeship.

The League of Nations has been frequently condemned as unrealistic. Its institutional possibilities, however, were already appreciated in 1924 as providing a key to Germany's resurgence by so realistic a statesman as Stresemann. This is a measure of the League's development in the brief period between the ratification of the Treaty of Versailles and the end of the year which saw the adoption of the Dawes Plan. And in the end, the influences making for war in the nineteen thirties did everything possible to undermine the League of Nations precisely because it offered the best hope for international co-operation and the preservation of peace. Had the League had time to revise certain portions of the peace settlement, its objects would have been fulfilled; revision *against* the League was destructive revision, spelling the ruin of Europe which already depended on what had been constructed at Geneva.

Chapter III

THE PROSPEROUS FIVE YEARS
1924-9

The British elections in December 1923 brought Labour into office for the first time, although without an adequate majority. When Ramsay MacDonald went to 10 Downing Street and to the Foreign Office at the beginning of 1924 this was felt to herald a new era. In fact the Conservatives were back in office in November 1924. The MacDonald interlude perhaps helped to break some ice, for MacDonald's speeches, full of hazy international benevolence, were conciliatory towards the League of Nations. Thus while he was Premier Britain seemed ready to accept the Geneva Protocol drafted in 1924 to mend the " gap in the Covenant " by making arbitration automatic. The Conservatives not unwillingly yielded to pressure from the Dominions in dropping the Protocol. To the Foreign Office they brought Austen Chamberlain whose pro-French sentiments presumably gave the Quai d'Orsay greater confidence. Chamberlain, too, although he was not felt fully to appreciate the spirit of the League of Nations, regularly went to Geneva. Indeed one of the essential characteristics of the prosperous five years was the increased tendency for Foreign Ministers to represent their countries there, the tendency in fact which made this into the Briand-Stresemann period.

The victory of the Left in the French elections of May 1924 brought, though not quite immediately, Herriot into power. Édouard Herriot represented everything that was best in liberal Republican France between the wars. He had the intellectual equipment of the *normalien*, wide interests, a flexible mind. He had been Mayor of Lyons since 1905 and held this position—except for the break from 1940 to 1945—until 1955, two years before his death. With all his commitments in Paris, he found time to do great things for Lyons. He had been elected President of the French Radical Party immediately after the war, and remained its President all his life; not even Herriot could arrest its decline. He was warm and true, a king too among epicures. In 1924 he became Prime Minister at the fitting age of fifty-two. This event led to a great leftist manifestation in November when the ashes of Jaurès were brought from Albi in the south to be deposited in the Pantheon in Paris. The ceremony was exploited by Communist demonstrators who were said to have forced people to take their hats off before the Red Flag. Hence the occasion was used by the press to attack the machinations of the extreme left, against for instance the power of France overseas, especially in North Africa; one Communist deputy notorious for this kind of activity was called Jacques Doriot. At this time the Rif rebellion in Morocco was not yet suppressed.[1] At this time also a deputy called Taittinger founded the rightist *Jeunesses patriotes* which appealed to the student world, and although the Republic did not seem to be in serious danger before February 1934, from this time onwards, that is nearly ten years earlier, its enemies began to organise themselves more seriously, and the royalist *Ligue des Camelots du Roi* which was attached to the *Action Française*, was among the associations which profited from the Jaurès ceremony to increase its membership. Herriot's *de jure* recognition of Soviet Russia towards the end of 1924 gave the Right another pretext for agitation.

In April 1925 Herriot's Government, having proved unable to deal with the financial situation, was succeeded by a Cabinet led by Painlevé. The significance of this change was contained in the appointment of Aristide Briand to the Quai d'Orsay where, while governments came and went, he remained until 1930. Thus he was installed in time for the negotiations at Locarno, and in partnership with Stresemann gave his name to the years of prosperity.

[1] Not until 1926.

Although the President of the Council of Ministers seemed frequently to change, the actual Cabinets in France in this period changed relatively little : they were rather, as this process was pejoratively described earlier in Italy, "transformed" into similar combinations. This fact, together with the existence of a Civil Service chosen from the most intelligent and best educated Frenchmen, gave the Government of France greater stability than was generally appreciated. The most striking example of "transformation" was the emergence in July 1926 of a Cabinet headed by Poincaré once again, with Briand as Foreign Minister, Painlevé as Minister of War and Herriot for Education: Louis Barthou, recently President of the Reparations Commission, Tardieu who had been Clemenceau's right hand, and Albert Sarraut, were also in this Government. This coalition had been brought about by the threat of the collapse of the French franc. The man who had been blamed abroad for the collapse of the mark was felt by French public opinion to be essential as the saviour of the franc. The occasion caused Poincaré to mark his recognition of the new standing of the French trade unions by consulting with Léon Jouhaux. After an extremist beginning Jouhaux had become a moderate Socialist; he was now the Secretary-General of the *Confédération Général du Travail*, or French T.U.C., a post he was to hold honourably for many long years. Income tax was now raised, the budget carefully balanced and the franc pegged low enough at 120 to the pound sterling to bring back much of the capital which had been exported from France. Poincaré summoned the Chamber and the Senate to meet as the National Assembly at Versailles on 10th August, 1926; in this way the state sinking fund, which he had planned in order to deal with the floating debt, was guaranteed by constitutional law and was thenceforth free from parliamentary interference. It was not until June 1928, after the elections in April of that year which favoured a centre-right policy (*union nationale*), that the franc was finally stabilised at 124 to the pound. This meant that the financial experts had defeated the traditionalists who wanted to protect the savings of the middle class. The governor of the Bank of France had the last word when he said " However much we respect the past, we must think of the future of France." By this time the country was restored to prosperity. Its economic development, however, continued, as in the later nineteenth century, to proceed at a slower tempo than that of Germany. Industrialisation and social welfare lagged behind, but France did not depend, as Germany did in these years, on American and British loans, often short-term ones.

Apart from the state's finances and the congresses of the political parties, the perennial quarrel between State and Church, a quarrel which potentially challenged the republican form of the lay State itself, flared up occasionally; since the Treaty of Versailles the Alsatians had reinforced the clerical side. The inheritance of the Most Christian King had its importance abroad, and it was said that anti-clericalism was not for export. Diplomatic relations with the Vatican had been restored in 1921. Although Herriot expressed disapproval of this fact in June 1924 and withdrew his representative in February 1925, late in 1926 the Papacy confirmed its condemnation of the monarchist, Charles Maurras, and his *Action Française.* The French clergy was thus brought into line with the Republic against this most articulate and interesting of the nationalistic extremists, hero of the anti-Dreyfusards years before. The financial law of 1928 sanctioned Catholic missionary bases in France and returned some of their property to the Catholic associations. In consequence the new Radical leader, Herriot's pupil Daladier, on 28th October, 1928, made a fiercely anti-clerical speech at the inauguration of a monument in Paris to Emile Combes, the man responsible for separating Church and State in 1905 and earlier. The sequel to Daladier's speech was the damaging of the monument by *Camelots du Roi*, one of whom was mortally wounded by the police.

On the other side of the coin interesting changes were

undertaken in French history textbooks under the influence of Herriot as Minister of Instruction. From the years (1929-1930) of the publication of the new books, history was taught more objectively in the state schools. Thus a fresh division appeared between clericals and anti-clericals, the former reproaching the latter for the pacifism or the cynicism of many recruits in the following period. In practice it was to be, above all, the influence of the self-conscious patriots on the Right more than that of the lay schoolmasters which demoralised young Frenchmen in the later 'thirties.

After a stupendous three months as Chancellor in which he had effectively stopped his country from falling to pieces and helped to prepare an international rescue of its currency, in November 1923 Gustav Stresemann was defeated in the Reichstag; this was due to the defection of the Social Democrats. Although never again Chancellor, in every successive German Government, until his death in October 1929, Stresemann was Foreign Minister. Thus he enjoyed continuous control of foreign policy even longer than Briand. It was the distinguishing mark of the period that their partnership was possible for four and a half years. Both were complicated characters whose interaction must be summarised later. But it will not make sense not to indicate something of Stresemann's social and political provenance. He came from a nationalistic businessman's world. He had been sure of German victory by ruthless means and in favour of exploiting it, and he never abandoned the war-aim of a German *Mitteleuropa*. To Lord D'Abernon, the first British Ambassador to Berlin after the war, Stresemann seemed like a German Winston Churchill. Augustus John, visiting Berlin in March 1925, was so much attracted by Stresemann's vivacity that he asked to paint his portrait. When completed, the portrait, D'Abernon said, "makes Stresemann devilish sly, but extremely intelligent." There can be little doubt that Stresemann had resilience, finesse, an ability to learn by experience and great courage. Probably he remained an intense, even a romantic, nationalist, but he saw that German nationalism might be better served by subtle diplomacy than by showing one's teeth.

As a good German patriot Stresemann regarded Germany's post-war cession of territory to Poland or, as at Danzig, for Poland's advantage, as intolerable. D'Abernon wanted to wean Germany from the Rapallo policy by reconciling her with France and he made the most of Stresemann's rare silence while sitting for that portrait. Stresemann, to whom the double understanding with Russia was invaluable, was clever enough to respond to D'Abernon in order to come to terms with France. Germany had actually applied for admission to the League of Nations on 24th September 1924 as a corollary to the Dawes Plan. Then, after various preliminaries, a German proposition was made to Paris on 9th February, 1925, in favour of a joint guarantee of the Franco-German frontier by Germany, France, Britain and Italy; Stresemann believed that a guarantee of Germany's western frontier was an essential preparation for revision in the east.

Events in Germany in the next month or so were not reassuring. A New Cabinet was formed under Hans Luther, a former mayor of Essen and a financial expert. By Stresemann's desire a group of members of the chauvinist *deutschnational* Party was brought into office. In February the unhappy Elbert died after particularly unscrupulous attacks from the Right on his innocent past. After an indecisive first round, Admiral Tirpitz, who had been elected to the Reichstag in May 1924, persuaded Field-Marshal von Hindenburg, already in his seventy-seventh year, to stand on the final election day for the Presidency on 26th April, 1925: to Stresemann's dismay Hindenburg was duly elected.[1] This was a deplorable event. In the first place it only occurred because the German Communists put forward their candidate, Thälmann, without whom the figures made clear that the

[1] H. A. Turner in his *Stresemann and the Politics of the Weimar Republic* has shown that Stresemann could have prevented Hindenburg's election.

ex-Chancellor Wilhelm Marx, a moderate member of the
Catholic Centre Party, would have been elected. Instead
an old man, born in the first half of the nineteenth century,
imbued with the notions prevalent in Bismarckian and
Wilhelmine Germany, was given a preponderant position
in the Weimar Republic. He took an oath to the Weimar
constitution which, while things developed fairly easily, he
surprisingly kept, but yet his very being was anti-Republican
and a disloyal paradox. Moreover the partial equilibrium
which Ebert had established between his, the civil power,
and that of Seeckt was abolished with a Field-Marshal as
President. Of course a person (though scarcely at seventy-
seven) can be moulded by the office they hold, and the
election of Hindenburg did not necessarily seal the fate of
the Weimar Republic : but it was jeopardized at a moment
when the outlook was relatively unclouded.

The election of Hindenburg almost exactly synchronised
with the appointment of Briand to the Quai d'Orsay : for the
time-being more would be heard of Briand. Already in
January. Herriot had expressed his desire to see the United
States of Europe. Indeed since he had replaced Poincaré
French policy had become genuinely favourable to the League
of Nations as such and therefore to a League which in every
sense contained Germany. Briand intensified this policy, so
that his name came to symbolise French support of Geneva.

After a series of Franco-British consultations it was finally
arranged that the representatives of the Powers concerned
with Germany's proposal of the previous February should
meet on 5th October, 1925, at Locarno in Italian-speaking
Switzerland. On 16th October a series of treaties was
signed there, the chief of which was usually referred to
as the Rhineland Pact. According to this Germany, Belgium
and France agreed to regard their existing frontiers and the
demilitarised zone of the Rhineland, which included a fifty-
kilometre strip of territory to the east of that river, as
inviolable : Britain and Italy guaranteed this arrangement,

and the peaceful settlement of all possible disputes through the Council of the League of Nations was provided for. Two Arbitration Conventions between Germany and France and between Germany and Belgium confirmed these undertakings. Two further Arbitration Conventions were signed between Germany and Poland and Germany and Czechoslovakia providing for arbitration over possible disputes; there was, however, no guarantee of the frontiers between these countries.

Except for the Russians, who were uneasy over what might spell German defection from Rapallo, public opinion in Europe seemed delighted with the Treaties of Locarno. Naturally the chauvinists everywhere displayed anger or scepticism or both. Mussolini, who signed for Italy, seemed neglected and bored on 16th October at Locarno : he failed to persuade the others to guarantee his Brenner frontier. Even the optimists were bound to recognise that the whole thing depended, as had been planned, upon bringing Germany into the League of Nations. But the signatures of Locarno were felt to constitute a long step precisely towards that and true Franco-German reconciliation. This had been initiated by, not forced upon, Germany, and France could consider herself secure at last. Indeed large amounts of sentimental satisfaction with the ' Locarno spirit ' were expressed in the press and elsewhere. The Germans now felt free to work openly for eastern revision. Stresemann always emphasised, in private also, that the methods to be pursued could only be peaceful. The French, on the other hand, were bound to hope and to work for an eastern Locarno. But such a diversity of aim might be fruitful rather than fatal. In the February Briand characteristically said " *A Locarno . . . nous avons parlé européen. C'est une langue nouvelle qu'il faudra bien que l'on apprenne.*"

Just before this, on 8th February, 1926, the German Government submitted its formal demand for admission to the League of Nations. One of the German conditions, made with an eye on Moscow, had already been dealt

with at Locarno. For Stresemann had claimed that a disarmed Germany could not undertake the obligations involved
in Article 16 of the Covenant (about joint military action
against an offender and affording passage for troops). In
the Protocol of Geneva a formula had been devised to
meet the case of disarmed Denmark which had then been
offered to the Germans; at Locarno therefore Germany
agreed "to co-operate loyally and effectively in support of
the Covenant and in resistance to any act of aggression in
the degree which its geographical position and its particular
situation as regards armaments allow." In April 1926 at
Berlin a fresh Russo-German treaty was signed, effectively
prolonging Rapallo : owing to the delays at Geneva described
below, this treaty actually preceded Germany's entry into the
League.

Meanwhile the Assembly of the League of Nations was
convoked for 8th March, 1926. The fact that Germany, on
admission, was immediately to be given a permanent seat
on the Council aroused some jealousy which expressed itself
in the demand that Poland should be honoured with the
same promotion. Thereupon Spain and Brazil developed
similar ambitions. Although Luther, the German Chancellor,
and Stresemann came to Geneva by special train, thanks to
the crisis over permanent membership of the Council, they
had to go home with empty hands. After this a reform of
the Council of the League of Nations was worked out. Its
membership was increased from ten to fourteen, the number
of the elected members being increased from six to nine,
while the number of permanent members went up from four
to five to include Germany. Although this plan led to the
temporary resignation of Brazil from the League, it was carried
through. At last on 8th September, Germany was voted
unanimously into the League of Nations, and two days later
her delegates, Stresemann, Schubert and Gaus, were given a
tremendous ovation both by the Assembly of the League,
over which Beneš that day presided, and by the Genevese.
Stresemann, visibly much moved, spoke in simple and straight-

forward fashion, in German. But it was Briand who expressed
the emotions of the day. Putting his beautiful hands before
his face as if to banish a nightmare, he said "*Arrière les
canons, les fusils et les mitrailleuses!* ... *Arrière les voiles de
deuil!* ... *Place à l'arbitrage, à la sécurité et à la paix!*"
and he went on to plead that France and Germany should
in future seek successes far from the battlefield. When he
sat down the applause was so enthusiastic that it was decided
to avoid the anti-climax of the usual translation into English.
It was a curious thing, and a temporary advantage, that
behind Stresemann and Briand, there loomed the symbolic
figures of Hindenburg and Poincaré. "*Seul Poincaré peut faire
adopter la politique de Briand,*" wrote Etienne de Nalèche on
21st September, 1926.

A week later Briand invited Stresemann to lunch with
him to enjoy the cooking at a certain restaurant near Geneva
at Thoiry in France. No one else was there although Austen
Chamberlain was, he maintained, kept fully informed by
Briand. Thoiry probably led nowhere, but it was one of
those moments in history which it is perhaps worth trying
to recapture. The mark was stabilised, the franc scarcely
on its feet again, so that Stresemann, strangely enough, had
financial offers to make to Briand. Serious journalists con-
jectured, and they were not contradicted, that while Stresemann offered rapid payments to France and Belgium, Briand
considered the return of the Saar and Eupen and Malmédy to
Germany, and the evacuation in the following year of the
Rhineland. These offers proved ephemeral because they went
too far for French opinion, and anyway the franc grew
stronger. Apart from this a real personal relationship was
established between Aristide Briand, a humble provincial
politician from Nantes, of Socialist origin like so many of his
colleagues, and the Berlin beer-purveyor's son, a graduate
of Berlin and Leipzig Universities, sixteen years his junior.
Briand had immense charm, eloquence, imagination and certainly fascinated Stresemann as Frenchmen have often
fascinated Germans. But he in his turn appreciated the

intelligence, the realism, the gusto and the flexibility-cum-persistence of this man of the rather unpromisingly Germanic appearance. Although Austen Chamberlain liked to think of a Briand-Stresemann-Chamberlain trio, there can be little doubt that the Englishman did not become involved with the others as they did with each other. It was an involvement which, so long as it lasted—till Stresemann's death in October 1929—did not spell hostility towards others and thus had genuinely fertile possibilities. That Stresemann could have turned Briand against the Poles is unlikely; we may feel certain that Briand could not have reconciled Stresemann with them. What we shall never know precisely, since he did not record his later thoughts, is whether Stresemann in the last years of his life did become less narrowly nationalistic. Certainly he appeared to enjoy Geneva by comparison with Berlin where bitterly nationalistic opposition pursued him: people felt that his declining health softened his natural prejudices.

It is of some interest that the International Steel Cartel was founded on 30th September, 1926, a fortnight after the lunch at Thoiry: its chief objectives were to check overproduction and to stabilise steel prices. Its earliest members were France, Germany, Britain, Belgium, and Luxembourg: early in 1927 it was joined by Austria, Czechoslovakia and Hungary. The links thus provided led to later political repercussions, Schneider-Creusot of France and the *Comité des Forges* becoming associated with the big German steel firms but also with Škoda at Pilsen in Czechoslovakia.

Mussolini of Italy was the aggressor of the later 'twenties though the aggression was not yet serious. Since the beginning of his real dictatorship in January 1925, although he had taken surprisingly conciliatory steps towards Greece, he had quickly changed his tone towards Yugoslavia. The latter country, and to some extent its partners in the Little Entente, were disagreeably startled by the Italian Treaty of 27th November, 1926, with Albania, followed by a second treaty a year later: by and large these provided for the

Italian economic penetration of Albania which Mussolini seemed likely to treat as his Balkan spearhead. On 5th April, 1927, his first treaty with Hungary added to the disquiet of the Little Entente which was partially reassured by the signature of a French-Yugoslav treaty on 11th November, 1927. Since January 1924 a French-Czechoslovak treaty of friendship and alliance had been in existence too.

Developments in Czechoslovakia between 1924 and 1929 were on the whole happy ones, involving a measure of reconciliation between the Czechs and their so-called activist Germans. In more backward Roumania there was some progress thanks to the redistribution of land inaugurated by the land law of 1921. In Yugoslavia, unfortunately, as in Poland, and to some extent in Austria, the attempt to work a western system of democracy flagged and broke down. Yugoslavia was possibly the most problematical of the successor states, containing such different Southern Slavs as the Catholic Slovenes and Croats and the Orthodox and economically more backward Serbs of Serbia and Montenegro. But Yugoslavia, the Triune Kingdom of the Serbs, Croats and Slovenes, also contained the major part of Macedonia, much more recently Turkish than Serbia, and also Bosnia and Hercegovina with their Moslem inhabitants some of whom were Turks. There were two official scripts, Cyrillic and Latin—when the Croats or Slovenes went to Belgrade they could not read the names of the streets unless they had learnt Cyrillic. Finally there were substantial minorities of Germans, Magyars and Albanians: the latter, some half million in numbers living around Serbian Kossovo, looked to the strange little state of Albania. This had emerged from the Balkan Wars in 1913 and was racially distinct from its neighbours, with a rough million of inhabitants within its narrow frontiers. It was a mountainous country nearly as infertile as Montenegro, and economically one of the most backward corners of the Balkan peninsula. It was ruled through most of the inter-war period by a local chieftain called Zogu who made himself King in 1928.

Before this, it has been seen, Albania had become the protégé of Italy.

There was no inherited social question in Yugoslavia because it was a peasant country without an aristocracy once it had cut free from Austria-Hungary. The most violent conflicts in Yugoslavia arose between the more chauvinist Serbs who regarded the new kingdom as an extended Serbia, and the Croatian peasantry and its leaders, in particular Štepan Radić and his brother, Antun. It was true that the Croat peasants had a highly developed community life with a pacifist tinge to its ideology: it was true that they would never willingly have joined in the Yugoslav State unless their autonomy had appeared to be guaranteed. It was true that the officials serving the Karageorgević, formerly Serbian, King Alexander, constantly interfered with Croat village life. It would not, however, be realistic to accept all the Croat objections, for the Croats are traditionally ' more Irish than the Irish.' Throughout the inter-war period it was interesting to see that the Slovenes, who were just as Catholic and more highly educated than the Croats, were always on better terms with the Serbs than the Croats were. It seemed unlikely that the only explanation of this fact was that Serbia and Croatia-Slavonia were adjacent or that the Slovenes were a smaller group. At all events the Serbo-Croat quarrel culminated in the murder of Štepan Radić in the Skupština or Parliament in June 1928 by a Serb desperado called Račić who was never punished; Radić died six or seven weeks later. Just over six months after this, on 6th January, 1929, King Alexander, after ostentatiously consulting the new Croat leader, Vladko Maček, declared that parliamentary government had broken down irreparably: therefore he found it necessary to announce his own dictatorship. In succession to the Slovene, Korošec, who had resigned, the King appointed a Serb of his own school as Prime Minister. Maček, who had openly demanded Croat autonomy from the King, was arrested towards the end of the year. No more was heard of the Triune Kingdom.

In neighbouring Austria 1927 had been the year of most acute political crisis until then. In spite of the economic recovery the political evolution of the first Austrian Republic was unfortunate from the beginning. Two big political parties quickly emerged, bitterly hostile to one another. One was the clerical Christian Social Party, led throughout the 'twenties by the ascetic and single-minded priest, Ignaz Seipel, who was the Chancellor of Austria through nearly the whole period. The other was that of the Social Democrats, which dominated Vienna where a third of the Austrian population lived. Vienna was desperately in need of new housing at the end of the war, and the Socialist municipality proceeded to build big blocks of workers' flats the rents of which were subsidised by the other houseowners in the city. From the beginning the enemies of the Socialists declared that these blocks were intended as military citadels as well. The Socialists were themselves divided between moderate revisionists such as Karl Renner and his friend Karl Seitz who was Mayor of Vienna on the one hand, and on the other determined revolutionaries such as Otto Bauer and Julius Deutsch who won their party the special appellation of *Austromarxisten*. Bauer was a brilliant and fascinating Jew who was determined never to be seduced by the notion of compromise, and Deutsch was essentially a soldier who may well have thought of the workers' flats in military terms from the start. Usually the Christian Social Party polled a little better than the Socialists; it represented the provinces and the countryside as against the capital with its huge mass of industrial workers. There were elections on 24th April, 1927, when Seipel's party obtained seventy-three seats in the Chamber, a loss of nine, and the Socialists seventy-one, a gain of three. At the same time the Pan-Germans went up from ten to twelve seats and the Peasants' *Landbund* from five to nine—both these groups were anti-Socialist. Deutsch had already organised the Socialist para-military *Schutzbund*, while the people on the Right were organising para-military formations of *Frontkämpfer*. A clash between Leftist and Rightist volunteers on 30th January, 1927, ended in the acquittal on 14th July of the Rightists who had been up for trial; as in Germany the courts were hostile to the Left. This acquittal unleashed a formidable uprising in Vienna on 15th July when the Palace of Justice was burnt down to the tune of large-scale civilian casualties. The first Austrian Republic never quite recovered from 15th July, 1927. After this all the para-military groups on the Right united in the *Heimwehr*, and Deutsch and the *Schutzbund* began to prepare for the Civil War which was to come in February 1934. It was characteristic of the Weimar Republic to be ruled by coalitions, but in Austria Bauer consistently vetoed Socialist co-operation with the predominantly Christian Social Governments. After 1945 the two countries reversed their political habits.

Austria was disturbed in the 'twenties not only by internal clashes but also by the *malaise* of all the Germans in the successor states who had been used to regard themselves as the ruling race but were now dethroned. In those days, apart from Bavaria, the Germans of the Weimar Republic were only genuinely aware of grievances on behalf of the Germans in Poland and the Baltic States; the *Bund Deutscher Osten* concerned itself specially with these, the "German East" meaning all Eastern Europe to the Germans. There was an *Auslandsinstitut* in Stuttgart and the *Verein für das Deutschtum im Ausland*, and of course Hitler's Pan-German Party agitating here and there. But Vienna was still, as it had been in Habsburg days, the headquarters of the Bohemian and Moravian Germans, of the Germans in Hungary and Roumania and Yugoslavia, and of course of the former Austrians in the now Italian South Tyrol or Alto Adige.

Italy as a Great Power was not bound by a Minorities Treaty; in any case her Yugoslav and her smaller German-speaking minorities (rather over five hundred thousand and two hundred thousand respectively) were condemned to ruthless Italianisation under the Fascists. After Locarno, Austrian and German opinion became indignant over Mussolini's treatment of the South Tyrol, and on 4th February, 1926, the Bavarian Prime Minister, not quite correctly, delivered a speech of protest. After a truculent answer from the Italian leader or *Duce*, Stresemann on 9th February replied, referring to Italy's abortive attempt to have the Brenner frontier guaranteed at the time of Locarno; after Stresemann had spoken of his warlike threat as "a crime and an absurdity," Mussolini climbed down. By 1927 it has been seen that he was beginning, though unsteadily, to veer towards support of the revisionist powers. His attitude, however, remained one of opportunistic vacillation until 1936. Indeed in response to a conciliatory speech from Briand on 30th November, 1927, Franco-Italian negotiations on North African controversies were put in train. Already on 3rd September, 1927, France and Italy had arrived at a *modus vivendi* with regard to the anti-Fascist Italian refugees in France, people like Saragat and Nenni who wished to be politically active. And when Mussolini addressed the Italian Senate on 5th June, 1928, even he achieved one of the rare feats of conciliatory equilibrium of this period by referring with moderation to the possible revision of the Peace Treaties according to Article 19 of the Covenant of the League of Nations.

In addition to the merciless italianisation of the minorities and an ominous hovering over South-Eastern Europe, in the period between Mussolini's speech of January 1925 and the crash on Wall Street Italy was pounded into Fascist shape. All locally elected bodies were abolished in favour of nominated officials, and in 1928 it was decreed that the Fascist Grand Council would choose four hundred names from lists presented to it by approved bodies, and that these four hundred were to be accepted (theoretically they could have been rejected) by the nation as its representatives in the Chamber. In 1927 the Charter of Labour approved of private enterprise, but subjected it to state interference when the state chose. This was the period, too, of the political trials of outstanding anti-Fascists who had not escaped from Italy—Radicals like Riccardo Bauer, Carlo Rosselli, Feruccio Parri and the Communist, Antonio Gramsci, who had returned from Russia in time to be arrested in 1927. The anti-Fascists defended themselves valiantly before the courts.

Economically Italian development was considerable, thanks particularly to the increasing production of hydro-electric power. Textiles developed favourably, adding artificial silk to their list. In 1927, however, partly in order to air the prestige of it by contrast with the new level of the French franc, Mussolini did Italy the disservice of stabilising the lira at ninety to the pound, thus hampering Italian exports. Late in the prosperous years—relatively prosperous in Italy—Mussolini achieved what many have regarded as his greatest, his most constructive success; in February 1929 the Lateran Agreements reconciled the Papacy and the Italian State after all but sixty years of enmity. At the time the treaties appeared rather as a Fascist success though in the long run the Vatican has gained greatly from them: at all events they fitted well into the picture of the settling of old quarrels in 1928 and 1929.

The culmination of international development following the Treaty of Locarno was the Kellogg-Briand Pact. On 6th April, 1927, the tenth anniversary of America's entry into the war on the Allies' side, Briand had sent a message to the American people suggesting that the occasion be celebrated by a mutual engagement in favour of " the renunciation of War as an instrument of national policy." It was finally arranged with the American Secretary of State, Kellogg, that a treaty incorporating this renunciation should be signed at Paris on 27th August, 1928, at the Quai d'Orsay by the Americans, the French, the British, the Germans, the Italians, the Japanese, Belgium, Czechslovakia, Poland, the five British self-governing Dominions and India.

The occasion was not entirely fortunate for Briand allowed

himself to invent a slightly ridiculous ceremony which gave
the French evening press the opportunity to mock at "the
celebration of Briand's spiritual wedding with peace." Stresemann, signing for Germany, looked very ill and was said by
Madame Tabouis, one of the most remarkable journalists
of the period, "to be dying visibly." The willing involvement
of the United States was, however, of the greatest importance.
All along the Allies' debts to America had involved her
involuntarily with the reparations question. Now on 17th
January, 1929, the United States was the first of the above
fifteen signatories to ratify the Briand-Kellogg Pact. By this
date only two (Argentina and Brazil) out of the sixty-four
states which had been invited to become parties to the Treaty,
had taken no action. After an invitation from the French
the U.S.S.R., although not yet recognised by the United
States, had adhered to the Pact on 1st October, 1928. The
Americans had in practice returned to Europe with the
Dawes Plan and the personnel—men like Parker Gilbert—
entrusted with carrying it out. The Briand-Kellogg Pact
seemed thus to plaster over the Russian as well as the
American gap at the same time at Geneva. In fact the
Russian gap had narrowed earlier. After their four years'
quarrel with the Swiss on account of the assassination of
their envoy, Vorovsky, at the Lausanne Conference in May
1923, the Russians came to terms with them in April 1927.
At this point Stalin's policy had completely ousted that of
Trotsky, and Moscow had officially ceased its conspiracy
against the world for many years. One month later a
strong Russian delegation arrived at Geneva to take part in
the League's first general economic conference. In December
of the same year Maxim Litvinov made his first appearance
at Geneva to participate in the Preparatory Commission of
the Disarmament Conference: this was the beginning of the
long League career of another remarkable personality, a
Russian Jew who had spent many years in London and had
married the daughter of Sir Sidney Low. Thus a Russian
representative was actually at the centre of the European

scene many months before the signature of the Briand-Kellogg Pact.

Briand with his fascinating eloquence had set tremendous things in motion, perhaps only quite superficially. It is time to see how the situation in the German heart of Europe had developed since the abortive conversation at Thoiry. The end of 1926 and the year 1927 were not without alarming prognostications. For on 3rd December, 1926, the *Manchester Guardian* referred to the manufacture of military aeroplanes for Germany in Russia, ironically enough in the very month when the Allies recognised that Germany had fulfilled her disarmament obligations. (These did not, as it happened, affect what she did outside German territory).

More than once in 1927 Parker Gilbert, the American Agent-General for Reparations, pointed out to the Germans that they were allowing their local authorities to be rashly extravagant: indeed foreign visitors to Germany at this time were astonished to see how much more building went on there than in the countries of the victors. Nevertheless the general impression of the consolidation of the Weimar Republic was confirmed by the elections held in May 1928 just after those in France in April. The extremists having lost (only twelve followers of Hitler were elected) and the Social Democrats having gained, a coalition Cabinet with the Socialist, Hermann Müller, as Chancellor was appointed. At the beginning of the year both Hindenburg and Stresemann had pressed for the evacuation of the Rhineland in return for Germany's fulfilment of her obligations to the Allies; in July Müller returned to this demand as did Stresemann when he came to Paris to sign the Briand-Kellogg Pact. The Dawes Plan had admittedly been only provisional.

Already in his report on the third year of its operation Parker Gilbert had said ". . . the very existence of transfer protection, for instance, tends to save the German public authorities from some of the consequences of their own actions, while on the other hand the uncertainty as to the total amount in reparation liabilities inevitably tends everywhere in Germany to diminish the normal incentive to do things and carry through the reforms that would clearly be in the country's own interests."

If a final settlement of Germany's financial obligations could now be negotiated the French Government agreed that the sanction of the occupation of German territory, envisaged in the Treaty of Versailles as lasting until 1935, might duly be curtailed. A committee of financial experts was appointed early in 1929; by 7th June they had drawn up the plan called after the American, Owen Young. This aimed primarily at converting the whole matter of reparations into a commercial, rather than a political, obligation. Later it was stated that from 1st September, 1924, to 31st August, 1929, Germany had paid 7,970,000,000 gold marks or nearly four hundred million pounds sterling; of this France had received half, Britain about a fifth and Italy and Belgium about one-fourteenth each; the other Powers concerned had only received very small fractions.

The Labour Party had returned to power in Britain in May 1929 with MacDonald again as Premier and with Philip Snowden as Chancellor of the Exchequer: Arthur Henderson went to the Foreign Office. When the representatives of Germany and her creditors met at the Hague on 6th August Snowden immediately protested against the Young Plan as having abandoned the Spa percentages to Britain's disadvantage. By the end of the month he had won notable concessions from the other Powers, particularly France. On 31st August a Protocol and financial agreement were signed, and a joint note to Stresemann about the evacuation of German territory. A second and final session of the Hague Conference took place from 3rd to 21st January, 1930, which the representatives of all Central and East Europe also attended. The final sum fixed for Germany's reparation debt was agreed at 110,735.7 million Reichsmarks to be paid in sixty annual instalments ending in 1988. A Bank for International

Settlements was to take over the functions of the Reparations Commission and provide any other machinery required to implement the Young Plan: the latter went into operation on 17th May, 1930, when the Bank for International Settlements opened its doors at Basle. The last foreign soldiers were to evacuate Germany by 30th June, 1930. Fourteen agreements had been signed which had also settled the reparations liabilities of Austria, Hungary and Bulgaria, and consolidated or cancelled the so-called liberation debts of Czechoslovakia, Yugoslavia, Poland and Roumania. In the British Blue Book containing the texts of the agreements they were said to "represent 'a general liquidation of the financial questions raised by the War and the subsequent Treaties of Peace,' which, as the Experts declared, was required to 'ensure the definite return of Europe to normal financial and economic conditions,' so that it may be said that the aim of the Conference has been fully and satisfactorily attained."[1]

The end of the Briand-Stresemann partnership, and with it the end of the period of hope, had however come three months earlier, in the autumn of 1929. At the Tenth Assembly of the League on 5th September, Briand brought forward his cherished scheme for the United States of Europe, hitherto considered only interesting to visionaries like the Austrian-Greek, Coudenhove-Kalergi. Briand's warmest support came from Stresemann who, in his last speech at Geneva, emphasised the need above all for European economic unity. The League as a whole was perhaps embarrassed by so much emphasis upon one Continent, even though it were that Europe which then seemed still as central and as dominant as it ever had. In 1930 a Commission of Enquiry into European Union was set up; its activities merged into the anxious searching for solutions in the 'thirties, but at least it was able to include representatives from Russia and from Turkey—until then Kemal Pasha's

[1] _Survey of International Affairs 1930._ p. 522.

Turkey had held entirely aloof from the Europe to which it had insisted on returning.

The death of Stresemann on 3rd October, 1929, at the age of fifty-one, immediately preceding, as it did, the collapse of confidence in New York, had already ended the five prosperous years. These events cut the ground from beneath Briand's feet; they made his optimism, which had been based on earlier realities, seem as hollow as that of the British Blue Book. In fact he did not suddenly lose his backing in France. It was in June 1931 that he made the mistake of standing for the Presidency, a formal position for which he was quite unsuited and in which his gifts would have been wasted. It was said that a malevolent intrigue of Laval overcame Briand's opposition to the plan. At any rate he failed; in 1932 he died in his seventieth year, three years after the death of Clemenceau and Asquith and two years before that of Poincaré. Newer names like those of Édouard Daladier and Pierre Laval were now to be more frequently heard in France. The former was a Provençal of peasant origins, a pupil of Herriot's who had become a schoolmaster: the bull, they called him because of his thick neck, but he seemed often more like a helpless child. Laval, originally a Socialist, half-educated and soon mysteriously rich, was shortly to become the instrument of those who feared social change more than national humiliation. The successful Presidential candidate against Briand was Paul Doumer, who was, however, assassinated on 7th May, 1932, by a half-mad Russian counter-revolutionary.

According to Herriot, Briand was no merely facile speaker nor vanity-ridden. "*Si puissant par ses moyens d'expression, Briand, toute sa vie, ne sera pas moins agissant par sa force de réflexion et de silence. En quelque endroit qu'il doive intervenir désormais, il explorera longuement le terrain.*"[1] Thus there was nothing in Briand's gifts to compare with the evil oratory soon to triumph in Germany.

[1] E. Herriot. *Aristide Briand.* p. 8.

As for Stresemann it seems clear that his death helped to intensify the crisis of confidence which reached its nadir in Wall Street on 29th October, 1929, Black Friday. The symbolism of the prosperous years had been destroyed, and Briand alone could do little to stem the tide of the Great Depression.

Chapter IV

THE PERIOD OF THE GREAT DEPRESSION

1929-33

I VIOLENT CHANGE IN RUSSIA

During the prosperous five years Russia played a less important part in European history because a prosperous Europe was much less concerned with revolution, and because Stalin's slogan formulated in the autumn of 1924 of "Socialism in one country" meant the surrender of a main source of the inspiration of the Bolshevik revolution itself, the idea that the revolution in backward Russia was a mere beginning of a more intense and technically advanced revolution in the whole world. Between 1924 and 1928 under the New Economic Policy, which aimed at keeping Russia going without creating further friction, the industry of the country picked up to about pre-war production by 1927. At the same time, owing to the breaking-up of the big estates in favour of the peasants, agricultural production fell; the N.E.P. meant that the richer peasants were free to exploit the situation to their own advantage and they naturally did so.

The acceptance of "Socialism in one country" was the negation of Trotsky's "permanent revolution" and the period from 1924 to 1929 spelt above everything the decline and fall of Trotsky; the in some ways *laissez-faire* character of the N.E.P. was also something of which Trotsky was bound to disapprove. The way in which Stalin exploited first Lenin's death to create a cult of Lenin quite alien to that leader's nature, and then the hostility of Zinoviev and Kamenev to Trotsky to oust all three of them, although all three were better Leninists than Stalin, is the theme of

Russian internal politics in these years. It is an extraordinary story, in some ways stranger than the success of Hitler. Trotsky was so evidently brilliant, so devoted to the revolutionary cause and yet so personally ambitious that it seems unintelligible that the stolid, apparently simple Stalin should have beaten him each time; it seems all the stranger when one remembers that Trotsky was the creator and chief of the Soviet Russian Army. Trotsky never used this instrument precisely because he was determined not to be a Bonaparte; indeed it was their loyalty to Communism which Stalin seemed ever ready and able to exploit in the case of all those whose power or position he was unwilling to accept. It was already in January 1925, the month in which Mussolini declared his dictatorship, that Trotsky resigned from the Commissariat of War, although he was not expelled from the Politburo until October 1926 nor from the Russian Communist Party until a year later (November 1927). In January 1929 the Politburo allowed Stalin to exile Trotsky to Turkey. It is a measure of standards in 1929, in Russia as elsewhere in Europe, that exile should then be the extreme punishment meted out to a political rival.

Exactly a year before the expulsion of Trotsky from Russia, in January 1928, the Russian Government found itself short by two million tons of the minimum amount of grain required to feed the urban population; that is to say the country was threatened with serious famine again. Partly this was due to hoarding by farmers who could afford to do so. At all events the food crisis galvanised Stalin, hitherto just the Party organiser, and against extreme measures of any kind which might ruffle organisation, into becoming a violent extremist. Before the end of 1929 he had launched two major inter-related social revolutions. On the one hand there was the drive against the kulaks and in favour of the collectivisation and mechanisation of agriculture, and on the other a sudden decision in the Five-Year Plan of 1929-33 to industrialise Russia at top speed; the production of pig-iron, for instance, was scheduled to increase from three and a half million tons per annum to ten million in 1933, Stalin originally demanding a much sharper rise still. The actual increase was, of course, much less, while the results of the whole economic offensive were at first chaotic. In their resistance the better-off peasants slaughtered their livestock wholesale, while the landless peasants were egged on to attack and betray the kulaks. The whole apparatus of the Russian Government, which had never lost the character of a police state, was mobilised to push through the ruthless modernisation of Russia at whatever cost: when labour became short it was roughly conscripted, so that socialist dreams about labour conditions were parodied, and slave-labour camps inaugurated. At about the time that Hitler became Chancellor of Germany—just before—Stalin betrayed a brief lack of confidence in what he was doing. He continued, nevertheless, with Russia's merciless transformation. When Hitler began his anti-Communist propaganda in the days of N.E.P. or earlier, it had far less justification beyond the fact that Trotsky was a brilliant Jew. By 1933 things were happening in the Soviet Union which were likely to cause the revision of the notion of socialism in one country in the not too distant future, since an industrially advanced, as well as Socialist, Russia might be far more infectious. People outside Russia said to each other that no great depression was possible in a Communist state.

Towards the end of the 'thirties Russian industrial power began to catch up with that of Germany, but it was less efficient, using more labour less well. Isaac Deutscher has compared the cruelty of unplanned industrialisation in Britain earlier with the cruelty of planned industrialisation in Soviet Russia: opinions will differ as to which was the more merciless. What happened to Russia in the nineteen-thirties was at any rate a "take-off": it contrasted sharply with what happened in the rest of Eastern Europe.

11 DEMOCRACY BREAKS DOWN IN POLAND 1924-32

The troubles of inter-war Poland, like those of Yugoslavia, have been the play-thing of German and Communist propagandists. Essentially both countries were under-developed; they were not unlike the new African countries of to-day. The liberating war had brought advanced Western ideas, so that societies which were largely illiterate and completely without positive political experience were expected to work advanced democratic constitutions. The liberating war had, moreover, used Poland as one of its major battlefields. At the end of it land reform was introduced in order to break up the big estates in the interests of the peasantry. German owners of big properties liked to claim that it was only operated at their expense: this was not true though it was clear that the Polish authorities had less hesitation where German-owned land was concerned. Elsewhere the reform worked out slowly. The high Polish birthrate, particularly in Western Galicia, brought concealed unemployment in spite of land distribution. Thus Poland not only had to start from the political zero of non-existence; she was plagued by acute economic difficulties as well as the bitter hostility of the Germans and Russians, and of her huge Ukrainian minority.

Pilsudski had retired into private life in 1923. By 1926, however, he was so angered by what he condemned as the futility of parliamentary democracy that he staged a military *coup d'état*: from then onwards Ministers were his nominees and he himself was always Minister of War and sometimes Prime Minister as well.

The big Peasant Party led by Witos, who had been Prime Minister in 1926, particularly resented Pilsudski's interference; so did Korfanty and his Upper Silesians, who disliked this semi-military centralisation based on Warsaw. In

1930 Witos and Korfanty, and others who shared their views, were imprisoned in the fortress of Brzesk (Brest-Litovsk) where they were maltreated. By 1931 they were liberated on bail and tried, and later they went into exile in Czechoslovakia where they were befriended by Beneš.

From 1926 onwards Poland was governed arbitrarily rather than despotically. This type of régime became the rule rather than the exception in Eastern Europe between the wars: it was perhaps halfway to Italian Fascism but more like Prussia or Austria in the 1860s. People were not on the whole odiously humiliated nor grossly tormented nor completely silenced, as they were by Stalin or Hitler. Different political parties with their newspapers survived precariously. It was worthwhile for the opposition to try to hit back, to make the facts known if they could, but all the trumps in the hands of the governments were used against them. This applied to the Poles in Poland.

It was different for the Polish Jews of whom there were at least three million out of a population of thirty-two or thirty-three million. These Jews provided a large proportion of the small middle-class; they were often the *entrepreneurs*, the bankers and the professional men. Sometimes Poland was proud, sometimes ashamed, of them. They were mostly practising Jews among the Catholic Poles and not in general assimilated as the German Jews were. Thus they tended to feel insecure and to be unpopular.

It was different, too, for the Ukrainians and White Russians whose autonomy, promised by Warsaw in 1922 to the Conference of Ambassadors before the latter recognised Eastern Galicia as Polish in 1923, never materialised. The Poles set out to polonise the Ukrainians without scruple, so that fierce opposition was aroused which in turn led to brutal military suppression in 1930, the so-called "pacification of the Ukraine."

It was different for the Germans in the towns of Western Poland or for the German landowners or industrialists in Polish Upper Silesia. For one thing they had their own resources. For another they could appeal to the League of Nations, with greater effect after September 1926 when Germany became a permanent member of the Council. There was endless trouble, of course, over the German city of Danzig within Poland's customs area and represented abroad by Poland. This situation caused the Poles to achieve one of the best jokes in the history of inter-war Europe. Since the Danzigers were unhelpful over the facilities of their port, the Poles built themselves a new one with better facilities at Gdynia on the very edge of the territory of the Free City. This obliged the Germans to step up their subsidies to Danzig. Unwillingly they had to admit that Gdynia was a technical success in spite of the Poles' proverbial incompetence (proverbial in Germany).

Gdynia was something of a show-piece. Elsewhere the difficulties were great. Although the French invested a fair amount in Poland there was a serious lack of capital and of skilled labour. With the help of the League of Nations Upper Silesia weathered its partition, but, just when there should have been expansion, in 1925 Germany denounced her trade treaty with Poland.

Somehow the Poles shared with the Italians an exuberant vitality that rose to occasions. An important opportunity came in 1926 with the British miners' strike which opened new markets for Upper Silesian coal. The economic depression hit Poland hard in 1931, and her agriculture never quite recovered from the contraction of demand for foodstuffs : the high birthrate meant that concealed unemployment on the land increased persistently. To the east Russia was a negative neighbour, after 1928 more cut off from Poland than before. Except in the Polish Ukraine, Polish and Russian history seemed hardly to touch one another in these years. Neither workers nor peasants in Poland were attracted by Russian Communism which had enrolled only a few individual Polish Jews of great distinction—such as Rosa Luxemburg[1]—

[1] See footnote p. 40.

who left Poland. As for the Ukrainian nationalists, they were as hostile to Stalin's Russia as to Poland.

Pilsudski, at least until the last few years of his life, had a certain flair. He brought with him to be President of the Polish Republic the distinguished chemist, Moscicki, and he appointed as Foreign Minister August Zaleski, a man who made Poland respected at Geneva. There he stood up with dignity to Stresemann over the issues about which Stresemann, at the zenith of his career, felt most bitterly. Zaleski remained at the Polish Foreign Office for six years until in November 1932 he was succeeded by Joseph Beck.

III GERMANY AND AUSTRIA:
HITLER CHANCELLOR OF GERMANY 1933

Although the economic recovery of Germany between 1924 and 1929 had been remarkable, Parker Gilbert's admonitions had been too modest. Local budgets often remained unbalanced because unpopular taxes were not carried through. While surprisingly large numbers of people were gathered into employment, too many people always remained without work. In 1927, when the system to relieve unemployment was worked out and became law, assumptions were made which were too optimistic; in other words a maximum unemployment figure of 1,100,000 was allowed for when in fact there had seldom been fewer at any season, and nearly always more at the unfavourable times of year. The winter of 1928-29 was very severe and the unemployment figure rose to about two and a half million. Stresemann made no secret in the last year of his life over his anxiety about the economic situation: he was, moreover, as he said to Jules Sauerwein, a French journalist, in July 1929, haunted "by the spectre of a violent dictatorship." In the United States from which so much money had been lent to Germany, confidence was beginning to crumble. In October crashes on Wall Street became the order of the day: it seems obvious that Stresemann's death at the beginning of that month had helped to destroy American confidence in Germany. The Young Plan of 1929 had been intended to consolidate an improving economic situation, bringing about German payments to France, Britain and their former Allies, and in turn facilitating the payment of Allied debts to the United States. Instead it was launched after the second session of the Conference at the Hague in January 1930. The circumstances now made it unlikely, especially with sharply falling prices, that the process of consolidation could properly be set in motion by the fulfilment of Germany's new, restricted obligations.

An attempt had been made to poison the German atmosphere in November 1929 by Alfred Hugenberg, the leader of the party of the *Deutschnationalen* or German Nationalists. On the right-wing of his right-wing party Hugenberg, now sixty-four, was a stock example of German Conservatism. As a young man he had been a Pan-German and employed on a commission for settling Germans in a predominantly Polish area, Poznania or Posen. From 1909 to 1918 he had been a director of the great Krupp concern, in 1916 acquiring a controlling interest in a group of newspapers together with the famous UFA film concern. He had been elected a deputy in 1919 but only became leader of the Nationalist party in 1928. A few weeks after the death of Stresemann, and before the final session of the Hague Conference, he sponsored a plan to hold a referendum condemning the Young Plan or the payment of any reparations at all—all such payments were branded by him as the "Enslavement of the German people." Six million votes were cast against this "enslavement," but these were not enough to bring about a referendum. In some ways quite as menacing was the publication early in December 1929 of a memorandum by the President of the Reichsbank since 1924, Dr. Hjalmar Schacht. The memorandum condemned the final version of the Young Plan (which Schacht himself had signed) and attacked the wasteful financial structure of

the Reich, its *Länder* and communes. After resigning from
his office, this *enfant terrible* proceeded to give a series of
lectures in the United States prophesying the collapse of the
Young Plan, and by doing so jeopardising its success.

The winter 1929-30 brought some three million unemployed
in Germany which was more immediately and sharply hit by
the American depression than any other country in Europe
thanks to all the American short-term credits. The finances
of Germany were thrown out to a much greater extent than
hitherto, while the Socialists in the Cabinet felt unable to
sponsor a deflationary policy which was unacceptable to the
trade unions. Although Keynes was beginning to work on
the subject, no one in power in those days could devise an
alternative to deflation as a remedy for economic depression.
In March 1930 Hindenburg sanctioned the implementation
of the Young Plan by Germany almost simultaneously with
the resignation of Hermann Müller and his Cabinet. The
President forthwith appointed the leader of the Centre
Party, Heinrich Brüning, to be Chancellor, keeping Stresemann's successor, Curtius, at the Wilhelmstrasse. At the time
the appointment of Brüning seemed quite normal, the more
so since he was known to stand for fiscal economies, lower
salaries and sterner taxes. The fact that Brüning had seen
Hindenburg shortly before this and been assured of Presidential support for his financial policy did not reveal the
fact that Brüning was backed at this time in Army circles
close to the President, and particularly by General Kurt von
Schleicher. Schleicher was a personal friend of Hindenburg's
son, Oskar; he had acted for Seeckt in some of the secret
negotiations with the Russians. He became notorious as a
political intriguer but he also represented an influential state
of mind. He and his kind saw the salvation of Germany in
making the President as powerful as the Emperor had been
before the Republic and in appointing Ministers to govern
independently of the Reichstag. Schleicher was younger and
more flexible than Oldenburg-Januschau, the tough old Junker
who had intrigued for the presentation of the East Prussian

estate of Neudeck to Hindenburg on his eightieth birthday
in 1927. Neudeck gave the President the personal interests
of an East Prussian landowner beyond the 'Corridor'.
Schleicher was more aware of the present. He was of the same
generation as Brüning in whom he saw a politician with
a soldierly respect for the President. Thus Brüning, it was
thought among the Generals, might be used to pervert
the democracy of the Weimar Republic : it is probably
true to say that Brüning himself was only half-aware of
this intention, if as much. He by no means stood on the
Right, having had a lot to do with the Catholic trade
unions with which he sympathised. Brüning was unfortunately one of those intelligent and upright people whose
practical judgment is constantly bad. He introduced the
financial programme in which he believed with disastrous
consequences. The Socialists were bound to oppose it, so
that it could not be got through the Reichstag. In July
1930 the President, as he had earlier implied that he
would, signed an emergency decree according to Article 48
of the Weimar constitution; this gave Brüning's financial bill
the force of law for the moment. Ebert had used Article 48
in his day, but now Schleicher and his set planned to use it
systematically to destroy the constitution instead of preserving
it. The country was badly demoralised by depression-cum-
deflation, except for Brüning himself, the Nationalists, Hitler's
National Socialists and the Communists. Brüning then made
the further mistake of dissolving the Reichstag so that a
general election was held on 14th September, 1930. It was
nearly seven years since Hitler's abortive *putsch* of November
1923, and the typical sober Berliner, for instance, had lost
track of him. This was pardonable but mistaken.

After his arrest in November 1923 Adolf Hitler had
exploited his trial in 1924 to the full to attract publicity
for his " Movement." He was then condemned to a nominal
five years in the fortress of Landsberg where he was treated
with such indulgence that he emerged positively fatter when

released at Christmas 1924. During this time he had not only received many visitors, but he also began to dictate his book *Mein Kampf* in which he defined his doctrine. It was a primitive declaration of a belief in nothing but force of different kinds. The strong, who were the Aryan or German race, were to be strengthened at the expense of the usurping weak, the Jews and Slavs. While he took for granted as he always had that the Germans would dominate the Danubian world, he now urged for the first time that they should "go back six hundred years," as he saw it, resuming the colonisation of North-East Europe and Russia. Thus they would acquire power and *Lebensraum*—which were complementary—absorbing or exterminating the indigenous population as best served their power purposes: it was important to destroy completely whomever one regarded as dangerous. Hitler identified the Jewish menace to German society, which he claimed to perceive, with the Communist threat of which most Germans were excessively afraid.

On emerging from prison he refounded his party of National Socialists, called Nazis for short, and he began the extremely serious organisation of his para-military formations, the Sport or Storm Troopers (the *S.A.*)[1] These, he insisted, were to be a political, not a military, instrument. They began ostensibly to protect National Socialist meetings from Communist interruptions. Hitler intended to gain power without at first attempting to use force directly or collectively. He intended to gain power by the perfection of propaganda which above everything would *threaten* the use of force; it was to threaten and persuade at the same time. Hitler devoted much thought to the technique of propaganda, learning where he could from the Communists, from D'Annunzio, from Mussolini, as from the former Mayor of Vienna, Lueger, and from Northcliffe. The flags and uniforms of the *S.A.* were planned accordingly, red flags being taken from the Communists but branded with the Swastika.

The S.A. men were clothed in shirts of a peculiarly dis-

[1] Standing for *Sturm Abteilungen*.

agreeable light brown with military caps on the imperial
Austrian model: a small bodyguard within the S.A. wore
the same brown shirts with a black uniform and peak-
caps decorated with a skull and crossbones; they were
called *Schutzstaffeln* or *S.S.* Both S.A. and S.S. inevitably
wore jack-boots, and the sound of marching boots gradually
acquired a sinister and demoralising significance for those
not wearing them. Increasingly the people wearing these
uniforms attacked and beat up people whom they chose to
regard as their opponents or as " Reds." It was characteristic
of Hitler that, until practically necessary, he did nothing to
acquire citizenship of the Weimar Republic or to become a
member of the Reichstag, both institutions he venomously
abused. His headquarters remained at Munich and he avoided
Berlin.

In his propaganda Hitler promised everything to everyone.
Now that it is easy to see what he intended, the credulity of
his audiences seems difficult to explain. Originally it was
due to his strange fascination as an orator, his appeal to the
most primitive mass emotions in a country where national
arrogance had been followed by the humiliation and
bewilderment of the early 1920s. In Wilhelmine Germany,
moreover, the way had been prepared by a good deal of
talk about the superior Aryan race and the incompleteness
of German *Freiheit* even then. Many people such as
Rauschning himself[1] at the beginning, felt that the vitality
of Hitler's movement combined with its rejection of the stiff
class system of pre-war days, was something which could
and must be turned to good account. They were sure that
the awful threats meant nothing. In particular they regarded
Hitler's movement as salvation from decadence.

To many a German with quite good traditions behind him
the change from the discipline of imperial days to the outburst of modernism in the arts and education after the war
was disturbing and shocking. The provincial, in particular,

[1] President of the Senate of Danzig for a short time. See p. 153.

was startled by the licence of Berlin, and it was true, although the explanation is obscure, that with the exception of Brecht and Gropius nearly all the new artists and writers were Jewish. A simple person therefore felt Hitlerism as a protection against alarming and exotic innovations. National Socialism also appealed to technicians, engineers, chauffeurs and so on; unlike the traditionalists they welcomed it as more modern, more efficient than democracy. It should also be noted that many people in Germany at this time, particularly belonging to the younger generation, were *Auslandsdeutsche* : they had left their old homes in the new Successor states where they felt, rightly or wrongly, that they were unfairly treated, to seek their fortunes in Germany itself. Naturally they were delighted by the Nazi attitude which proposed to incorporate all Germans in Germany without saying how this could be done : this was one of the 25 points in the early National Socialist programme.

With the autumn of 1929 Hitler's prospect improved marvellously. The S.A. had provided a haven for adolescents who, in other times and countries, have formed into fighting gangs; it now provided a haven for the jobless whom it supplied with soup and boots. The grim economic situation exacerbated class relations and increased the anti-Communists' fear of growing Communism. Some industrialists, losing faith in Hugenberg's obviously declining strength, began to subscribe money to the Nazi Party. Hitler, as he once implied to Otto Strasser, was only anti-capitalist where the capitalists were Jews. He continued, however, to make much of the Common Good before that of the individual, which sounded modern, uplifting and socialistic to those searching for a faith; at the same time an industrialist, who gave money to him as the most likely barrier to social revolution, was given the agreeable sensation of behaving altruistically. Particularly since 1870 at the German Universities the more vociferous professors and students had expressed strongly nationalistic and often anti-Semitic emotions, and academics had shown themselves eager to prove racialist theories true;

thus the organised intellectuals wanted to believe in Hitler although isolated intellectuals often saw to the depths of his wickedness without being Jews. The social group which scarcely surrendered to him at all was that of the elder generation of the industrial working-people; their younger generation, finding no work after 1929, was of course inclined to follow this Pied Piper. Indeed the younger men and women often voted Nazi and Communist by turns, Communism having the new attraction of isolating Russia from the effects of the slump.

Thus it should not have been surprising that in the elections of September 1930 the Communists increased from fifty-four to seventy-seven deputies, while the Nazis shot up from twelve to one hundred and seven, becoming the largest party in the Reichstag after the Socialists. From this time onwards, certainly until November 1932, everyone to the right of the Socialists felt, often uneasily, that the Nazis must somehow be brought into the government: there was a widespread feeling that this was the only way in which they could be " tamed." To the left of the Socialists the Communists sponsored the suicidal slogan that the sooner the Nazis came to power the better, as this would be the last bourgeois phase before the Communist state. Blindly Moscow and the Third International preached hatred of and opposition to the Social Democrats whom they called the Social-Fascists. Far from having weathered the storm, as he naturally hoped, Brüning was faced with catastrophe upon an apocalyptic scale in 1931. Before this descended upon him there occurred, early in that year, the crisis precipitated by the plan for an Austro-German Customs Union.

The Republic of Austria, small though it was, occupied a key position in Central Europe. It has been seen that it was particularly susceptible to economic dangers and German racial nostalgia. The fact that the Christian Social and Social Democrat parties were nearly equal in strength and diametrically opposed in ideology caused the former to tolerate more and more *Heimwehr* activity in order to intimidate the

Socialist *Schutzbund* into passivity. Yet although the *Heim-wehr* chief, Prince Starhemberg, a former *Freikorps* fighter, was made Minister of the Interior in September 1930, in the elections in November of that year the Socialists came out top with seventy-two seats in the Chamber to sixty-six Christian Social members; the Pan-Germans increased from twelve to twenty and a group of eight *Heimwehr* deputies appeared. In the presidential election at the end of the year a moderate and democratic member of the Christian Social Party, Wilhelm Miklas, gained 109 votes against 93 for the moderate Socialist leader, Karl Renner, whom we already know. Meanwhile a Cabinet had been formed with the Pan-German, Johannes Schober, as Foreign Minister. The collapse of the *Bodenkreditanstalt* bank, which was merged in the *Creditanstalt* towards the end of 1929, was one immediate indication of the disastrous consequences of the American slump for Austria, which, like Germany, depended upon foreign credit and markets abroad.

Schober naturally supported the closest possible collabora-tion between Austria and Germany, and it was well-known that not only the Socialists, but also young people at the Austrian universities and in general were *grossdeutsch* in sentiment. In addition to those who called themselves Pan-German there were pockets of National Socialists, a party which originated in Austria before 1914 as the *Deutsche Arbeiterpartei*; it was represented in Vienna at this time by Walter Riehl who had, however, broken with Hitler some years earlier since Hitler brooked no rival. After the elections of September 1930 in Germany, Brüning and Curtius were looking for some nationally gratifying expedient; they could not be indifferent to the fact that the first of the twenty-five points in the Nazi Party programme was a demand for the absorption of Austria into a greater Germany. Thus when on 3rd March, 1931, Curtius visited Vienna he naturally fell in with Schober's proposal for an Austro-German Customs Union which was made public later in March: anyone else who wished to join this union, it was stated, would be free to do so. The reaction in France and in every country sensitive to the re-appearance of a *Mitteleuropa* plan was sharp. In the French Chamber Briand defended his policy in the past with spirit, and on 18th May Germany accepted the French challenge to submit the Customs Union project to the judgment of the permanent Court of International Justice in the Hague. Later on this court condemned the plan by one vote, but the plan had in any case been blocked. It had achieved little but to discredit Briand's attitude. In the French Chamber on 8th May Herriot defended Briand "*qui à voulu substituer à l'antagonisme des forces l'équilibre des droits*"; he went on to say that the Austro-German plan had denied the spirit of the League of Nations after Austria had undertaken to preserve her complete independence not only at St. Germain but also when the League came to her financial rescue in 1922. This, then, was the French point of view, and it appeared that French action in Vienna had accompanied its expression.

On 11th May, 1931, the *Creditanstalt für Handel and Gewerbe* in Vienna failed. This bank had been the financial centre of the economic life of Central Europe pretty well since its foundation in 1856. In spite of the disintegration of Austria-Hungary it had remained in close relation with banks and industries in most of the Danubian countries which were therefore shaken by its fall. It seems probable that French financial manœuvres, in protest against the plan for the Customs Union and in order to make the Austrians choose dependence upon France, contributed to the collapse. Inevitably the effect was alarming in Germany whence further funds were withdrawn. On 5th June Hindenburg signed an emergency decree imposing further increases in taxation and cuts in salaries and unemployment benefits; protests against reparations payments became louder. There was a feeling that there would soon be nothing from which to pay salaries and that government would break down. Indeed normally light-hearted social gatherings were to be found in Berlin at this time anxiously discussing the collapse of civilsation.

On 20th June, 1931, owing to the tremendous outflow of foreign exchange from Germany, the *Reichsbank* decided to suspend private discount business. On that same day President Hoover of America brought general respite by proposing that all payments both of interest and of principal on inter-governmental debts should be postponed for one year. The French were at first disturbed by this suggestion since they stood to lose so much in reparations; they felt that the distinction should be retained between conditional and unconditional annuities under the Young Plan. A compromise formula was arrived at, more or less accepting the distinction required by the French. The respite proved little but an illusion, for on 13th July one of Germany's three great joint stock banks, the *Darmstädter und National Bank*, DANAT for short, closed down. The crash on Wall Street less than two years earlier seemed like child's play in comparison with the situation in Europe in July 1931. Hitler had always said that the Republic of the "November Criminals" would lead to disaster[1]: quite innocent and sensible people now thought that they recognised a prophet.

While the bankers of the world patched things up here and there to keep them going, those who could took their summer holiday, stunned though they felt. Brüning and his colleagues searched frantically for expedients to hold down the huge unemployment figures, proportionally higher in highly industrialised Germany than elsewhere in Europe. They made plans for labour service which the French suspected as plans for another para-military formation. They made plans for settling people on failing estates in East Prussia which made Junker hackles rise. Reich plans clashed with Prussian plans. Prussia was in effect ruled by two Socialist Ministers, Otto Braun, who had been its able Prime Minister since 1920 almost without interruption, and his friend, Carl Severing. Schleicher and the people round

---

[1] "November Criminals" was the label Hitler attached to the Socialists and Erzberger who had agreed to the armistice in November 1918.

Hindenburg felt that the Socialists still had too much to say; they wanted Prussia to be fully absorbed into a more authoritarian Reich. It was time, it seemed, for Brüning to modify his Cabinet and to drop the democratically-minded Wirth from the Reich Ministry of the Interior. In October Brüning's second Cabinet also dropped Curtius, the Chancellor himself taking over the Wilhelmstrasse: ominously General Groener, Minister of Defence, became at the same time Wirth's successor. Groener was the most moderate and civilian of the Generals, but he was inevitably influenced by his colleagues.

Brüning had refused to invite any Nazi into his Cabinet but he could not prevent Hindenburg from receiving Hitler together with his lieutenant, Göring, on 10th October, 1931; this was Hitler's first meeting with the President who appealed to him without success to support a more presidential régime. After this on 11th October Hitler arrived with fresh prestige at Bad Harzburg for a joint demonstration with Hugenberg's Nationalists against the Government. All kinds of former celebrities, including Seeckt (who had resigned in 1926) appeared at Harzburg. But Hitler made it clear that he regarded it rather as the end than the beginning of a Nazi-Nationalist alliance. The Harzburg meeting, however, provided the occasion for a demonstration by Schacht who threw all his international reputation throughout 1931 into declarations that only Hitler could save Germany. When the brilliant and independent Schacht said this at every lunch-party he attended in the banks and embassies, he probably did more than any other individual to smooth Hitler's path both at home and abroad.

In 1925 Britain had returned to the gold standard. When Labour came to power in May 1929 this was in good time for Black Friday on Wall Street in the following October. After the Austrian and German crashes between May and July 1931, Britain's financial position became critical, and on 21st September she abandoned the gold standard. This situation extinguished the Labour Government, Ramsay

MacDonald going into coalition with the Conservatives to form a National Government in August 1931. Labour as such disappeared from the Government benches until after war had broken out in 1940, although Stanley Baldwin did not actually succeed MacDonald as Premier until 1935.

London was still the world's financial capital in 1931, and the British abandonment of the gold standard set off a chain of reactions throughout the world, particularly strong ones in Scandinavia. Strangely enough Germany and Austria maintained the gold standard, having even begun, during August, to pick up. For another year Germany more or less stagnated economically. With Brüning's Cabinet patched up the next problem to be faced, apart from that of somehow containing the Nazis, was the election of a new President of the Republic; this fell due in 1932. Brüning, Schleicher and Groener agreed to avoid controversy by organising the re-election of Hindenburg who was now eighty-four and unlikely to survive for another seven years' term. Uneasily the Social Democrats agreed too, whereupon Hugenberg turned against the idea. Hitler was still not a German citizen but here was his chance. Through the Nazi, Klagges, who was a Minister in Brunswick, he got himself a Brunswick appointment which made him into a German. The absurd situation now arose that Hindenburg found himself supported by the Catholic Centre and the Socialists, whom he distrusted, and opposed by his own kind, the Nationalists, as by the Nazis: it is believed that he blamed Brüning for this discomfiture. On 13th March Hindenburg polled 18,661,736 votes to 11,339,285 for Hitler, the Nationalist candidate Düsterberg gaining less than Thälmann, the Communist: Hindenburg just missed the necessary absolute majority. In the second vote on 10th April Hindenburg was duly elected with 19,360,000 votes to 13,418,000 for Hitler. But the opportunity had been richly exploited by the Nazis who flew Hitler from place to place to address the people, calling their campaign " Hitler over Germany "—electioneering by air was a novelty in those days. On 24th April, 1932, elections fell due in a number of *Länder* including Prussia; in that other Germany with its good Socialist—and other non-Nazi—Ministers, the Nazis were now elected to be the biggest party in the *Landtag* though not big enough to form a Nazi Government alone : consequently the Social Democrat Prime Minister, Otto Braun, remained provisionally in office.

The German situation had been constantly confused by the conflicting policies of different *Länder* and the Reich towards the Nazis. The Prussian police might act in Berlin according to different directives from those guiding Reich officials in the same city. In July 1930 the Prussian Government had forbidden Prussian officials to be Nazis or Communists; this meant that a school teacher in Berlin or Cologne might not join the Nazis although a railwayman appointed by the *Reichsbahn* might do so. After the so-called Boxheim documents, and other evidence that the Nazis were seriously planning a reign of terror, had been found by the police, the Prime Ministers of the *Länder* were able to convince Groener that the Storm Troopers must be banned throughout the Reich. As luck would have it, the first noteworthy action his Ministers asked Hindenburg to take, after his re-election as President, was to sign an emergency decree suppressing the S.A. on 13th April. Neither Hindenburg nor his advisers, such as Schleicher, could believe that the Nazis—being nationalistically-minded—were really dangerous, nor that the Socialistic formation of the *Reichsbanner*, which existed to protect the Republic, was preferable. The banning of the S.A. eleven days before the Prussian and other Land elections raised a howl of Nazi anger as political discrimination. Brüning and Groener now lost Schleicher's confidence as well as Hindenburg's; Schleicher had met Hitler several times by now and was busily planning a new government more to the right, more authoritarian, and at least tolerated if not supported by Hitler. Hindenburg spent Whitsun at Neudeck where his neighbours convinced him that Brüning's few settlers on the land spelt a policy of what they called *Agrarbolschevismus*. After attending the

Disarmament Conference in Geneva towards the end of April, at the end of May Brüning resigned.

The man chosen by Hindenburgh and his 'court' as Brüning's successor was Franz von Papen. As German Military Attaché in Washington in the First World War he had got into notorious scrapes: more recently, in 1928, he had been expelled from the Centre Party. He was to do a great deal of mischief in the next few years. Papen now headed what was quickly nicknamed the Cabinet of the Barons; they were all nominees of the Hindenburg court. Schleicher was appointed Minister of Defence and Neurath went to the Foreign Office.

The first thing Papen did was to legalise Nazi activity. Hitler was not to be placated so easily. Knowing that Papen's Government was only supported by the dwindling Nationalist Party he attacked it as reactionary. When elections were held on 31st July the Nationalists lost ground again but the Nazis more than doubled their votes. On 20th July Papen had taken the dubious step of dismissing the Prussian Government, and, to the accompaniment of martial law, had declared himself to be Chancellor of the Reich and Reich Commissioner of Prussia at the same time. As the Nazis said, this saved them the trouble of suppressing the Prussian Government themselves. Otto Braun was away and Severing decided that with so much unemployment it would be useless to try to organise resistance as at the time of Kapp's abortive attempt in 1920. Many experts feel that 20th July, 1932, was the day on which the Weimar Republic committed suicide; organised resistance to the Nazis was almost impossible after this, they believe, but could still have been effective on that day.

In August 1932 Papen and his colleagues began to realise that they had sown dragon's teeth. On 9th August by emergency decree they announced severer punishment, including the death penalty, for political violence. That same night nine Storm Troopers murdered a Communist miner at Potempa in Upper Silesia in a particularly horrible way.

On 13th August Hitler was again received by Hindenburg who, however, refused to give him the Chancellorship with full powers as he demanded. The Nazi Press had, since 9th August, condemned the new emergency decree as not enough; on 14th August it attacked it as arbitrary. On 22nd August five of the Potempa murderers were condemned to death whereupon Hitler sent them an outraged telegram to express his " solidarity " with them. What he stood for was made clear to all the world that day, but liberal voices were still raised in liberal protest against the death penalty.

Desultory manœuvring for position continued. The Reichstag was dissolved once more, and elections held early in November in the midst of a traffic strike in Berlin which was backed by Nazis and Communists in collaboration. The unemployed were increasing less quickly this autumn than they had for three years and the Nazis lost two million votes. Nevertheless 50.7% of the new Reichstag deputies were enemies of the Weimar constitution. Papen resigned and early in December Schleicher took his place as Chancellor, hoping to win support from both the trade unions and the more moderate wing of the Nazis represented by Gregor Strasser. At the Disarmament Conference at Geneva the formula of German equality of military rights was accepted. People in Berlin began to breathe again. But the irrepressible Papen now chose to intrigue with Hitler against Schleicher. This was fatal because Hindenburg had a weakness for Papen, and Schleicher had made many enemies. One of the latter was General von Blomberg, a weak character susceptible to Nazi pressures who represented Germany at the Disarmament Conference. Later in January 1933 Hindenburg, shaken but still unwilling to give power to Hitler, agreed to do so when Blomberg, returning from Geneva, volunteered to be Hitler's Minister of Defence. Thus, almost by accident, Hitler became German Chancellor on 30th January, 1933: Papen was Vice-Chancellor and most of the Ministers were Nationalists.

Hitler had power: now he would use force still at first

with circumspection. He had demanded the right to hold
an election on the first Sunday in March. He and his
friends said there need never be another for they would
terrorise the German people into giving them full powers.
To start with he had only brought two Nazi colleagues into
the Government with him, Göring to be Minister-President
of Prussia controlling the police and Frick as Reich Minister
of the Interior. At the end of February the strange affair
of the Reichstag fire[1] gave the Nazi leaders a marvellous
pretext. They said the fire had been meant as the signal for
a Communist revolution, and they arrested whom they chose
and suppressed all criticism in the press. The S.A. were
enrolled as auxiliary police and beat up anyone obviously
hostile to their barbarous notions; such people began to
disappear into camps at Dachau, Sachsenhausen and Oranien-
burg.

The non-Nazi half—more than half—of the German nation
showed remarkable courage on 5th March, 1933. In spite of
the Nazi reign of terror the Socialists and Centre lost relatively few votes that day and the Nazis failed to win the 51%
they had gone all out for; they gained only 44.5% of the
votes recorded. Thus even in coalition with the Nationalists'
8% they controlled only 52.5% of the seats in the Reichstag.
By suppressing the Communist Party and deceiving and
frightening the Centre, Hitler passed an Enabling Act with
the necessary two-thirds majority in the Reichstag on 23rd
March: only the Socialists opposed it. He could now decree
whatever he chose. It took him another fifteen months to
consolidate his power to his own satisfaction, and to speed
up re-armament, inside Germany now, not in Russia. He
dissolved all organisations that stood in his way, the trade
unions especially: the autonomy of the *Länder* was suppressed, Germany becoming a highly centralised unitary

[1] It is usually supposed that the Nazis were responsible for this,
but it is possible that the young Dutch half-mad revolutionary,
Marinus van der Lubbe, who was charged with the crime, fired the
Reichstag alone. See F. Tobias. *The Reichstag Fire*, 1963.

state, ruled by the Nazi *Gauleiter*. It became impossible to pursue any profession or practise any art without conforming to Hitler's standards; anyone with a Jewish grandparent was excluded from all office. The flowering of new art and literature in the Weimar period was killed by the frost of National Socialism. On 10th May, 1933, the Nazis ceremonially burnt all the books they could think of by writers of whom they thought ill. Nazis were put in key positions, Goebbels as Minister of Propaganda, Himmler, the chief of the S.S., in command of all police organs which were reorganised under the control of the Secret State Police (*Geheime Staatspolizei* or *Gestapo*). Although a number of industrialists had helped Hitler, particularly as they lost faith in Hugenberg, they were now subjected to arbitrary interference whereas in the days of the Weimar Republic they were sometimes Ministers and in any case had done very much as they chose; then the state and the trade unions had only restricted their authority to a negligible extent, but now the Nazi state dictated to them.

In the last resort Hitler was appointed Chancellor because Blomberg, and his right-hand man, the keenly pro-Nazi General von Reichenau, wished it, after Schleicher (whom they disliked) had turned against him. Thus he owed a debt to the chiefs of the *Reichswehr* as he also did to the S.A. and their chief, Ernst Röhm, who had intimidated all Germany, including if only indirectly the chiefs of the *Reichswehr*. One of Hitler's cleverest operations was then to destroy his dependence on Army and S.A. at one and the same time. He allowed the secret police to suggest to each that it was plotting against the other. Then suddenly on 30th June, 1934, he used Army assistance to arrest Röhm and all the outstanding S.A. leaders who were shot by S.S. men : during that same week-end everyone still at liberty whose existence Hitler found irksome was murdered. In this way he disposed of Schleicher and Gregor Strasser and of two protégés of his own Vice-Chancellor. These two had helped Papen to criticise the Nazi régime in an interesting speech he delivered at Marburg University on 17th June. Thus the Army was made to condone a week-end of massacre. In July Hitler declared that his will had the force of law and that he had saved Germany on 30th June: this gave a death-blow to the pre-Nazi judicature which, in spite of its Wilhelmine attitude—perhaps because of it—had acquitted three Bulgarian Communists (including Dimitrov) arrested on the charge of having helped to fire the Reichstag. When Hindenburg died in August 1934, by pre-arrangement with Blomberg Hitler became President, though he never used the title: each soldier in the German Army now swore an oath of fidelity to the *Führer* and *Reichskanzler* personally.

The effect of Hitler, the Austrian Pan-German, becoming Chancellor of Germany stimulated the aspirations and grievances of all the Germans outside Germany, the *Auslandsdeutsche*. Although some individuals preserved their sanity, they were apt to be reproached as traitors by the rest of their group, whether it were Germans in Poland, Czechoslovakia, Yugoslavia or Roumania. Most disturbed by the Nazi *Machtergreifung* were the Germans of Austria whom Nazi propagandists henceforward addressed as if they were citizens of Nazi Germany. Yet the Germans of Austria were more divided than the German minorities elsewhere because the Austrian Socialists (Pan-German though they in a sense were) now inevitably became hostile to the *Anschluss*. The Christian Social Party, though its position was always befogged by phrases about a common German civilisation, felt some suspicion towards Hitler; the small Legitimist Party was of course opposed to him, as was also the important Jewish intellectual élite of Vienna. On the other hand upholders of the *grossdeutsch* spirit of the Austrian Universities and the Austrian tradition of German dominance in *Mitteleuropa* applauded Hitler; this was in addition to the direct approval of the Austrian Nazi movement.

In 1932 the Lausanne conference had organised a fresh loan to Austria in return for the dismissal of Schober and his ideas. In May the young Christian Social Minister Engelbert

Dollfuss became Austrian Chancellor, with a certain majority of only one in the Chamber. In July the Triestine, Suvich, was appointed Mussolini's right-hand at the Italian Foreign Office. In January 1933 the Austrian Socialists made public the fact that old Italian arms had been sent from Italy to the Austrian arms factory at Hirtenberg partly to be used by the *Heimwehr*, partly to be sent on to Hungary : Starhemberg, it seemed, had arranged this with Mussolini. Thus by the time of Hitler's coming to power the Austrian authorities were beginning to rely upon Italian Fascist support : they were more than ever estranged from their own Socialists at a moment when all Austrians had a new reason to hold together.

The Four-Power Pact between France, Italy, Britain and Germany made in June 1933 seemed to establish some kind of truce, though Austria was greatly disturbed by Nazi agitation and terrorism. Hitler had nominated Habicht, his *Gauleiter* in Wiesbaden, to be Inspector of the Austrian Nazis, and then at the same time the German Press attaché in Vienna, in order to organise disturbances. In October the Four-Power Pact fell to pieces when Germany left the League of Nations after being asked to show patience over her "equality of (military) rights." By this time Mussolini was urging Dollfuss, who had dismissed the Austrian Parliament as unworkable in March 1933, to suppress the Austrian Socialists. When it came to the Civil War of 12th to 16th February, 1934, it seems likely that the first shot was fired by the Socialists in Linz, but it had been made clear enough to them by the then Vice-Chancellor, Fey, that they were about to be attacked. Most of the fighting was in the working-class areas, Floridsdorf especially, of Vienna, the workers' flats being bombarded : after this new non-Socialist municipal officials were imposed upon Vienna. The memory of February 1934, more than thirty years later, still reconciles the hostile parties of the coalition government of the Second Austrian Republic. At the time the civil war was suicide. The Nazis triumphantly mocked at brutal Dollfuss who shot down the workers. When Dollfuss launched his corporate state on 1st May it had a hollow ring. Many rank and file Austrian Socialists, always a little more racial in attitude than the German Socialists, felt Hitler was better than Dollfuss and the priests. Traditional Austrian contempt for Italians discredited Dollfuss' dependence on Mussolini. When Hitler first met Mussolini at Stra and Venice on 14th and 15th June he knew that his own position was stronger than the world believed. At the end of July, when his agents in Vienna had murdered Dollfuss but failed to seize the Government, Hitler's relations with Mussolini reached their nadir; Italian troops moved towards the Brenner frontier and the Italian press denounced the Nazis. This was humiliating for Hitler but not decisive.

Thanks partly to assistance from the Italian Legation to the Austrian Government the Nazi *putsch*, which cost Dollfuss his life, failed otherwise. The Nazis had planned to murder the whole Austrian Cabinet, but its meeting was postponed so that Dollfuss was the only victim. The whole attempt had been touch and go, for many in the Austrian Police and Army were uncertain as to the loyalty they felt. Miklas, the Austrian President, now appointed Kurt von Schuschnigg to succeed Dollfuss, with Starhemberg as Vice-Chancellor again. Schuschnigg represented the clerical trend, and Starhemberg the *Heimwehr*; the latter consisted of Austrians not wholly hostile to Hitlerism but yet wishing to preserve the identity of Austria. Schuschnigg's more mystical attitude was difficult to define or comprehend.

One of the strangest things about this phase of Austria's history was the appointment of Papen, immediately after he had been in disgrace with Hitler for his speech at Marburg on 17th June, to be the Führer's special envoy to Vienna. Papen stood for cultural pressure and economic penetration rather than the open use of force by Germany against Austria. By now the industrial workers, largely concentrated in Vienna but also in some provincial towns such as Steyr and near the iron mines of Styria, were sullen, or they defected to the Nazis.

The Rome Protocols of March 1934, however, helped the Austrian timber trade, and altogether Austria's economic situation improved. Indeed the Nazi contention that an independent Austria was not economically viable became out-dated, although as propaganda it continued to be repeated. This thesis was due not least to the Dutchman, Rost van Tonningen, who was the financial representative of the League of Nations in Vienna. Later, in the war, he became second in command of the Dutch Nazis.

Chapter V

THE DECLINE OF FRANCE
1933-6

I CRISES OF FEBRUARY AND OCTOBER
1934

Financial and economic collapse had been dramatic in Vienna and Berlin in 1931 : in September sterling had been devalued. France had appeared less vulnerable. In fact the depression attacked her more slowly but not less profoundly. The Austro-German Customs Union and the Japanese defiance of the League of Nations in Manchuria in 1931 had shocked French public opinion : ministries changed hands more often now. Then suddenly Hitler was in power in the winter when French unemployment figures shot up. France was ominously split from 1933 onwards. The left declared itself against everything for which Hitler stood, but on the right the industrialists and the patriotic leagues began to search for a French Mussolini or Hitler : even the French Socialist Party produced its National Socialists such as Marcel Déat. In 1933 the Veterans' Association of the *Croix-de-Feu* decided to recruit younger people who would be called *Volontaires Nationaux* (VN). The leader of the *Croix-de-Feu* was Colonel de la Rocque. " He was not a good speaker and he wrote badly, but he inspired confidence and his troops believed in him : they seemed willing to be led towards a goal which he was careful never to define." He really seems not to have known what he wanted.

On Christmas Eve 1933 a municipal banker was arrested at Bayonne for malpractices : he declared that the Vice-Mayor, Garat, was responsible. A day after Garat's arrest, on 8th January, 1934, a crook called Stavisky killed himself. It turned out that he had enjoyed considerable protection in high places. The Chamber met on 9th January and the battle was joined. The deputy Philippe Henriot accused Eugène Raynaldy, the Minister of Justice, of irregularities, and on 27th January the Prime Minister, Chautemps, and his Cabinet resigned. The ever maladroit Daladier undertook to form a new government, causing a storm by transferring Jean Chiappe, the Prefect of the Paris Police, unloved by the Socialists, to be Resident-General in Morocco (which Chiappe refused), and making another police official director of the Comédie Française. Indignation became feverish. On 6th February in the Chamber Daladier gained a vote of confidence after furious protest and much skirmishing, and the Chamber rose at 8.30 p.m. Since two o'clock however, Paris had seemed full of rioters demanding the Government's resignation. Between 7.30 and 8 p.m. it was reported in the Chamber that the police were shooting. The next day it was known that 170 civilians had been injured and six killed, while 412 police of different categories had been wounded. Well-known Republican figures like Herriot only just escaped being thrown into the Seine. According to the report drawn up by a Commission of Enquiry in 1946: " February 6th was a revolt against Parliament, an attack against the régime. It was hoped through a popular rising to disperse the deputies, to seize the Chamber and proclaim at the Hôtel de Ville of Paris an authoritarian government." This intention has, however, been questioned more recently. Certainly important industrialists such as Ernest Mercier (in control of the key commodities of the period, electricity and petrol) had been preparing for action since early in 1933, and de la Rocque afterwards claimed that he could have seized power. Disturbances all over the country continued for days and a general strike was called for 12th February. By 9th February, however, the former President, Gaston Doumergue, had emerged from his retirement to form a government of national union: he achieved the essential combination in that both Herriot of the left and Tardieu of the right (who was suspected of encouraging the 'patriotic' leagues) agreed to serve in it: the veteran Minister, Louis Barthou, went to the Quai d'Orsay and Marshal Pétain to the War Office.

The French crisis of 6th February, 1934, paralysed France internationally; in particular many believed that the Austrian Socialists would not have been so easily destroyed otherwise. The encouragement provided to Hitler and all enemies of the Treaty of Versailles was immense. Internally it was notable none the less that, unlike that of Weimar, the French Republic had survived: on the other hand it was clear that certain constitutional reforms were overdue while the economic outlook was bleak.

Before rising for two months in the middle of March the Chamber appointed an all-party Commission of forty-four members to reform the state of France; they did good work, some changes being proposed which were adopted after 1945. Several administrative adjustments were made at once by decree, but the vital constitutional reforms which were proposed were constantly delayed. Although Doumergue adopted a policy of direct contact with the people by broadcasting, confidence sagged again: it was not reinforced by the frequent, highly justifiable demands for the devaluation of the franc made by a clever Radical deputy called Paul Reynaud.[1] While the Leagues continued to agitate, Socialists and Communists drew together in a " *front commun* " against the Government.

The most brilliant member of this Doumergue Government was Louis Barthou, the contemporary of Briand and Poincaré. From the Quai d'Orsay, in spite of his seventy-two years and the despair in his heart,[2] he revivified French foreign policy. He travelled to Czechoslovakia: he visited Poland whose non-aggression pact signed with Germany in January 1934

---

[1] The French, followed by the Swiss, the Dutch and others, devalued their currency in 1936. See below.

[2] See Geneviève Tabouis: *Vingt Ans de " Suspense" diplomatique* (1958) describing a conversation between Barthou and Alexis Léger shortly before Marseilles.

had caused dismay in France. He was partially successful in re-asserting French friendship with Poland; for he was able to encourage the Poles to make a non-aggression pact with Russia, and spoke in favour of the Russians joining the League of Nations which took place in September 1934. An eastern Locarno began to become credible. In order to take advantage of Mussolini's annoyance with Hitler over Austria Barthou decided that he must first re-emphasise French fidelity to Yugoslavia : King Alexander was therefore invited to visit France in October 1934. Barthou went to meet him at Marseilles on 9th October. A Macedonian revolutionary incited by a fanatical group of Croats far to the right of Maček assassinated the King, and Barthou was struck down at the same time. " These were the first shots of the Second World War," Lord Avon has written.

The murder at Marseilles was one of the most appalling events of this inter-war period and it was most injurious to France which had been unable to protect its royal visitor; Barthou's death was said to have been due only to delay in supplying medical care. Albert Sarraut resigned as Minister of the Interior, and the soiled and sinister figure of Laval moved from the Colonial Ministry to the Quai d'Orsay : according to Madame Tabouis, who must have been present, he told the press that he intended to come to terms with Germany as well as Italy. The days of the Doumergue Cabinet were now numbered and it scarcely needed Herriot's personal dislike for Doumergue to bring it down on 7th November. A Flandin ministry succeeded, not really very different in membership; although the Minister of the Interior (Marcel Régnier) had forbidden de la Rocque to let his people demonstrate over the change of government, the internal condition of the Republic remained deplorable. Bitter rivalries, however, between Maurras, La Rocque and other rightist leaders, kept its enemies divided.

The immediate question of the day was that of the Saar. It has been seen that, according to the Treaty of Versailles, the Saar coalmines had been ceded to the French state, and the Saar territory, economically linked with the ore of Lorraine, had been placed under the rule of a Commission of the League of Nations for fifteen years. At the end of this period, that is in January 1935, the Saarlanders were to vote between returning to Germany, becoming French or preserving the *status quo*. Only a few French people could be expected to vote for France. But since Hitler had been Chancellor of Germany the Socialists and the small group of Communists had begun to support the *status quo*. It was a strongly Catholic area and during 1934 some Catholics in the Saar also began to feel doubtful about the return to a Germany which had become National Socialist. Goebbels staged a tremendous propaganda campaign with the distribution of cheap wireless-sets in the Saar. The League of Nations might promise that voting would be secret, said the *Flüsterpropaganda*, but the Nazis would know exactly how every Saarlander voted—let them beware. When Max Braun, the Socialist leader in Saarbrücken, preached support of the *status quo*, meaning, it was obvious, only for the duration of Hitlerism, the Nazis denounced him as an appalling traitor who would mislead simple people to vote away German territory forever. On the morning of the plebiscite on Sunday 13th January the German wireless announced that Max Braun had run away to France: he drove through the streets of Saarbrücken in an open car to little purpose—people said that must be an impostor.

Thus, although there was no German *coup de main* against the British, Italian, Dutch and Swedish troops who protected the plebiscite personnel of the League of Nations, there was a 90% vote for Germany. No one can say what it might have been without Nazi terrorism: certainly well over 50%, so what did the inflated figure matter? It mattered a good deal, for it justified the boasting of Hitler and Goebbels, humiliated the French and alarmed non-Nazi Germans in Austria and elsewhere in Central and Eastern Europe. Although the League of Nations managed the whole affair, the outcome was unflattering for its representatives.

II THE ITALIAN ATTACK ON ETHIOPIA AND THE RE-MILITARISATION OF THE RHINELAND
1935-6

On 15th March, 1935, the French Chamber debated the prolongation of military service in France to two years. Paul Reynaud had discussed the whole matter with a Colonel de Gaulle who had made clear to him that, since the French Army could not rival the German one in numbers, it should aim at surpassing it in quality. Already the Treaty of Versailles had helped the Germans to a highly professional army. "The French problem," Paul Reynaud said in the debate, " is to create a specialised corps, capable of reacting in lightning fashion to any attack. We have a policy; what we need is the army to carry it out. And this policy is general international assistance and solidarity. Does anyone believe that this assistance can be limited to passive defence of our own territory while Herr Hitler marches about the length and breadth of Europe? The slowness of intervention means the facilitation of aggression." The Chamber voted by 350 to 196 for the Government and against the advice of Reynaud and de Gaulle.

On 16th March, the very next day, Hitler defied the military clauses of the Treaty of Versailles, reintroducing conscription into Germany; there were to be twelve Army Corps or thirty-six divisions. Herriot now exerted all his special influence as the first French Premier to have recognised the U.S.S.R. to bring to fruition a military pact, within the framework of the League of Nations, with Russia : this was signed on 2nd May, 1935. If either power were attacked by a European state the other would come to its assistance; Stalin now caused the French Communists to drop their hostility to the French Army bill at last. With the meeting of French, Italian and British representatives at Stresa in April, Germany seemed to be encircled or contained, although only until the Anglo-German naval treaty on 18th June. Municipal elections in France on 5th May strengthened the tendency towards co-operation between Radicals, Socialists and Communists in France, but the emergent *Front Populaire*, as the *Front commun* had become, caused capital to be withdrawn from France, worsening the country's economic condition.

Thus the rift in French political life continued to be profound. When Laval succeeded Flandin as Premier in June 1935 he attempted to deal with the economic crisis by decrees which were angrily attacked from the left. His attitude of condonement towards Mussolini's attack on Ethiopia in October 1935 increased the indignation felt against him, and soon after the débâcle of the Hoare-Laval Plan he was forced to resign. A ministry headed by Albert Sarraut at last saw the suppression of the *Action française* and of the *Camelots du Roi*: Charles Maurras, who had published an odious attack on the Socialist leader, Léon Blum, on 9th April, 1935,[1] was condemned on 21st March, 1936, to four months' imprisonment for incitement to murder. On 27th February the Chamber had ratified the Franco-Soviet Pact; the Senate followed suit which gave Hitler his pretext for re-militarising the Rhineland. The French parliamentary election in April and May brought an increase of forty-nine Socialist deputies and sixty-two Communists, although the Radicals lost: this heralded a government of the *Front populaire* led by Léon Blum, a Parisian Jew of great intellectual distinction. Blum took office on 4th June in time to be faced with the outbreak of the Spanish Civil War. It is probably worth noting that

[1] Maurras had written in the *Action française* of Blum:
"*C'est un monstre de la République démocratique. Détritus humain, à traiter comme tel . . . C'est un homme à fusiller mais dans le dos.*" In prison Maurras lived as comfortably and freely as Hitler in his German prison in 1924. See E. Weber. *Action française.*

Déat, the National Socialist, lost his seat in 1936, while the former Communist, Doriot, went into alliance with the bitterest enemies of the *Front populaire*.

III ITALY, GERMANY AND THE ANSCHLUSS

In these years Fascist Italy may be said to have matured. Mussolini in 1932 had committed himself to a definition of Fascism for which "the state is an absolute before which individuals and groups are relative." It should be noted that in 1931 the poet, Lauro De Bosis, lost his life in a flight to Rome to drop anti-fascist leaflets there. It should be noted that several of the country's most distinguished professors refused to take the oath imposed upon them by the Fascist state in that year. On the whole, however, Italy had settled down to Fascism, which, in its turn, tolerated the hostile criticism of the philosopher, Croce, and his pupils, a dissident intellectual centre in Naples.

In some ways the world depression suited Mussolini since it justified the *autarchia* which he wished in any case to adopt : further it justified the state control of the economy which the Fascists were endeavouring to establish. The economic troubles of Central Europe seemed to give Italy new opportunities to extend her influence, particularly over Austria and Hungary. The Rome protocols of March 1934 arranged for Italy to provide a much-needed market for their goods. It has been seen that in this year Mussolini took the initiative in championing Austrian independence against Hitler. The threat from Germany appears to have persuaded him to hasten his preparations for expansion at Abyssinian expense : certainly from 1934 onwards he was mainly preoccupied with the Abyssinian question. Much depended upon the attitude of the French masters of the Maghreb, powerful in the Middle East and with a key position in East Africa in French Somaliland. What would Barthou have said to Mussolini? Might he not have found a formula? But he was killed and it was Laval who went to Rome in his stead at the beginning of 1935. There on 7th January an agreement was signed according to which Italy made notable concessions, but Mussolini presumed that Laval was giving him in return a free hand in Ethiopia when Laval was almost certainly thinking only in terms of Italian economic penetration. The tripartite meeting at Stresa did nothing to disabuse Mussolini: conscription in Germany spurred him on. In February and March 1935 two divisions of Italian infantry had been shipped to Africa and by the end of May nearly a million Italians were under arms.

Opinion in France and Britain, upon which their governments genuinely depended, was deeply pacifist: in Britain, particularly, there was a sincere desire to make the League of Nations work without fully apprehending, as the peace ballot in June 1935 demonstrated, that it could not be worked by pacifism alone. In Britain, however, there was a tendency to condone German misdemeanours or to protest far less over threats to a member of the League like Austria than those to a member like Ethiopia. Was it instinctive naval rivalry with Italy when the French instinctively dreaded the new German Army? On 18th June, 1935, the British naval agreement with Hitler seemed to the French an act of supreme treachery, and to Mussolini, receiving Eden to discuss Ethiopia a few days later, an act of folly. His determination was clinched; at the beginning of October Italy attacked Ethiopia.

Within a few days Italy was condemned as an aggressor by the League of Nations and the question of sanctions against her was raised. This made it easy for Mussolini to arouse Italian enthusiasm for the Ethiopian war, the Fascist Grand Council denouncing sanctions as a " plan to suffocate the Italian people economically." Meanwhile De Bono's army had captured Adowa and advanced to Makalle by 8th November, 1935. Mussolini, wishing to push more quickly ahead, sent Badoglio to replace De Bono. In December Laval, together with Baldwin's new Foreign Minister Sir

Samuel Hoare, worked out a compromise which was however indignantly rejected by British public opinion, to the marked relief of Hitler. It seems possible that Mussolini would have accepted it. When it collapsed he was naturally more aggressive than before. On 12th January, 1936, Badoglio began the advance which ended in the Italian capture of the enemy capital, Addis Ababa, on 5th May. "On 9th May, 1936, Mussolini from the balcony of the Palazzo Venezia in Rome proclaimed to a delirious crowd the annexation of Abyssinia and the assumption by the King of Italy of the title of Emperor of Abyssinia. It was the moment of his life in which he savoured his greatest triumph . . . possibly for the first time he was enjoying the unqualified admiration and support of the whole Italian nation "[1]—well, nearly the whole.

In the meantime, after threatened isolation in the spring of 1935 and then again at the time of the Hoare-Laval plan, Hitler had staged his biggest challenge so far to the Western Powers. On 22nd February, 1936,[2] it was conveyed to Mussolini from Berlin that Hitler intended to emasculate the Franco-Soviet Pact by re-militarising the Rhineland in the spring of 1936—until then he had planned this move for spring 1937. Hitler originally suggested that Mussolini should be the first to denounce the Franco-Soviet Pact as a violation of the Treaty of Locarno, the *Führer* then appearing to follow his lead. In spite of his anger over sanctions Mussolini did not fall in with this insinuation. In fact the French Chamber ratified the Franco-Soviet Pact on 27th February by 353 to 164, and the Senate followed suit with a bigger majority on 12th March. Hitler moved on 7th March in reply, it seemed, to the ratification of the Pact by the Foreign Affairs commission of the French Senate on 5th March, 1936. It was Hitler who was breaking the Treaty of Locarno, although he had himself undertaken more than once to observe it. His military advisers were opposed to ill-prepared amateurish German soldiers being

[1] I. Kirkpatrick. *Mussolini.* p. 317.
[2] D.G.F.P. series C. vol. IV. no. 579.

sent into the hitherto de-militarised zone. The friction between Paris and London over the Abyssinian war, however, made this an irresistible moment for Hitler to take the risk; perhaps he knew with his sixth sense that British popular opinion, being incensed against Mussolini, would be lenient towards Hitler's "moving troops about in his own country," and it was impossible for Eden, now British Foreign Secretary in succession to Hoare, to convey to his public the menace and the treachery involved in Hitler's action. Thus France was left without support from Italy or Britain or Belgium.[1] The French Prime Minister at the time was Albert Sarraut again, with Flandin at the Quai d'Orsay. It is only right to add that Sarraut, having made his famous speech about not exposing Strasbourg to the fire of German guns, found his own generals, including his Minister of War, Maurin, as unhelpful as his allies: even among his cabinet colleagues there was indecision, division, hints that the elections were too near. The accounts differ as to which Ministers stood firm; it is not questioned that Sarraut himself and Georges Mandel, who had been Clemenceau's Secretary, favoured strong French action. After futile inter-Allied discussions in Paris the Council of the League of Nations met in London where the Nazi Ribbentrop, about to be Ambassador there, represented Germany; on 19th March it was confirmed by the Council that Germany had broken her treaty obligations, but no practical measures were suggested by which she might be penalised.

On 7th March, 1936, Hitler added to his announcement that he had invaded the Rhineland a statement that elections to the Reichstag would be held on 29th March. In the plebiscite and elections held on 12th November, 1933. when Germany had left the League of Nations, and again in the plebiscite held to confirm Hitler's succession to Hindenburg on 19th August, 1934, the pro-Nazi vote had been just about 95% of the whole, leaving five to six million hostile votes. On 29th March, 1936, after a campaign of propaganda which surpassed anything staged even by Goebbels and his

[1] See Avon. *Facing the Dictators*, pp. 334, 338.

team hitherto, 99% of the Germans voted for Hitler. Now there were only 543,926 hostile votes, the highest proportion being as usual in Hamburg, with Berlin second on this roll of honour. The French Ambassador, who appreciated the tremendous intimidation exerted by the Nazi Party, sent home one of his most brilliant despatches about the ' election ' of 29th March. " *C'est ce gain de cinq millions de voix,*" he wrote, " *qui, s'ajoutant aux 39 million déjà assurés, constitue aux yeux des nationaux-socialistes ce qu'il y a d'innouï, de prodigieux, de fantastique, de phénoménal dans le scrutin du 29 mars.*"[1]

Looking back nearly thirty years it is easy to see clearly what many people knew then, that the successful re-militarisation of the Rhineland, in destroying the framework and the hopes of the main inter-war period, opened the way to all Hitler's outrages. Treaty links between West and East Europe lost their meaning. Germany would have to be broken before the West could implement a guarantee to Poland, and by then it would be too late for other reasons. From 7th March, 1936, onwards Hitler could carry out the programme he had defined in *Mein Kampf* over ten years earlier. The League of Nations, which, in its first twelve years of life had achieved so much in so brief a period, in the Saar, in Upper Silesia, even in Danzig, was shaken by events in the Far East after 1931, then by the Abyssinian war. Until 1936, however, if immature it was alive and growing. From 1936 onwards nearly all the smaller powers lost faith in the League; they sought refuge either in neutrality, or, following Italy's example, by courting Germany; sometimes they compromised in courting only Italy. The last alternative allegiance could but be to Soviet Russia under Stalin who was now involving himself in hectic persecution of all the rival leaders of the Russian revolution.

Hitler's re-militarisation of the Rhineland did not, as some supposed, represent the first piece of Nazi-Fascist collusion;

[1] *Documents Diplomatiques français 1932-9*, series II. vol. I. no. 543.

Mussolini had been pre-informed but he had not been encouraging. Indeed, there is reason to believe that he was disagreeably startled. Not only would his troops not return to Europe in time to "contain" Hitler; thanks to the Ethiopian affair the Italian economy was becoming dependent on Germany, particularly for coal which was still all-important. Early in May 1936 Mussolini must just have learnt of the success of the *Front populaire*, and particularly of the Communists, in France when he appears to have sent a message to Vienna proposing that Starhemberg, by now paradoxically the most anti-Nazi member of the Austrian Cabinet, should be dropped from it. This duly occurred on 13th May, four days after the announcement of the new Italian Empire; it was as good a birthday as any other for the Rome-Berlin Axis. It was now fairly obvious that Italy would as quietly as possible drop her championship of Austrian independence[1] in order to satisfy Hitler who was ready to recognise the new Italian Emperor of Ethiopia, King Victor Emmanuel. There followed the Austro-German Agreement of 11th July originally planned as a press truce: it rendered Austria defenceless by allowing the big Nazi newspapers into Austria, by bringing two crypto-Nazis, Glaise-Horstenau and Guido Schmidt, into the Austrian Government, and in other ways. Thus Austria had lost her independence in all but name. In October Ciano, Mussolini's young son-in-law and new Foreign Minister, went to Germany. There secret Italo-German agreements, the October Protocols, were signed, pledging the two powers to co-operate against Communism in general and against the Spanish Republic in particular. On 1st November in a speech at Milan Mussolini first referred to the Berlin-Rome line as an "axis around which can revolve all those European states with a will to collaboration and peace." In September 1937 the Axis was strengthened by Mussolini's visit to Germany: Hitler felt sure now of Mussolini's support, and the impasse, as it

[1] Mussolini first tentatively offered to Germany to abandon Austria in January 1936.

seemed, in Spain, encouraged him to crystallise his plans.

Little did Europe know, but her fate was blue-printed by Hitler at his secret meeting with his military chiefs on 5th November, 1937, recorded five days later by Colonel Hossbach. Hitler always remained an old-style Austrian chauvinist of an extreme kind; he therefore regarded Czechoslovakia and Austria as the essential core of the *Mitteleuropa* which he envisaged as the basis of his Great German Empire; this was also, as we know, to extend eastwards into Russia. The crux of his statements on 5th November, 1937, was that "our first objective . . . must be to overthrow Czechoslovakia and Austria simultaneously."[1] As it happened the undermining of Schuschnigg's authority raced ahead of events in Czechoslovakia. In preparation for the forceful action he was planning, on 4th February, 1938, Hitler took over the Supreme Command of the German Army. On the same day the completion of his total power over Germany was illustrated by the dismissal of Neurath, a typical member of the old ruling-class, and his replacement as Foreign Minister by Ribbentrop, Hitler's obvious tool. A week later, on 12th February, Schuschnigg was summoned to visit Hitler at Berchtesgaden and was so fiercely threatened there by the Führer, who ostentatiously displayed the presence of Generals Keitel and Reichenau, that he provisionally agreed to accept Hitler's orders. They included the appointment of a Nazi, Artur Seyss-Inquart, as Austrian Minister of the Interior. On the evening of 14th February Hitler approved Keitel's suggestion that the Germany Army should be made to appear to be preparing action against Austria. On 9th March Schuschnigg, in spite of this mounting pressure from Germany, announced that on Sunday 13th March a plebiscite would be held throughout Austria of approval for a "free and German, independent and social, Christian and united Austria." Only people of twenty-four or over were to be entitled to vote. On 10th March, after four years in the wilderness, the Viennese Socialists expressed support for Schuschnigg—at last he had

[1] D.G.F.P. series D, vol. I, no. 19. (The Hossbach Memorandum.)

made advances to them. But it was all too late. Far too many
wooden horses had entered the Austrian Troy since July 1936;
police, army and administration were riddled with Nazis.
Mussolini conspicuously disapproved of Schuschnigg's plebiscite. Eden had been edged out of office by Neville Chamberlain some three weeks earlier; in Paris Blum was vainly trying
to form a new government after Chautemps' resignation.
Deserted on all sides Schuschnigg was overthrown by a stream
of impossible demands pouring in from Berlin—they were
sponsored by Seyss-Inquart. He abandoned his plebiscite and
resigned. In any case the German Army had instructions to
occupy Austria as from daybreak on 12th March, 1938. Those
who witnessed both the *Machtergreifung* in Berlin on 30th
January, 1933, and the Nazi occupation of Vienna on 12th
March, 1938, said that Vienna showed more enthusiasm although it had always been less Germanic in spirit than Innsbruck, Salzburg or Graz. The relatively large Jewish community in Vienna was subjected to all kinds of Nazi baiting.
On 10th April a plebiscite was held in Austria to sanction the
Anschluss with Germany before the Austrians had realised
that they were to be subjected to the highly centralised authority of Hitler's Germany. Thus the Austrians were conquered
before the Czechs; the second part of the Czech-Austrian
operation had yet to be performed.

Chapter VI

THE THIRTIES ELSEWHERE

I THE BALKANS AND HUNGARY 1929-36

The transitional period between the first signs of the great
depression and the advent of Hitler was in Yugoslavia the
period of the consolidation of King Alexander's dictatorship.
On 3rd September, 1931, a new constitution was proclaimed
which tightened royal control. A mockery was made of the
advanced political forms which the new Yugoslavia, far less
hampered by feudal survivals than the other new States, had
attempted to adopt; voting for the National Assembly or
Skupština was in future to be open instead of secret. The
only other country in Europe where open voting legally
obtained at this time was Hungary; it prevailed there only
outside the towns which, except for Budapest, were small,
and the urban population in a minority. It was thus in-
sured that in the villages the Hungarian peasants would
vote as the local magnates or gentry wished. Elections were
held in Yugoslavia on 8th November, 1931, in terroristic
conditions. All serious politicians who were not the King's
men tried to publish protests, but they were prevented from
every political activity and even from moving about the
country. The royal Government condoned the most brutal
police methods; declining prosperity, collapsing prices in
agriculture, did not increase its popularity. It should be
added that in the spring of 1931 the King had shown
interest in the Austro-German Customs Union, thus giving
the first sign of Yugoslav infidelity towards the Little Entente.
Despotic Serb though he was, it would be misleading to
ignore the fact that Alexander tried intermittently to feel his
way towards the Croats: more than once he discussed their

problems with the sculptor, Ivan Meštrović, who was a Dalmatian and a Croat patriot.

Although the Croats were inclined to damn the royal dictatorship as a matter of Serb savagery directed against them, serious opposition to the system of government arose in Serbia itself in 1932. It arose in the person of a Professor of Economics at Belgrade University, a man of peasant origins who came from Pirot near the Bulgarian frontier. His name was Dragoljub Jovanović and he devoted his life to the conception of a genuinely democratic peasant federation which should bind together all the Southern Slavs, Serbs, Croats, Slovenes, but also Bulgars. Jovanović was arrested because of the views he had expressed, abominably treated by the police, then condemned to a year's imprisonment. His protest and his ordeal created the nucleus of a real Yugoslav opposition, not merely regional, to the King; and it greatly influenced the students of Belgrade University which preserved a certain autonomy all the time. The royal dictatorship pushed many students beyond the ideas of Dragoljub Jovanović towards Communism. The Serbs, like the Bulgars, had ingrained Pan-Slav traditions, and young people were indignant over the King's refusal to recognise the U.S.S.R.; indeed no one did more to prepare the ground for Tito than King Alexander Karageorgević with the Tsarist mementoes he kept at his palace gates in Belgrade. In 1932 political conditions in Yugoslavia were perhaps the worst in Eastern Europe, with the possible exception of Russia itself. In their own ways, nevertheless, all the different Yugoslavs showed great spirit; this spirit was never broken.

The history of Bulgaria was less interesting because Stamboliski, the peasant leader there, was murdered much earlier, that is in 1923, and King and Army manipulated the political scene after that: thus there was no one in Bugaria to respond to Dragoljub Jovanović in 1932. Like Hungary, Bulgaria was negatively disturbing because it was revisionist in all directions. As in Hungary the emotions which this revisionism engendered could be exploited by the Bulgarian Government to ward off criticism; they could also be exploited by Communist agents, the more easily because of Bulgaria's Pan-Slav inheritance. It was a Bulgarian Communist, Georgi Dimitrov, who was the hero of the Reichstag Fire trial in Leipzig in the autumn of 1933; having been falsely accused he defied Göring in court. He was soon to be the head of the Comintern.

Between them Yugoslavia and Bulgaria, but also Greece, provided the framework of the Macedonian question, the unsolved riddle of Macedonian nationality—if there was such a thing—which in itself prevented the tranquillity of the Balkan peninsula. The major part of the territory which the nationally conscious Macedonians believed to be theirs had now been allotted to Yugoslavia though some was in Greece. Yet since the Bulgars regarded the Macedonians as a species of Bulgar, they claimed all Macedonia and protected the Macedonian patriots. Some of the latter had been organised since 1896 in the Internal Macedonian Revolutionary Organisation (or I.M.R.O.) which was thus able to direct its assassinations from Bulgarian territory. The Macedonian was almost more puzzling than the Ukrainian notion for there had been virtually no social development, no spread of education to create it; it seemed to illustrate the naked force of the political ideas of the French Revolution in their own right or else the facility with which one could equate them with primitive tribalism. Since the Macedonians aimed at cutting away the southern portion of Yugoslavia, they were the allies of any bitter enemy of the régime in Belgrade. The more the political struggle between King Alexander and his protesting subjects was exacerbated, the more the extremists among the latter were willing to collaborate with the Macedonian terrorists.

Hungary's revisionism was spiced in 1932 by the appointment of Gömbös, previously Minister of War, as Prime Minister. This put an end to the predominance of the magnates under Bethlen in favour of a new man, a soldier who was half German and highly susceptible to Nazi influence. Horthy in the background could only put a brake upon Gömbös' inclination to look to Hitler after 1933 rather than to Mussolini. On the other hand it should not be forgotten that the small and weak Liberal and Socialist Parties were tolerated in the Hungarian Parliament until 1944. With his Austrian way of thinking, Hitler was to take for granted that Hungary's wheat production and Hungary's control of the Danube should be at his disposal. His interest in Hungary was not diminished by the increase in her production of textiles and chemicals in the years of prosperity.

In Roumania, in view of the huge territorial problems which had to be dealt with, a fairly successful period preceded the depression and a notable redistribution of land gave many small peasants their own property. The peasant leaders in old Roumania and in Transylvania had combined in one National Peasant Party in 1926. Its leader, the Transylvanian, Maniu, who became Prime Minister in 1929, allowed the new properties to be sold which brought an increase in landless labourers again : in 1929 he also began to encourage foreign investment in Roumania.

Roumania was in fact the first country in Europe where crude oil was produced as far back as 1857, just before the Danubian Principalities were united. Now foreign capital flowed in, French, American, British and Dutch, oil having become one of the most important of all raw materials since the invention of the internal-combustion engine : Roumanian production at Ploesti rose to its inter-war maximum in 1936.

While this development made Roumania of particular interest in peace and in war, Yugoslav metals attracted much foreign investment. The copper at Bor financed by the French was important, the lead of Trepča financed by the British (both in Serbia) and the bauxite in Dalmatia. But there were many ores besides, including coal and iron. No individual in Yugoslavia had the capital to develop the various mines, so that the way was clear for French, British, Swiss and Czechoslovak investors. In spite of the fact that the Yugoslav state was the biggest investor of them all, there was thus in Yugoslavia, perhaps more than in the rest of Eastern Europe, what would nowadays be called a "colonial" situation. The East European peoples, poor though they were, had little class feeling, but they were emotionally anti-Russian in Poland, Hungary, Roumania, Finland and the Baltic States, and therefore willing to be told that Communism was bad because it was Russian. But in Czechoslovakia, Yugoslavia and Bulgaria popular feeling was pro-Russian; this was true even in Slovakia and Croatia, though less so than in Bohemia and Serbia. And since the régime in Yugoslavia had made itself hated and since it was demonstratively anti-Communist, opinion in Yugoslavia adopted a near Communist resentment against the foreign capital upon which the country's development depended. Here, too, the way was prepared for Tito. After the depression, as war came in sight in the middle 'thirties, Yugoslav metals increased in importance, but there was a change in capital investment.

The news of Hitler in power in Germany following the effects of the depression—above all the collapse of grain prices—at first caused the smaller powers, as it were, to close their ranks. In February 1934 with the motto of "the Balkans for the Balkan people," and at the instigation of Titulescu and the Turkish Government, Roumania, Turkey, Greece and Yugoslavia formed the Balkan Entente for mutual defence. In May 1934, partly in response to pressure from Belgrade, the Bulgarian Government expelled the Macedonian terrorists, and it appeared as if Bulgaria would join the Balkan Entente. In September 1934 the King of Yugoslavia visited Sofia. Exactly what this visit meant may never be clear. At the end of July, after the murder of Dollfuss, Austrian Nazis took refuge in Yugoslavia, while anti-Italian feeling there was fanned by the Italian troop movements towards the Brenner. It seems to have been Italian pressure on Bulgaria and Albania which prevented these two from joining the Balkan Entente. Soon after his visit to Bulgaria, Alexander of Yugoslavia set off on his ill-fated visit to France. Can his allegiance to France and the Little Entente have been shaken by Hitler's anti-Communism? We shall probably never know this.

Turkey, much more Asiatic than European now, was instrumental in bringing the Balkan Entente into being: she was also instrumental in bringing about the Conference of Montreux in 1936 which allowed her to re-militarise the Straits. Kemal Pasha cleverly kept on good terms with Turkey's traditional enemies, Russia and Greece. The Greeks had absorbed their Anatolian refugees, but their merchant fleets were hard hit by the world depression, and Greece itself with all the islands was painfully underdeveloped. After years of squabbling between Monarchists and Republicans the Monarchy was restored in 1935 only to tolerate the establishment of a dictatorship in the following year. The new dictator, General Metaxas, claimed to have eliminated a grave Communist danger; although this was suspected of being little but the rebelliousness of very poor people, developments during the Second World War showed that Communism had struck roots in Greece.

11 THE NORTHERN AND LOW COUNTRIES AND SWITZERLAND

Of the Scandinavian countries Denmark was hit by the great depression because she had built up a world market for her butter, bacon and eggs. Sweden, with her timber, iron-mines and electrical industries, was also severely hit, and when the Swedish match king, Ivar Kreuger, killed himself in 1932, there was widespread panic: from this situation the Swedish Socialists emerged reinforced because only theirs among the political parties had steered clear of Kreuger's wealth. Norway was less affected by the slump. The three countries, in spite of the tangle of their political parties and the high social demands upon their budgets, recovered with relative ease. They neither abandoned the welfare systems they had contructed nor their political democracy. While the Danes were faithful to their disarmament, developments in Germany after 1933 caused the Swedes to re-arm; like the Swiss they wished to defend their neutrality if it came to it. German re-armament, incidentally, made heavy if stimulating demands upon Swedish iron.

Holland and Belgium were in most ways more exposed and less united: together they were the most densely populated area of Europe which made them vulnerable; on the other hand each still ruled an extra-European empire, Holland mainly in Indonesia, Belgium mainly in the Congo. In Holland the normal clash between left and right was complicated by friction between Protestants and Catholics, in Belgium by friction between Walloons and Flemings. The slump had severe repercussions which worked out more slowly in Belgium. It was not until 1935, the year after King Albert's death, that the main crisis occurred there. After a policy of deflation had done no good a Cabinet of National Union was formed by Van Zeeland in March 1935; in it Liberal and Catholic Ministers were joined by Socialists such as Emile Vandervelde, who was President of the Second or Social Democratic International, and the Fleming, Henri de Man, a Marxist whose conception of Socialism was a tortuous one—so much so that when the war came he was willing to collaborate with the German occupying authorities. In April the Belgian franc was devalued by 28%. World economic conditions had by this time, it has been seen, largely recovered, and unemployment in Belgium now rapidly diminished. In Holland unemployment after 1931 increased Communist opinion; at this time, too, the first was heard of a small group of Dutch Nazis led by Mussert. The Dutch followed the Belgian example in devaluing their currency eighteen months later.

The most anomalous of all the West European States was Luxembourg. It had only some three hundred thousand inhabitants, but its iron foundries were some of the most important on the Continent. In the last twenty years of the nineteenth century, after the Gilchrist processes had been adopted, Luxembourg had produced fantastic amounts, more than half its population being employed in the foundries; after 1900 the rate of increase had dropped but it was still high in 1914. Whereas the Swiss by then knew very well that they were neither German nor French, the history of Luxembourg was such as to make its bi-lingual inhabitants still uncertain. In the eighteenth century they had belonged to the Habsburgs, then from 1795 to 1815 to France. From 1815 to 1867 they were attached to the kings of Holland, but Luxembourg was garrisoned by Prussia and was from 1842 a member of the Prussian *Zollverein*. In 1867 the Powers guaranteed the neutrality of Luxembourg, the Prussian garrison being withdrawn. Between 1871 and 1914 Luxembourg remained in the German Customs Union. During the war it was occupied and exploited by the Germans. Then in January 1919 the Allies expressed a certain displeasure towards the Grand Duchess, Marie Adelaide, who abdicated in favour of her sister Charlotte: the latter reigned as Grand Duchess of Luxembourg until she resigned in favour of her son, Jean, in 1964. A referendum in September 1919 gave a majority in favour of economic union with France. The French, however, refused, and on 1st May, 1922, Luxembourg entered into a customs union with Belgium. Soon after this, thanks to its able Foreign Minister, Bech, Luxembourg was allowed to join the League of Nations. Luxembourg was anomalous in every way. With its relatively huge industrial resources it did not seem highly industrialised because so small a population did not lose its roots in the land. It was on the contrary an example of how an area might be highly developed without being over-industrialised: consequently, though it felt the slump, it did not experience the shock felt by its bigger neighbours. It should perhaps be added that the owners of the most important iron foundry in Luxembourg were people of remarkable enlightenment.

Switzerland, also a highly industrialised country dependent on foreign tourists as well as on foreign markets, suffered from severe unemployment in the early 'thirties. Under Nazi influence some younger people grumbled over Swiss traditionalism or stuffiness. On the whole the German-Swiss recognised the Nazi menace to the independence of their country : by 1936, however, the French-speaking bankers of Geneva affected the slogan of "Rather Hitler than Blum." When, in that year, the Swiss Socialists for the first time approved military credits, the gulf between workers and middle class, which had yawned since the General Strike of 1918, began to narrow. In October 1936 the Swiss devalued their currency in the wake of France; this contributed to their economic recovery.

In the tiny Baltic States, depending as they did upon exporting farm produce, the world depression was perturbing, and after 1933 external pressures were intimidating. The three Republics drew together in a Baltic Entente in 1934, but the same years also saw the collapse of democratic government in Riga and Tallinn, and the establishment of dictators in each of them. In Lithuania—enfeebled by its unending feuds with Poland and Germany—democratic government had collapsed eight years earlier.

Finland had developed well in the 'twenties and was not unduly disturbed after 1929. Her most obvious trouble took the form of violent anti-Communist agitation here and there by the so-called Lapuans; in 1930 laws were passed against the Communists. In 1932, and later, the Lapuans and other pseudo-fascist bodies were suppressed, and the régime emerged with Scandinavian imperturbability.

III RUSSIA 1933-7

After the upheavals between 1928 and 1933, in 1934 Stalin "wavered between intensified repression and liberal gestures."[1] At any rate there was a pause for breath. The men of his own generation, though uneasy or distressed or shocked by what was happening, were too tired and too

[1] I. Deutscher—*Stalin.* p. 354.

loyal to the party to resist Stalin in any serious way, although the full force of his later reign of terror had not yet been approached. They believed that there was no going back and that if they could somehow criticise effectively this would be counter-revolutionary in any possible result. The next generation was beginning to think in the terms of revolutionary students in the nineteenth century. This led to the same kind of tragedy. In December 1934 Sergei Kirov, Stalin's man in Leningrad, was assassinated by a young Communist revolutionary called Nikolayev. Kirov had been sent to Leningrad to combat Leningrad's critical spirit which had, however, bitten him. This had made it easier for his murderer, for Kirov objected to excessive police protection. Kirov's death transformed Stalin into the monster of the great purges, for he now decided that every vestige of opposition to him, Stalin, must be crushed in the spirit of the worst Tsar but with greater skill.

For he provided cover for himself early in 1935 by asking his colleagues to help him to draft a new, enlightened constitution, to be named after him, Stalin. It was officially adopted in November 1936; in fact this constitution did not operate, but on paper it was, as it was called, "the most democratic in the world." As an experienced political prisoner himself Stalin knew how to destroy the human safety-valves of the Tsarist police system. The prisons were no longer the 'universities' of the revolutionaries, for political prisoners were not allowed to read, but were worked to death or nearly so. Mass trials were staged. They were used, not to provide the prisoners with a political platform, but by the police using threats and torture to jockey the accused into discreditable and humiliating confessions. The most important of these trials were those of Zinoviev, Kamenev and fourteen others (the Sixteen) in August 1936, of Radek, Sokolnikov and fifteen others (the Seventeen) in January 1937, and of Rykov, Bukharin and nineteen others (the Twenty-One) in March 1938. Nearly all the recent leaders of the Soviet world were thus indicted and slaughtered, not omitting the two police chiefs, Yagoda and Yzhov, who had provided the 'evidence' against most of the rest.

The whole horrible process was accompanied by other circumstances of which at least two must be emphasised. The continuing economic revolution necessitated the spread of literacy which occurred at an astonishing pace. At the same time literature and the arts were so shackled by Stalin as to become, in so far as they survived, farcical. Whereas revolutionary Russia had been in living and rewarding touch with the world outside Russia in the 'twenties, in the 'thirties she was cut off in what seemed an Asian isolation.

In June 1937 there took place in secret the trial of Tukhachevsky and others of the highest officers of the Red Army which Stalin had recently re-equipped with the status and discipline of Tsarist times. In this case there was the justification that Tukhachevsky and his colleagues had in fact decided that they must act against the mad dog, Stalin. It was also true that the Russian Army had long collaborated secretly with the Germans[1]; they did not break off the connection when Hitler came to power though the collaboration rather petered out. At first Stalin had been unsure what to make of Hitler in power, and in a sense he always remained so. It is interesting that Trotsky had no doubts. And it is perhaps worth emphasis that Trotsky, the arch-enemy of both, was murdered in Mexico in 1940, the period of the Soviet-German rapprochement. On the other hand it cannot be neglected that the great purges took place in the period between Hitler's re-militarisation of the Rhineland and the German annexation of Austria; thus they were possibly in part a reaction to developments in Germany. When Stalin had begun his dragonnading of the peasants Nazi propaganda did not seem to interest itself particularly; but now it made full use of the great purges to try to demonstrate that there were worse tyrannies than that of Hitler.

The murder of Kirov had followed closely upon the admis-

[1] See above p. 42.

sion of the U.S.S.R. to the Council of the League of Nations in September 1934. This astonishing change was followed by the treaties with France and Czechoslovakia in May 1935. Ironically enough the period of the purges synchronised with that initiated by the seventh congress of the Third International or Comintern in August 1935, when the policy—so useful to Hitler—of hostility to all "bourgeois" parties especially to Social Democrats, was reversed in favour of the idea of Popular Fronts. It was with the slogan of the Popular Front uniting all the parties on the left that Soviet Russia met the Civil War in Spain which broke out a month before the trial of the Sixteen and over four months after Hitler's march into the Rhineland.

Chapter VII

THE SPANISH CIVIL WAR
1936-9

Throughout the nineteenth century Spain and Portugal had signally failed to catch up with the rest of Western Europe: in the first quarter of the twentieth violence and instability had prevailed in both. The Portuguese had earlier lost Brazil but astonishingly maintained a hold over big territories in Africa where the Spaniards preserved only their Moroccan foothold and the Canary Islands. Both countries were wretchedly poor. After the murder of the King of Portugal and his heir in 1908 a Portuguese Republic was established in 1910. Between 1910 and 1926 Portugal experienced sixteen revolutions and forty changes of ministry. Then in 1928 the dictator of the day, General Carmona, persuaded Oliveira Salazar, a youngish Professor of Economics at Coimbra University, to become Minister of Finance. Salazar has often been regarded as a fortunate Schuschnigg. In 1933, having become Prime Minister in 1932, he provided Portugal with a corporative constitution; for better and for worse he created a narrowly Catholic authoritarian state which has lasted for well over thirty years. Thus stability was attained without any real conquest of Portuguese poverty. In May 1936 Salazar opportunely took charge of the Portuguese Ministry of War.

In so far as Spain had been industrialised this process had been centred upon Barcelona or the mining districts of the north: thus economic development had intensified the problem of Madrid's relations with the Catalans and the Basques. The industrial working-class, more persistently than the Italians or the French, tended to be anarchists or syndicalists, and many of them had been organised in the syndicalist *Confederación Nacional del Trabajo* or C.N.T. since 1911.

Within this body there existed the secret and extremist union of anarchists, the *Federación Anarquista Ibérca* or F.A.I. The workers were in the most bitter conflict with the rigid conservatism of the Spanish Church. A running fight with the Berbers of the Rif in Morocco added to Spain's troubles until 1927, and helped to justify the military dictatorship of General Primo de Rivera from 1923 to 1930. After his collapse confusion reigned and feeling mounted against the Monarchy. Municipal elections having been held in April 1931, and bringing strong Republican voting in the towns, King Alfonso XIII renounced the crown and went into exile. The great depression was unfortunately at hand. A liberal Government (headed by Zamora) took over and held national elections in June, "undoubtedly the fairest that had been held in Spain."[1] Apparently a big majority supported the liberal Republic and the Government proceeded to draft a liberal constitution which enfranchised both sexes. The new constitution was so unrelentingly anti-clerical that it split the Government itself : at the elections in November 1933 held according to this, the rightist parties including the Monarchists, did well, and of them the *Confederación Española de Derechas Autonomas* or C.E.D.A. based on Catholic Action and led by Gil Robles, emerged as the biggest party in the new Cortes. This was a clear rejection of the liberal constitution drawn up by the deputies of 1931 which was never implemented again. It was typical that, when in October 1934 members of the C.E.D.A. were included in a new Government, a general strike was called and there was insurrection in Catalonia and the Asturias; in the latter province it appeared to be successful, all the leftist parties, including the Anarchists, holding together for a time. So alarmed was the liberal Government that it sent the Foreign Legion led by General Franco to suppress the miners of the Asturias. Much revolutionary violence was more than paid for by the cruelties perpetrated by the Foreign Legion. This fresh rift between Left and Right has never yet been bridged. In Spain,

[1] Hugh Thomas. *The Spanish Civil War.* 1961. p. 45.

moreover, the rifts within the groupings were often profound
—on the right between Monarchists, Clericals and Primo de
Rivera's son, José Antonio, the founder of the *Falange
Española* in 1933, on the left between various kinds of
Radicals and Socialists, and the Anarchists, whose creed had
mostly forbidden them to vote so that they were electorally
concealed. The Communists were at this time still a small
group, but after the Comintern meeting of August 1935
they put forward the notion of a Popular Front in which all
the leftist parties should combine for the new elections to
be held in February 1936. The semi-Trotskyist and keenly
revolutionary Workers' and Peasants' Alliance, soon to be
renamed the *Partido Obrero de Unificación Marxista* or
P.O.U.M., although on the worst of terms with the Communists, also supported the Popular Front. The P.O.U.M.
was later the heart and soul of Republicanism in Barcelona
where it created perhaps the most enthusiastic atmosphere
during the civil war, the feeling that a social revolution had
really been achieved.

In the elections of 1936 the Popular Front obtained
4,176,156 votes, the National Front (Monarchists, Catholics,
landowners, etc.) 3,783,601; in addition the Basque Nationalists and some small moderate parties gained a little support.
The C.E.D.A. (within the National Front) was still the
largest party of all, next to it coming the Socialists and the
Republican Left, both within the Popular Front. After the
election the well-known radical, recently Minister of War,
Manuel Azaña, at first became Prime Minister, but was later
chosen to be President: he was the leader of the Republican
left.

The elections had been fairly orderly, but Spanish political
life had entirely failed to achieve stability since the departure
of the King. Chaos and violence prevailed; it seemed impossible to exorcize them, and one crime led to the next. On
13th July, 1936, the police murdered the Monarchist leader,
Calvo Sotelo, in reply to a murder of one of their officers,
Castillo. Three nights later General Franco left the Canary

Islands to lead his expedition against the Republican Government and thus to initiate three years of civil war in Spain. The Prime Minister of the day, Casares Quiroga, thought Franco's was only a rising in Morocco and at first refused to arm the people; already on 18th July Franco's followers were defying the government throughout Andalusia. After the customary burning of churches[1] in Madrid the Popular Front successfully asserted itself there, as it did in Barcelona. By 21st July the country was divided between the Republic, which dominated the south and east and the mining and Basque provinces along the northern coast, and the Nationalists in the rest of the country centred on Burgos. Already each side, in spite of all Spain's national pride, had not hesitated to appeal for foreign help. The Republican Government had on 19th July asked Blum, who had been in power only just over six weeks, for French assistance, while on the following day Franco's emissaries were on their way to Mussolini and Hitler. It was thanks partly to the aeroplanes provided by Italy and Germany that Franco's army in Morocco, some of it Arab, could be transported to Spain. In Germany Blomberg, Fritsch and the Wilhelmstrasse were scared of intervention; for Hitler, however, there was little question since Göring was eager to try out the Luftwaffe in Spain, and Canaris, chief of the *Abwehr* or Military Intelligence, had old Spanish links and approved of Franco personally. For Hitler, too, within less than a fortnight of the Austrian agreement which marked Mussolini's surrender to him, an action which involved, as he must have known it would, German-Italian co-operation, was precisely what he needed: it would bring to fulfilment the Italian alliance upon which he was determined. Salazar eagerly provided Portugal as a base to be used against the Spanish Republic whose success would menace all that he himself had achieved.

Mussolini and Hitler ostensibly justified their intervention chiefly as part of their battle against Communism. The Spanish Government was supported by Radicals, Socialists,

[1] This was an extraordinary Spanish habit, unthinkable in Italy.

Anarchists and a small Communist Party of whom the most picturesque character was the woman always referred to as *La Pasionaria*. What was to be the attitude of Stalin? His own tyranny was about to culminate in the Trial of the Sixteen (Zinoviev, Kamenev, Smirnov, etc.) in August 1936. In his foreign policy, however, it has been seen that he had switched away from hostility to Social Democracy, and, using Georgi Dimitrov, the head of the Comintern, to expound it, had changed right about to the championship of Popular Fronts, precisely in fact what the Spanish Government comprised. On the other hand he was anxious that his alliance with France should not lose its meaning in spite of Hitler's re-militarisation of the Rhineland, and he knew that the Popular Front in France aroused fierce antagonism. So he now did two things. He sent some of his ablest Communists, notably the Italian Togliatti, to Spain; there they were to use the new situation to strengthen the Spanish Communists, and in doing so weaken the Anarchists and Syndicalists and emasculate Anarchist plans for revolutionary reforms. At the same time Stalin decided to support the French initiative in favour of non-intervention.

When Blum was first approached by the Spanish Republican Government for help (the Spanish Government also asked the Germans to help it) he was obviously greatly tempted to comply; both his ideals and his interests seemed to dictate aid to Republican Spain, and some of his Radical colleagues, particularly Pierre Cot, agreed with the idea. But Herriot, as well as the French President Lebrun, felt this involved too serious a risk of European war and entanglement with all kinds of sinister violence in Spain: it involved also grave risks in France itself where the Right and the big industrialists preferred Franco to Blum. The latter was, it must be repeated, a life-long pacifist and susceptible to arguments against risking war over Spain when one had not risked it over the Rhineland. Blum, further, was at one with Alexis Léger, the Secretary-General at the Quai d'Orsay, in believing that France must before everything keep in step with Britain over the Spanish question. Although, later, British opinion was to show itself perhaps more emotional about Spain than about any other political issue of the period, Baldwin's government clearly could not, and would not, be anything but neutral. On 2nd August, therefore, the French proposed that France, Italy and Britain should formally agree not to intervene in Spain. Italy concurred equivocally on 21st August and Germany agreed to non-intervention on 24th August. The U.S.S.R. had agreed on 23rd August. Early in September the *ad hoc* Non-Intervention Committee was set up at French suggestion in London. The League of Nations was deliberately avoided since Germany no longer belonged to it, and Italy was very much on the way out after Abyssinia. However at the League Assembly in September 1936 the chief Spanish delegate, Del Vayo, protested against non-intervention on two grounds : first that in theory it penalised the lawful Spanish Government as severely as it penalised the rebels : second that in practice it penalised the Government more, because the Powers from whom it might have bought arms kept their word, while Italy and Germany broke theirs with enthusiasm.

In the middle of October 1936 Russia, which had hitherto sent only food and raw materials, began to send military aid to Spain. The Comintern busied itself with organising International Brigades to go there; the Yugoslav Communist, Josip Broz, was sent to Paris to help expedite volunteers to the Spanish front. One of Stalin's motives may well have been to clear Communist *émigrés* out of Russia, at the time of the purges, by sending them to Spain. The International Brigades were sent to Albacete half-way between Madrid and Valencia; here they were under the command of the French Communist, Marty, and two Italians, of whom one was Luigi Longo. The first Russian ships to bring arms to Spain synchronised with the arrival of the nucleus of the International Brigades of volunteers, when Russia was officially demanding that the Fascist countries should be forced to respect non-intervention. Stalin had one advantage over

Hitler and Mussolini in that the Spanish Government sent him payment in gold before the end of October.

On 1st October Franco was declared Head of State at Burgos; his government was recognised by Mussolini and Hitler as that of Spain on 18th November. In October, when Ciano visited Berlin he and the Germans regarded the fall of Madrid as imminent, but Russian help, which included aeroplanes, seems to have been decisive towards the end of the year in saving Madrid from the Nationalist Army after a long period of near siege and siege. The morale of the Nationalists was, however, maintained by the arrival of more substantial help from the Axis Powers, as they were now called. Nine Italian battalions of so-called volunteers under General Roatta assembled north of Malaga which they helped to conquer early in February 1937. In the middle of March 1937 complicated fighting north of Guadalajara involved several international elements; in addition to Spaniards on each side, there were Italians, and in the end the anti-Fascist Italians (they included Pietro Nenni) got the better of Roatta's army, to the intense chagrin of Mussolini. The battle of Guadalajara was one illustration of the way in which Spain was being treated as a military dress rehearsal, a " European Aldershot." The Fascists, however, mismanaged their tank warfare, so that they drew wrong conclusions.

Almost more insolent were the exploits of the German Condor Legion of airmen which dive-bombed Durango on 1st March, 1937, and Guernica on 26th April. The attack on defenceless Guernica, a small town which was the pride of the Basques, on a market day was phenomenally cruel; it proved to be a boomerang in the long run. The greatest painter of the age was a Spaniard, Pablo Picasso. Between 1st and 11th May, 1937, he painted his indictment of Guernica, a magnificent picture which was exhibited in the Spanish Pavilion at the Paris World Exhibition early in June 1937. In the long run this became the accepted verdict on Guernica and helped to defeat Hitler. " Did you do that?"

the German soldier gaping at the picture, after Southern France was occupied at the end of 1942, was said to have asked. " No, you did " was Picasso's and the world's reply.

Unlike Mussolini, Hitler was not concerned to bring about a victory for Franco; on the contrary it suited him that the Spanish Civil War should continue indefinitely since he and Göring found it marvellously convenient to try out the Luftwaffe at other people's expense. A second matter of importance to Hitler was to procure as much Spanish iron and other metals as he needed to prepare for war; this was a need which would continue too.

Meanwhile the British and the French had been trying to work out non-intervention in practice, and it had been made illegal to volunteer to serve in Spain after the end of February 1937. Arguments in the Non-Intervention Committee when the representatives of Italy, Germany or Russia were speaking tended to take the form of indignant denials on the part of whomever was the culprit of the day. The representatives of any of the three invariably approved of non-intervention just after they themselves had got substantial reinforcements through. A final scheme was agreed on 8th March, but did not come into operation until the end of April 1937 just after Guernica. Naval control around Spain was distributed between Britain, France, Germany and Italy, Russia mysteriously agreeing not to be represented—was Stalin distrustful of his admirals? " This plan seemed inevitably to the Republic to add insult to injury. Not only were Germany and Italy bringing arms to the Nationalists without abatement, but they were now allotted a task policing the prevention of this. The mockery was complete."[1] At the beginning of 1937 Eden, with the approval of Baldwin and Halifax, had done his best to put through a plan for control all round Spain by the British Navy, but when put before the British Cabinet it was vetoed by the First Lord of the Admiralty, Sir Samuel Hoare. This was just after the rather

[1] Hugh Thomas. *op. cit.* p. 395.

meaningless Anglo-Italian Gentlemen's Agreement of 2nd January, 1937, when the British hoped they had persuaded the Italians to withdraw their ' volunteers '. Eden, who himself in August 1936 still thought it worthwhile to 'set a good example' to Hitler and Mussolini, six months later seems to have been the only member of the British Government who had become aware of what was happening. "At the outbreak of the Spanish Civil War," he has written, "I had no political sympathy with either side, but only wished that the Spaniards should determine their own fate. As the war progressed, however, I became more concerned lest the insurgents should win, because the foreign powers backing them were themselves a menace to peace. From the early months of 1937, if I had had to choose, I would have preferred a Government victory."[1]

The summer of 1937 saw the fall of Bilbao and Santander and at last in October the Nationalists' conquest of Asturias, the elimination, that is to say, of the Republic in northern Spain. The Italians and Germans continued to play the *enfants terribles* of the Non-Intervention Committee which Eden described as a leaky dam but better than none. When Santander fell in August Mussolini blatantly telegraphed his congratulations to the Italian Commanders there. At this point Italian submarines were shamelessly aggressive in the Mediterranean, sinking a number of ships likely to help the Republicans. In September, therefore, the French and British met at Nyon and decided to use their own navies really to prevent this piracy: they were successful for a few weeks. After this Eden was increasingly paralysed by Neville Chamberlain who had become Prime Minister on 28th May, at about the same time as Juan Negrin succeeded Caballero as Premier of Republican Spain. Negrin was a brilliant doctor of medicine with the briefest political career behind him. He was brought into power, not because he was a Communist as people said, but because he considered it essential that the

[1] Avon. *Facing the Dictators.* p. 435.

Republican Government should get as much help as it could from the U.S.S.R. Negrin was sensible and competent, but his high-handedness made him enemies. In November the French frontier was pushed half open on the Republicans' behalf, though it was not officially thrown open until 17th March, 1938, immediately after the *Anschluss*.

It has been seen that on 5th November, 1937[1] Hitler still preferred the Spanish war to continue indefinitely, for it was basically demoralising to all those he regarded as his enemies, most of all to those with liberal beliefs in democratic government and international negotiation, indeed in any practical compromise which could reconcile conflicting interests. Mussolini would all along have welcomed an acknowledged Axis triumph, but Hitler probably preferred its postponement until after Munich or at least until after the *Anschluss*. The Civil War in Spain—its ruthlessness, its subjection of all more enlightened thought to Communist or Clerical or Fascist coercion—became a threat to be brandished at the heads of Schuschnigg and Beneš. The German S.S. weekly, *Der Schwarze Korps*, was full of ideas in the winter of 1936-7 for a second Spain in Czechoslovakia where German, Hungarian and Slovak 'volunteers' could easily be organised. And although Hitler and Mussolini had different aims in Spain, and the Germans sent there continued to despise the Italians they met, the Rome-Berlin Axis was fortified by the Spanish situation. The insolence and effrontery of Hitler and Mussolini in Spain impressed the increasing number of people in Europe who lacked leadership. Those who were repelled were bound to be discouraged too, and tired before the real war came. Thus the war of nerves, with its extension of real, hot war in Spain, worked out just as Hitler wished it should. It was characteristic of the year 1937 that in June the Italian anti-Fascist, Carlo Rosselli, who had declared on the wireless in Paris that "To-day in Spain, to-morrow in Italy" Fascism would be defeated, was

[1] See above.

murdered in France by Cagoulards, the new type of terrorists employed by the *Action Française* since 1936, now instigated from Rome. International enlightenment seemed to be at the mercy of an evil conspiracy. The day mockingly chosen for Rosselli's murder was the thirteenth anniversary of that of Matteotti.

In spite of the opening of the French frontier and Hitler's pre-occupation with the Czechs, and in spite of the Nationalists' failure to conquer Valencia in July, gradually Republican territory was shrinking in 1938. It is true that in that summer many people, such even as the sceptical Azaña, thought that the Republic had consolidated its position. With the Czech crisis in September there was hope for the Republic that the Spanish war would be absorbed into a general one. After Munich, however, Hitler and Mussolini, and Franco in their wake, had gained enormous prestige: Franco's fifth column of sympathisers within Republican Spain was greatly encouraged too. Stalin, humiliated and scared of the future (though not sufficiently so), withdrew the external Communist contribution to Spain, including the International Brigades. Negrin and others secretly tried for a compromise peace, but Franco would make no concessions. Early in 1939 his armies conquered Catalonia, and, by the end of March when Madrid had fallen, Republican resistance had become negligible. France and Britain had recognised Franco on 27th February and the Non-Intervention Committee dissolved itself on 20th April: the first French Ambassador to Franco was Marshal Pétain. On 19th May, 1939, the Nationalists' victory parade took place in Madrid, the Italians taking their place in it. On 22nd May at Léon there was a farewell parade for the Condor Legion.

From the Spanish Republican point of view the whole struggle had been for nothing. The experiences gained, apart from their value to the Axis, profited only the partisan fighters in the Second World War. Franco established a centralised and Catholic dictatorship, built upon merciless reprisals; the social programme of his Falangist brother-in-law, Suñer, who in August 1939 became his second in command politically, remained on paper, the more so since for years the country inevitably suffered from abject poverty. The stability of Salazar's régime in Portugal was reinforced by the more military character of Franco's rule in Spain : violence had ceased except in the unmerciful treatment of political opponents. Modern economic development lay in the distant future.

Chapter VIII

THE MUNICH AGREEMENT
1938

The economic depression did not originally hit Czechoslovakia so severely as it hit Germany and Austria because the Czechoslovak Republic was less dependent upon foreign loans and because Czechoslovak agriculture and industry were better balanced. Yet in another way the slump hit Czechoslovakia more gravely as well as later. For its German population was mainly engaged in vulnerable and in many cases inessential or unfashionable light industries, textiles, glass and so on, whose foreign markets were immediately destroyed. Thus the Sudeten German population was terribly impoverished just when Hitler's advent to power in Germany caused Nazi propaganda to become exuberant. Here was a fertile grievance to exploit. Another one soon ripened. The Sudeten Germans lived round the edges of Bohemia and Moravia. Hitler obliged the Czechs to arm more thoroughly, and this provided a welcome stimulus to heavy industry. But one does not develop armaments industries in frontier districts. Hence the Nazi propagandists complained that the Sudeten Germans were deliberately kept out of the munitions factories. This became increasingly true as the Czechs had increasing reason to regard the Sudeten Germans as a Fifth Column from about the time when General Franco coined the phrase.

In October 1933, just when a big political trial which had compromised them was leading to the suppression of the Nazi Party of Czechoslovakia, a certain Konrad Henlein of Asch in the Egerland started what he called a *Sudetendeutsche Heimatfront* (S.H.F.) whose aims at first seemed loyal enough to the Czechoslovak Republic. Elections fell due in May 1935, and from the beginning of that year the S.H.F.

initiated propaganda along Nazi lines against Jews and
Socialists, while it became clear that Henlein, like Hitler, did
not think it worthwhile to try to become a member of Parliament himself. Generous funds were secretly supplied to the
S.H.F. from Germany, though this was fiercely denied at the
time.[1] Although scarcely 63% of the Sudeten Germans[2]
voted for Henlein's *Sudetendeutsche Partei*, as it had been
renamed, it polled 1,249,530 votes, thus becoming the biggest
political party in Czechoslovakia; the second and third biggest
were the Czech Agrarians (hitherto always in the lead) and
the Czech Social Democrats respectively. The Czechoslovak
election fell two months after Hitler had re-introduced conscription in Germany and seven since the Little Entente had
been startled by the murder of Alexander of Yugoslavia and
Barthou. At the end of 1935, Thomas Masaryk resigned,
and Beneš was elected President of the Republic in his
place. In May 1935 he had associated Czechoslovakia with
France in her treaty with the U.S.S.R.; only if Russia were
to be attacked by a European state and the French went to
her assistance was Czechoslovakia bound to do the same.
The German re-militarisation of the Rhineland made a
mockery of the whole plan, but Nazi propagandists complained that Beneš had made Czechoslovakia into an air-
base for world Communism at a time when the Spanish Civil
War was blowing up and the Austro-German press agreement imminent; he had done nothing of the kind.

It was not surprising that Henlein delivered a more
obviously Nazi speech at Eger on 21st June, 1936. This
helped to impel Beneš and the Agrarian Slovak Prime
Minister, Milan Hodža, to come to terms with the leaders of
the remaining activist Sudeten Germans in an agreement
signed on 18th February, 1937, guaranteeing the rights of
minorities in the new conditions of the time. It was a major
tragedy for Czechoslovakia by then that the Slovaks, under

[1] D.G.F.P. series c, vol. III. no. 509 shows that Henlein received
over 300,000 R.M. from Germany.
[2] Wiskemann. *Czechs and Germans*. p. 206 footnote.

their clerical leader, Hlinka, nursed increasingly bitter feelings against the Czechs, whom they blamed for everything, the fall in agricultural prices in particular. Inside Slovakia, the Magyar minority was rebellious; this meant that Hitler exploited Slovak and Hungarian, as well as Sudeten German, emotions against Prague. For the moment, however, the February Agreement was followed by divisions among the Henleinist leaders, and threats to stage another Spanish Civil War in Czechoslovakia. It was in these circumstances that Hitler on 5th November, 1937, told his military chiefs that he intended to destroy Czechoslovakia: on 19th November in a secret report sent by Henlein to Hitler it was stated that Henlein's party longed for nothing more ardently than for the incorporation of all Sudeten German territory in the Reich.[1] Hitler's conquest of Austria meant that Czechoslovakia was engulfed by her enemies; she had a long frontier with Poland, which, after Pilsudski's death in 1935, seemed almost more hostile to the Czechs. In the south-east there was at least one ally, Roumania, where, however, Nazi pressure was having its effect. Terror-cum-euphoria swept over the Sudeten Germans in March 1938 at the time of the *Anschluss* with Austria, and all but the Sudeten German Social Democrats joined Henlein's party. On 24th April at Carlsbad Henlein made eight demands which revealed a part of the truth; the eighth claimed " Full freedom to profess German nationality and the German *Weltanschauung*," to repudiate, that is to say, the political principles of the Czechoslovak State.

After 1936 at the latest the history of Czechoslovakia was in essence the history of her Germans, just as the history of Germany, and indeed of Europe, was the history of Hitler. In May 1938 the Führer visited Italy; he was back in time to be, as he saw it, " provoked " by Czech mobilisation on 20th May in reply to reported German troop movements. Then and there he ordered all preparations for the destruction of Czechoslovakia to be ready " as from 1st October at the

[1] D.G.F.P. series D. vol. II. no. 23.

latest." The Runciman Mission sent by Chamberlain to
Czechoslovakia in August 1938 to analyse the Czech-German
problem seems farcical in retrospect; it was well exploited by
the Henleinists whom it treated, not as a party in the
Republic, but rather as the Republic's partner.

Traditionally Hitler held rallies of the Nazi Party in
Nuremberg every September; the rally was held from 6th to
the 12th September in 1938, Hitler using the occasion for
a savage outburst against Beneš and his alleged treatment of
" these tortured creatures," the Sudeten Germans. Three days
later, on 15th September, Neville Chamberlain, stubborn,
vain, naïf and ignorant, but above everything eager to prevent
war, flew to Germany; the elderly Premier of the United
Kingdom made this pilgrimage to ask Hitler what would
satisfy him. Nothing could have been more futile, since
Hitler was insatiable, and he asked for everything in the
name of preserving the peace which he despised. France was
bound by treaty to come to the help of Czechoslovakia if the
latter were attacked. On 16th September, however, the French
warned Beneš that they could not be expected to go to war on
his account unless Britain, too, would fight. Then Daladier
and Bonnet went to confer in London where the French and
British did their best to unload the blame on to each other.
Beneš did consider ceding the Egerland as he had considered
it in 1919. Faced with losing all that Henlein, once so
dutiful to Czechoslovakia, now wished to join to Germany,
he was helpless, the more so since Hodža seems to have
spoken equivocally to the French Minister in Prague. On
21st September Beneš therefore accepted the so-called Anglo-
French plan of 19th September according to which predominantly German-speaking territory was to be ceded to Hitler:
on 22nd September Chamberlain went to Godesberg to
report to Hitler all that he had fixed for him. Now Hitler
demanded an immediate German occupation of the Czech
territory he claimed, and the satisfaction of the Poles and
the Hungarians at the Czechs' expense. At a second meeting
between Hitler and Chamberlain on 23rd September news

came that the Czechs had mobilised. On 21st September
there had indeed been nationalistic demonstrations in Prague
in which Nationalists and Communists were equally prominent.
In view of Hitler's further demands both London and Paris
had sanctioned the Czech mobilisation and they themselves
began more serious military preparations: the British Home
Fleet was mobilised on 27th September. At the very last
moment Chamberlain appealed to Mussolini, who persuaded
Hitler to postpone marching orders and to meet Chamberlain
and Daladier in conference at Munich on 29th September
1938. Daladier did not press his suggestion that Czechoslovakia should be represented, and Mussolini put forward
Hitler's latest demands as his own proposals. At 1.30 a.m.
on 30th September the Munich Agreement was signed. On
the very next day, 1st October, the Czechs were to begin the
evacuation of all territory where, according to German claims,
more than 50% of the population was German: this
evacuation was to be completed by 10th October, 1938.
Earlier Daladier had suggested a guarantee of what remained
of the Czechoslovak State, and the French and British now
expressed themselves in favour of this. Mussolini and Hitler,
however, were only prepared to consider this possibility after
Polish and Magyar claims upon Czechoslovakia had been
satisfied. On 2nd November Ribbentrop and Ciano in Vienna,
without consulting the Western Powers at all, put an end
to the wrangling between Magyars and Slovaks by drawing
a new frontier between them: this gave a noticeable slice of
territory to Hungary, still the protégé of Italy. Throughout
the Munich crisis Chamberlain seems to have felt successful,
while Daladier was too honest not to realise that France
was betraying the Czechs. Daladier's chiefs of staff had told
him that France could not fight and he made no attempt to
conceal this fact by bluff. Hitler, who detested the conception
of negotiating with equals, was filled with contempt for the
businessman from Birmingham and the Provençal farmer's
son. They for their part were glad to discount the already
glaring evidence that Hitler was a criminal: Mussolini, who

indulged in the same postures as Hitler, discounted that murderous evidence too.

The political importance of the Munich Agreement was immense. It was rather as if the Central Powers had won the First World War twenty years later. For Hitler now controlled the old Austrian territory, the core of the Pan-Germans' *Mitteleuropa*; the Czech interior of Bohemia and Moravia lay at his mercy and he was ready for his much-heralded expansion far to the East. The French had broken their long-standing treaty with the Czechs and lost their European standing; the Third French Republic was utterly humiliated. Life-long pacifists like Léon Blum knew that this peace was not worth having. In the last instance, as in 1936, it was the leaders of the French Army who had preferred the disgrace of France. Of course Britain had taken the lead but Britain had not been pledged by treaty: here, too, however, Hitler had won a notable victory in the war of nerves. He was a past-master of inflicting the pangs of humiliation upon his enemies, of extracting a shame-faced admission that it was not really worth trying to do the right thing.

Hitler himself was, however, disappointed by the Munich Agreement, disappointed not to have had an open war to extinguish Czechoslovakia. He had to wait nearly six months to be able to pick a quarrel that suited him with the now nearly neutral government of rump Czecho-Slovakia in which Slovakia had become autonomous. He set up his German protectorate in Prague on 15th March, 1939. Even Neville Chamberlain grasped that he was a liar when this happened, for on 26th September, 1938, Hitler had declared that he wished to rule over no Czechs. Nevertheless Daladier's suggested guarantee of post-Munich Czech territory was ignored. Hitler made two other changes in March 1939. He offered the Slovaks a nominal independence under German protection, and for six years Slovakia, enjoying various economic privileges, served as the model of a German-protected state. At the same time Hitler put an end to the farcical and ambiguous independence of Ruthenia. This was a small, backward and anomalous region in which the Czechs had for years failed to discover the competence which could make possible the autonomy they had promised there in 1919. After Munich until the beginning of 1939 the Germans had tried to utilise Ruthenia by treating it as a Ukrainian Piedmont, thus causing anxiety to the Russians, the Poles, and to a lesser extent to the Roumanians who ruled some Ukrainians or Ruthenes in the Bukovina. Ruthenia was now handed back to Hungary to which it had belonged before 1918. Thus Poland had lost any chance of annexing Slovakia but acquired for a few months the common frontier with Hungary for which she had hoped.

Having liquidated Czechoslovakia with no irritating mediation to rob him of his prey, Hitler was ready to deal with Poland, the more so since Stalin was showing signs of flexibility. Before betraying his intentions towards Poland Hitler wished for a full military alliance with Italy; this should help to make the Western Powers think twice about their guarantees to Poland. When the Führer had visited Italy in May 1938 Ribbentrop had proposed a military alliance between Italy and Germany, but Mussolini and Ciano had been evasive. A year later the *Duce* accepted the same general proposition from Germany, and Ciano went to Berlin to sign the Steel Pact on 22nd May, 1939. The Italians had left the final drafting to the Germans and were now bound to come to Hitler's aid if he " became involved in warlike complications." Hitler had inspired a frankly aggressive treaty : as Mussolini noted, there was no need for a defensive one, since no one intended to attack the Axis Powers. Originally the Germans had wished to include the Japanese. Now that the barriers between Germany and Russia might be melting, they were glad to forget Japan for the time-being.

An important part of the history of Europe in the 'thirties, and the key to the startling success of Nazi Germany, was her economic subjection step by step of under-developed eastern and south-eastern Europe. It has been seen how the great depression caused agricultural prices to collapse. Nazi Germany could make good use of cheap food supplies in carrying out her Four-Year Plan from 1936 onwards. Originally it was due to the initiative of Schacht that she offered to buy up the peasant countries' food produce in return, not for currency, but for the goods which it suited her to export. Already in 1933 Nazi Germany had come to the economic rescue of Bulgaria. In 1935 the imposition of sanctions by the League of Nations against Italy meant that a country like Yugoslavia lost its Italian market and was thankful to export the goods in question to Germany. In the following years the tension created by Hitler caused most countries to look to their armaments and to try to increase them and make them more efficient; in Eastern Europe resources might be scanty but the pacifism of Western Europe was unknown, the feeling of physical danger being too conscious an emotion. The rearmament of Austria, Hungary and Bulgaria was tacitly accepted now. Nazi Germany often paid for some of her imports from the Balkan countries by sending them weapons, even though she did not wish to export many nor the best: German weapons, instead of French or Czech ones, reversed a trend and began a conveniently dependent demand for German spare-parts.

With the absorption of Austria by Germany in March 1938 old banking and industrial connections between Vienna and Hungary and the south-east, connections which had survived the peace settlement and the great depression, came into German control. Thus the growing economic dependence of the smaller countries upon Germany was stimulated and extended. The absorption of Czechoslovakia, in the two stages of the Munich Agreement and the occupation of Prague, was almost more important economically than it was strategically. All along the leaders of Czechoslovakia had thought in terms of making the Little Entente into something fairly independent of the Great Powers. Czechoslovakia was sufficiently advanced economically to offer to her backward

Yugoslav and Roumanian partners : (1) invested capital; (2) some of the industrial goods they did not themselves produce; (3) a market for some of their agricultural goods and other raw materials, like oil, copper and lead. In 1937, for instance, Czechoslovak investment in Yugoslavia was only exceeded by that of France and Britain and was greater than that of wealthy Switzerland : further the Czech armaments industry at Pilsen supplied weapons to Yugoslavia and Roumania. Between September 1938 and March 1939 all Czechoslovakia's industry and investments fell into German hands. Thus a big shift in power was effected which extended to Belgrade and Bucharest; Bulgaria was already an economic vassal, and Hungary, which had hoped to preserve its independence of Germany by its links with Italy, was tricked by Italy's poverty—after the Abyssinian and Spanish Wars— into selling more to Germany. The whole operation of semi-annexation of the south-east by economic control linked the small countries' currencies to that of Germany in such a way that their freedom of economic movement seemed doomed. The German authorities—a Nazi journalist and financial expert called Walther Funk succeeded Schacht as Minister of Economics in 1937, Schacht continuing as President of the Reichsbank until 1939—now planned a series of long-term agreements to consolidate German control. Within just over a week after the Nazi seizure of Prague and on the same day as Hitler seized Memel, Funk had persuaded the Roumanians to accept what from the Nazi point of view was a model commercial treaty, reminiscent incidentally of a treaty imposed by the Central Powers upon Roumania in May 1918.

The German-Roumanian Treaty of 23rd March, 1939, was concluded for at least five years. Joint German-Roumanian companies were to intensify the exploitation of Roumania's oil and other natural resources, machinery and plant being provided by the Germans to whom " free zones " in Roumania were to be allotted. In other words Nazi Germany was seriously setting about the economic development of Roumania, the Balkan area most urgently requiring this in Hitler's own interest. Since he already directly controlled Austria and Czechoslovakia, and Hungary and Bulgaria depended upon him to a great extent, there remained the questions of Poland and Yugoslavia to be solved by Nazi methods. There were many indications of a " Roumanian " approach to Yugoslavia but no plan ever emerged for the Nazi development of Poland in spite of the coal and iron of Polish Silesia : this suggested that Poland, like Czechoslovakia, was marked down for destruction.

Chapter IX

THE FALL OF POLAND
1932-1939

Since 1930 Marshal Pilsudski, now an old man if indisputably a grand one, had ruled Poland mainly through certain of his former Legionaries, the "Colonels." Among these Joseph Beck, who had at an early stage been Polish military attaché in Paris, seemed to gain most influence over the Marshal. At the end of 1932 he succeeded Zaleski as Polish Foreign Minister. Beck had hated Paris and was as anti-French as Zaleski had been francophile; indeed Beck and his friends admired Fascist Italy. When Hitler came to power in Germany Pilsudski is believed to have approached the French secretly with a view to swift preventive war. It must have been at this point, at the beginning of March 1933, that the Poles reinforced their harbour police on the Westerplatte at Danzig. The League of Nations was obliged to point out that this was contrary to an agreement made in 1921 and the Poles withdrew. At the same time Pilsudski seems to have drawn a blank in Paris. If France failed to respond then the next best thing might be to come to terms with Hitler; after all, his anti-Russian agitation was acceptable to the Poles where the Rapallo policy had been a threat to them. In January 1934 a ten years' Non-aggression Pact was signed between Poland and Germany. Poland was thus the first country to come to terms with Hitler; Beck and indeed many Poles eagerly pointed out that Hitler was not a Prussian but an Austrian with a friendly tradition, therefore, towards their nation. When Barthou visited Warsaw that spring he seemed to have patched up the Franco-Polish relationship, but, according to Lord Avon, he could not quite resist taunting the francophobe Beck with Poland's aspiration after Great Power status. In September 1934 Poland seized this rank by repudiating her obligations under the Minorities Treaties. Since January there was more direct intercourse with Germany; hence League protection of the Germans in Poland and of the Poles in Germany might be less necessary in theory. Now in September the U.S.S.R. became another permanent member of the Council of the League of Nations and might well have raised the matter of Poland's Ukrainian and White Russian minority. In the following year Pilsudski died. The Colonels continued to rule but none of them were men of vision. Stalin's reign of terror seemed to justify their policy, and they dissociated Poland ostentatiously from the French-Czech-Russian combination.

After the Westerplatte incident Poland's relationship with Germany was still complicated by the status of Danzig. Elections there on 28th May, 1933, made the Nazis the biggest party (with 50.03% of the votes and 38 seats out of 72) and brought their local leader, Hermann Rauschning, into power. This man was a clever, flexible Nationalist—no Nazi—and made intelligent suggestions for Baltic co-operation to include the Soviet Union. Surprisingly Hitler took him into his confidence for a time with two interesting results. Rauschning was appalled, and abandoned Danzig; in addition he felt obliged to warn the world which he did in conversation with anyone who would listen to him and later in his *Revolution des Nihilismus*; this book, was, however, too long and involved and altogether too Germanic to reach a wide public. In 1934 Greiser had replaced Rauschning as President of the Senate of Danzig. At the elections in 1933 the Nazis had failed to gain a two-thirds majority and were therefore unable legally to alter the constitution of Danzig guaranteed by the League of Nations. Thus over Danzig there was a head-on collision between the League and National Socialism. This culminated in July 1936 with a visit of Greiser to Geneva; on leaving a council meeting he cocked a snook at the assembled journalists. This childish behaviour had been preceded by serious intransigence towards the council then presided over by Eden. The Polish Govern-

ment professed to believe that it could settle all it needed by
direct negotiation with Hitler, and it showed indifference
over the constitution of Danzig. At a secret Council meeting
Beck did, however, promise that Polish troops should protect
the League High Commissioner there if necessary. In fact
Polish and German interests over Danzig were so conflicting
that for the time-being the issue was not forced, and the
presence of the League's representative made him into both
sides' scapegoat. During this critical period a remarkable
Irishman, Sean Lester, was the High Commissioner of the
League in Danzig until he succeeded Avenol as Secretary-
General in Geneva in the autumn of 1936. Lester was
succeeded in Danzig by the Swiss diplomatist and historian,
Carl Burckhardt.

The Poles had not forgiven the Czechs for acquiring the
lion's share of Teschen in 1920. After 1936 Beck played up
the grievances of the Polish minority there in order to gain
easy popularity at home and to display solidarity with Hitler
against Beneš. Immediately after Munich the Poles were
rewarded with the booty of the Czech portion of the Teschen
territory; in the winter of 1938-9 their Government canvassed
the Polish annexation of Slovakia, still linked with Prague
until March 1939. The feeling grew, however, that Beck
and his friends were delivering Poland into Hitler's hands by
their jackal policy. The Teschen territory had slightly increased the German minority in Poland, and the Ukrainians
in Eastern Galicia were tentatively following Henlein's lead
in demanding autonomy, not without German encouragement.
Although its leader, Witos, was still in exile in Czechoslovakia, certainly from the beginning of 1937 the big oppositional Peasant Party was gaining ground; its leaders in
Poland, men like Professor Kot, together with General Sikorski who sympathised with them, urged upon their people the
mortal danger represented by Hitler. These leaders were
often under house-arrest but they remained exceedingly active
in spite of all obstacles, and they urged the need for Poland
to draw nearer to Czechoslovakia—while there was time—

and to the West. In December 1938 after Munich, the oppositional parties were strikingly successful in municipal elections in fifty-two cities; while Communist influence was negligible in Poland, the Socialist and Peasant Parties had at last drawn together. Naturally the Socialists were stronger in the towns while the Peasant Party had most influence in Western Galicia, the most over-populated area in all peasant Europe. This meant an indefinite supply of cheap labour so that even when industry in Upper Silesia (next door to Western Galicia) began to recover, labour conditions remained bad.

Hitler had begun to prepare his directive for the destruction of Poland not long after the Munich Agreement. It was on 24th October, 1938, that Ribbentrop proposed to the Polish Ambassador in Berlin that Danzig should be restored to Germany (politically, but not economically, he suggested) and that German extra-territorial railway-lines and a motor-road across Pomorze (the 'Corridor') should be built. The Poles refused to comply. Late in January 1939 Ribbentrop on a visit to Warsaw urged Beck to take compensation for Danzig in the Russian Ukraine, the area Hitler was most determined to germanise. Within a week of the German occupation of Prague, on 23rd March, Hitler forced Lithuania to surrender Memel to him. Beck at last took alarm. On 27th March a Nazi press campaign was launched accusing the Poles of atrocious behaviour towards their German minority, a campaign which was a disagreeable reminder, as Ciano said in his Diary, of the tone of the German press towards Austrians and Czechs at other times. On 31st March, Britain, in the person of Neville Chamberlain, pronounced a guarantee of the frontiers of both Roumania and Poland, countries more remote than the Czechoslovakia he had thought so far away so short a time before.[1] Thereupon Beck visited London early in April; he left there on the day, Good Friday 7th April, that Fascist Italy seized Albania,

[1] Similar guarantees were given to Roumania and Greece in the middle of April 1939.

Mussolini thereby adding to Chamberlain's slowly mounting anti-Axis indignation. On 28th April in the Reichstag Hitler repudiated his pact with Poland : it had lasted just over four years out of the envisaged ten.

On 23th May, 1939, the day after the signature of the Steel Pact and while Ciano was still in Berlin, Hitler again summoned his military chiefs to a secret conference and announced his decision "to attack Poland at the first suitable opportunity ". " Danzig," he said, " is not the subject of the dispute at all. It is a question of expanding our living-space in the East. . . ." He was sure there would be war this time, and perhaps not only against Poland. On 17th June Goebbels, speaking in Danzig itself, made a ferocious attack upon Poland. All the evidence suggests that the Germans in Poland and Danzig became almost as provocative during this summer as the Henleinists in Czechoslovakia a year earlier : among the Poles there was a general determination to resist the Nazis. The Polish police tightened things up in exposed areas, but not excessively. The Polish Army tried to prepare itself but had not the means nor the Spanish experience. Negotiations with the Western Powers with regard to the implementation of their guarantee dragged out; partly the task was insoluble without much greater air strength, but the Poles were also disappointed by the apparent unwillingness of Britain to lend them money. They for their part helped to wreck the negotiations for a military alliance between the Western Powers and Russia since they, like the Roumanians, refused to agree to the passage of Russian troops across their territory. It needs to be emphasised that this objection was not solely due to the prejudice of the governing Colonels but enjoyed wide popular support, owing to distrust of the Ukrainian minority, but also to genuine popular antipathy to both Russians and Communism.

The next thing, on 23rd August, 1939, was the Russo-German Pact which startled the world : secretly it provided for the partition of Poland between Germany and Russia.

On 24th August Forster, the local Nazi Gauleiter, was declared Head of the State of Danzig which spelt German annexation: the Poles did not react to this provocation.[1] Hitler had decided to attack Poland on 26th August. On the day before he heard two things: one was that Mussolini was not ready to fight and needed re-fitting with war material on a grand scale after his Spanish escapade which had only just ended: the other was the news of the signature of an Anglo-Polish Alliance pledging each country to help the other to the utmost if it were attacked. These two pieces of news caused Hitler to hold up his order to the German Army, but only for a few days. In the early hours of 1st September, 1939, the Germans invaded Poland: there was no declaration of war and the pretext was a feigned attack upon Gleiwitz wireless station by Germans in stolen Polish uniforms. Hitler wished to make the impression of a merely punitive expedition. On 3rd September Britain and France, as Poland's allies, declared war on Germany. At last the war which Hitler had begun when he re-militarised the Rhineland had been heated up into legal existence. Poland was over-run by the Germans within the first half of September, and, as far as they were concerned, deleted from the map once again.

[1] Burckhardt, the last High Commissioner of the League of Nations, did not leave Danzig until 1 Sept. 1939.

Chapter X

THE FALL OF FRANCE
1936-40

The predicament of France between the assumption of office by the *Front Populaire* early in June 1936 and the catastrophe of June 1940 was infinitely tragic. At first there was a euphoric occupation of the Parisian factories with jolly feasting. Then in the second half of 1936 Léon Blum struggled to put through in the Matignon Agreements long overdue social reforms including a forty-hour maximum week. But with the aftermath of the re-militarisation of the Rhineland and then the Spanish Civil War upon his hands, he struggled to little purpose : the main result was financial disarray, intensified by his political enemies who exported all the capital they could. The devaluation of the French franc on 1st October, 1936, was only an alleviation. "The basic cause of French financial and economic difficulties," it has been written, "was the fact that the French national income . . . was not large enough to maintain customary income standards at a time when the rapidly increasing burden of rearmament was superimposed upon a situation already rendered difficult by the attempt to achieve radical social reforms."[1] In truth France was by now overtaken by a frightening decadence. Her production was inadequate, her fiscal system vicious, her statistics inaccurate. The fantastic luck which seemed to bless Hitler from 1930 to 1942 would have it that on the very day of the *Anschluss*, 12th March, 1938, not only were eighteen more Russian political leaders on the eve of being sentenced to death, but France was without a government as she had been at the time of the suppression of the Austrian Socialists in 1934. At last in April 1938 Daladier's Ministry was appointed with Georges

[1] *Survey of International Affairs. 1938.* vol. I. p. 113.

Bonnet, prince of the appeasers, at the Quai d'Orsay. This brought Paul Reynaud, one of France's most brilliant financial experts, to the Ministry of Finance; but again it was too late. The demoralisation, which perhaps had its roots in the fearful losses between 1914 and 1918 and the falling birthrate after that, was nourished by the open division of the nation since February 1934. It fed also upon the prevalent scepticism expressed in literature and the arts, again led by Paris since they had been crushed by Hitler in Berlin and Vienna and by Stalin in Moscow. And it was deepened by such things as the bitter disillusionment of so distinguished a writer as André Gide when he returned from the U.S.S.R. in 1936.[1] With the fall of the Spanish Republic there was nothing left to believe in except the enemies of France. Such despair was duly exploited by the *Comité France-Allemagne* organised in close touch with Laval by Comte de Brinon and the German Otto Abetz, who became the German Envoy in France in 1940. Symptomatic of the decline from the 'twenties to the 'thirties was the history of the French Air Force, at first the most technically advanced in Europe, but by 1939 backward and too ill-informed to realise its own utter inadequacy. In addition to these fearful deficiencies and the humiliation of Munich which caused France, not Britain, to throw over a treaty obligation to her Czech ally, there came the Russo-German Pact of 23rd August, 1939, and the scrapping of the *Front Populaire* position by the Comintern. The French Communists and some French Socialists had really believed in this as the only practicable policy; now it lay in ruins and Moscow ordered opposition to the war effort when it should have been nationally initiated in France thirteen days later. National morale had been further debilitated by a famous article in *l'Oeuvre*[2] in this same August by the National Socialist, Déat, in which he mocked at the suggestion that

---

[1] See his *Retour de l'U.R.S.S.* 1936 and *Retouches à mon Retour de l'U.R.S.S.* 1937.

[2] This having been Madame Tabouis' paper, the publication of Déat's article was all the more striking.

any Frenchman should "die for Danzig." It is not really difficult to explain the military collapse of France in June 1940 after Hitler had bowled over Scandinavia in April and the Low Countries in May.

A 'Law for the Organisation of the Nation in War-time,' passed on 11th July, 1938, empowered the Prime Minister to govern by decree from the day the war began. The most essential need, a Ministry of Armaments, was not, however, created until 13th September, 1939, and it never caught up in any way with the nation's requirements. The outbreak of war did banish Bonnet from the Quai d'Orsay (which Daladier took over from him) to the Ministry of Justice. During the winter of 1939-40 rightist prejudices were fortified by the Russian war against Finland; yet the Russo-German connection helped temporarily to unite the French Right and Left. When the Finns made peace in March 1940 the Daladier Cabinet collapsed, and Paul Reynaud succeeded as Minister-President. Reynaud, who had condemned the Munich Agreement, and who had persistently demanded more dynamic leadership, seemed to be the right man at last: he still championed de Gaulle as against General Gamelin.

The German western offensive was planned with confidence and precision and was based upon the dynamic offensive and technically modern principles habitual to victors. The Allies could muster just about as many men, but it has been seen that the attitude of the French Command was purely defensive; faith in the Maginot Line had become the dogma of the French Generals other than de Gaulle whose writings had been read with admiration only by the Germans. The German plan in its first stage was to break any Dutch and Belgian resistance and encircle the Allied Left. The German Generals in command were Rundstedt, Bock and Leeb with a hundred and fifty divisions: they invaded the Low Countries on 10th May, 1940.

The Dutch were overwhelmed by the German combination of parachutists, bombers, tanks, in four days, and capitulated on 14th May; the next day saw a huge German breakthrough. On 18th May Reynaud finally replaced Gamelin by Weygand, who had been right-hand man to Foch in the First World War; Pétain, an older member of that generation (he was now eighty-four) who had been French Ambassador to Franco since France had recognised him, was made Vice-President of the Council of Ministers, and Georges Mandel came back into the Government as Minister of the Interior. (Daladier was moved from the Ministry of Defence to the Quai d'Orsay). A superficial optimism was generated by the conjuncture of such traditional names, but on 27th May King Leopold of Belgium asked for an armistice. This meant that there was a gap in the Allied line from Ypres to the sea, and considerable French and British forces were cut off in Belgium. After they had failed to break out of their German encirclement towards the south, their last hope was evacuation by sea from the Dunkirk beaches for which Eden, who was British War Minister, had ordered preparations. Rundstedt, supported by Hitler, felt it militarily necessary to pause and re-organise for about a week. This made possible Operation Dynamo, the evacuation from Dunkirk which began on 28th May and continued until midnight on 2nd June; 337,131 soldiers of whom a full third were Allied Nationals, not British, were rescued, but all their equipment was lost. Although the Germans were re-fitting, they harried their enemies. The British Navy and all the volunteer ships that joined up with it improvised magnificently, and Dunkirk was not the defeat the Germans claimed although six British destroyers and twenty-four smaller war vessels were lost. From the French point of view it could all be portrayed as not only defeat but desertion.[1]

For on 5th June the Germans began what was to be called the Battle of France, forcing the Somme and Aisne-Oise canal crossings. There was some stubborn French fighting which held up the German infantry, but the Germans started with favourable bridgeheads and their armoured cars rushed

---

[1] The very last British troops embarked from France farther west on 16th and 18th June: these included a Canadian contingent.

ahead. On that same day, 5th June, Reynaud re-shuffled his Cabinet again, dropping Daladier and bringing in de Gaulle as Under-Secretary of Defence. By 10th June it was clear that France was heavily defeated and Mussolini declared war. Worse than that, on 11th June the French Government withdrew from Paris to Tours, the Quai d'Orsay having made a bonfire of its papers : later the Government retired to Bordeaux. The French Army was now increasingly paralysed by the confusion created by refugees streaming west and south-west. A last blow to morale was the entry of the Germans into Paris on 14th June. On 16th June the British offered the French the political union of the two countries; this astonishing proposition deserves to be recorded although it is not clear how seriously it was made : it was certainly rejected. Reynaud, like the British Government, wanted to save the French Fleet from the Germans and to continue the war from North Africa. But on that very night of 16th June Reynaud was forced to resign in favour of Marshal Pétain. This spelt the success of the moderate Right which was anti-democratic and anti-British; on 17th June Pétain asked the Germans for their terms and broadcast that fighting must cease (" *il faut cesser le combat* "). Twenty-four deputies (including Mandel and Mendès-France) and a Senator who sailed in the S.S. Massilia to Casablanca were prevented from landing there by the authorities and sent back to Bordeaux.

This was the moment of Hitler's greatest triumph. France appeared to be broken and Germany had taken nearly two million French prisoners. The Führer could not resist the delight of summoning the defeated French leaders to meet him on 21st June in the railway carriage at Compiègne where the Armistice had been signed in 1918. On 22nd June France accepted Hitler's terms which involved the German occupation of Paris and the industrially important part of France, the French to pay the costs of occupation. The French prisoners-of-war were not released. France, however, was not totally crushed by Hitler as Poland had been, although she had fought no better; indeed there had been more division and far greater defeatism in France. But Hitler saw a political advantage in a small authoritarian France ruled by Pétain from Vichy, ostensibly on his side against Britain. In this way the French retained an autonomy limited in space as in quality, and were able to delay any decisions about the French Empire. (The French Navy was to be demobilised under German supervision, but this, too, was delayed). Hence the Armistice signed with Italy on 24th June immediately arranged for nothing but a demilitarised strip fifty kilometres deep along the French side of the Franco-Italian frontier. For the time being the defeat of France seemed overwhelming and the victory of the Axis Powers complete.

Chapter XI

THE DESTRUCTION OF YUGOSLAVIA

1936-41

Many sober judges had supposed that Yugoslavia could not survive the murder of King Alexander at Marseilles in October 1934. It was all the more remarkable to observe that real grief was shown over the King's death even by Maček's peasants in Croatia. In spite of a few extremists in Croatia and Macedonia, the Southern Slav idea proved to have some vitality when it was so sharply challenged. On the succession of the child-King, Peter, with his cousin Prince Paul as the chief of three regents, it was hoped to make a new start. Dragoljub Jovanović appealed again for peasant federation among the Yugoslav peoples. Prince Paul, however, made an unfortunate and unpopular choice in appointing the Serb banker, Stoyadinović, as Prime Minister. This man appeared highly susceptible to the trend towards dictatorship and towards getting on to the winning side, but he showed no inclination to tackle the Croats' claim to autonomy. Stoyadinović, indeed, drove the Serbs themselves on to the Croat side, so that Dragoljub Jovanović could join with Maček to form a Serbo-Croat United Opposition to the Government, an opposition which demanded the end of Belgrade's tyranny and the free participation of the peasants in the choice of those who governed them. It would perhaps have been too much to expect the conservative and timid Prince Paul to accept as fit for responsibility this spontaneous Serbo-Croat movement: the Prince was indeed alarmed by the big Serb demonstrations in Maček's favour when the Croat leader visited Belgrade in October 1937. Prince Paul succeeded only in dismissing Stoyadinović and appointing a more neutral figure, Cvetković, to be Prime Minister. This was in February

1939, after elections which had given the opposition no numerical success—this would not have been possible—but a striking moral victory in December 1938. Negotiations were then pursued which led to a half-hearted compromise between Belgrade and the Croats on 26th August, 1939, the *Sporazum* or Agreement which pleased no one.

It has been seen that since 1935 Nazi Germany had become an important commercial partner of Yugoslavia, taking her produce in return for what Germany chose to export—at one time it was notorious that Belgrade was choked with German aspirin. Funk made agreements which linked the Yugoslav currency with that of Germany. The German minority in Yugoslavia busily bought up land. Then in 1938 and 1939 Germany took over Austrian and Czechoslovak holdings in Yugoslavia. This situation made it easier for Hitler to exert other pressures on a poor peasant country of this kind.

The *Sporazum* was made the day after the signature of the Anglo-Polish Treaty and Mussolini's default as an ally for Hitler. The Führer's quick triumph in Poland was an object lesson to any small nations in eastern Europe which still preserved some independence. The collapse of France in June 1940 was all the more impressive. These developments helped to destroy the spontaneous rapprochement between the Serbs and Croats in the later 'thirties which had seemed to justify the Yugoslav idea. From the time of the *Sporazum* onwards the Serbs became increasingly defiant of the Axis; not even the fall of France, with whom they had felt a particular sympathy, changed their attitude. On the other hand much of Croat opinion—not all of it—decided that Croat desires could best be fulfilled by following the example of Slovakia. After Mussolini's unfortunate attack upon Greece in October 1940, Hitler, who was already beginning to plan his war against Russia in detail, decided that he must first put an end to Axis difficulties in the Balkan peninsula on his right flank. This meant that the German Army would move into Greece as soon as the winter was over; for this to go smoothly Hitler required

Yugoslav acquiescence. After gruelling negotiations between Hitler and Ribbentrop for Germany, and Prince Paul, Cvetković and the Foreign Minister, Cincar-Marković, for Yugoslavia, and after remarkable concessions to the latter, the Yugoslav Ministers signed the Tripartite Pact on 25th March, 1941 : this treaty, since its initiation in the previous September, had been offered to all satellite states to register their support of the Axis and Japan by signing it.

Among the Serbs and Montenegrins there followed a spontaneous mass protest in Belgrade which swept away Prince Paul and his Ministers. King Peter, now seventeen-and-a-half, was to rule himself with General Simović, the head of the Yugoslav Air Force, as his Prime Minister. For Hitler this was the signal for the merciless destruction of Yugoslavia. Once more the son of the Austrian customs official was incensed by the insubordination of a state constructed by the Slavs he had always despised as inferior : this time it was those same Serbian dogs who had perpetrated the murder at Sarajevo in 1914 : though they had killed the heir of the Habsburgs—whom he had hated—and provided the occasion of war which had delighted him, the Serbs had remained the villains of his piece. On 27th March, 1941, Hitler informed his military commanders that Yugoslavia was to be pitilessly destroyed with lightning rapidity. On 6th April German Stukas more or less wiped out Belgrade. The German Army arrived there on 13th April, the King and Government escaping to Greece. Thereupon Yugoslavia was as ruthlessly partitioned as Poland. Croatia was established, like Slovakia, as 'independent' under Pavelić, the notorious terrorist, as its dictator : he was a convenient tool of the Axis. The Croat Peasant Party remained faithful to Maček who was placed under house-arrest by Pavelić.

The curious and purely nominal agreement offered to the Yugoslavs by Stalin on the night preceding the Luftwaffe's attack had only helped to stimulate Hitler's anti-Slav rage in preparation for his attack upon Russia.

Chapter XII

STALIN AND HITLER
1936-41

The Spanish Civil War did not increase confidence in the
U.S.S.R.; still less did the elimination of Russia's leading
Generals in 1937. Another monster trial was staged in
March 1938; it opened on 2nd March, and on 13th March,
the day after the German Army occupied Austria, Bukharin,
Rykov, Krestinsky and fifteen others were sentenced to death
after grotesque confessions from them had been read out in
court : the three remaining accused were sentenced to long
periods of imprisonment.

The second Five-Year Plan in Russia, which had run from
1933 to 1937, had seen the completion of the collectivisation
of agriculture; it had also provided for rapid industrial
development which included armaments production. The
third Five-Year Plan was launched in 1938; again in this year
the harvest was as good as in 1937. The same ferocity with
which the Chief Public Prosecutor, Vyshinsky, attacked the
accused political prisoners in court made the Five-Year Plans
more effective than Western opinion could believe. To the
outside world in 1938 the U.S.S.R. presented " a phantas-
magoria of treason, plotting, arrests and executions . . .
impotent for any decisive action . . . the painted semblance of
a Great Power."[1]

For the trials in Russia had continued in the second half
of 1938, the period of the Czechoslovak crisis : it was in
these later months of the year that the two police chiefs,
Yagoda and then Yezhov, who was succeeded by Berya, were
tried and executed. Thus the period of the Munich Agreement marked the extreme isolation of the Soviet Union and
galvanised Stalin into a series of critical decisions. " One

[1] *Survey of International Affairs* 1938 vol. III. p. 400.

might think," he said a few months later, "that the districts
of Czechoslovakia were yielded to Germany as the prize for
her undertaking to launch war on the Soviet Union." Russia
for her part felt affronted in every way. A vital step had
been taken on the Western edges of Eastern Europe without
any reference to Moscow; indeed the whole system so carefully constructed by Litvinov of French-Czech-Russian collaboration within the League of Nations had been roughly
brushed aside. In the autumn the activities of the Germans
in Ruthenia became highly provocative to the Soviet Union
with its big Ukrainian Republic. When in January 1939
Chamberlain went to Rome to make his final bow to Mussolini, Stalin was informed that he, Chamberlain, had spoken
as if he would be glad to see the Germans advance from
Ruthenia further east into the Russian Ukraine in accordance
with Hitler's long cherished ambitions. It seems almost
certain that it was Stalin who more deliberately decided to let
the Germans loose upon the West while he himself gained
time. Clearly Hitler's next victim was to be Poland and over
Poland Russia's interest, it has been seen, always tended to
coincide with that of Germany.

As the spring of 1939 approached there were many
obscure indications of a reshuffling of the pack and Hitler's
fulminations against Asiatic Bolshevism were heard no more.
Early in March, the eighteenth congress of the Communist
Party of the U.S.S.R. met—the seventeenth had been held in
1935—in Moscow, and on 10th March Stalin made a famous
two-edged speech full of contradictions. It condemned the
appeasement of Nazi Germany, but it also derided the West
for egging on Germany to attack Russia, stating that there
were no "visible grounds" for a conflict between the
Governments of Berlin and Moscow. Five days later Hitler
marched into Prague and on 18th March Germany's action
was denounced by Litvinov. As he had immediately after
the *Anschluss*, the Russian Foreign Minister proposed a
Conference of Russia and the Western Powers with the
smaller countries in Eastern Europe threatened by Hitler. On

each occasion Chamberlain refused the suggestion: now in 1939 he revolutionised British foreign policy by giving guarantees to Poland, Roumania and also to Greece. Here were fresh affronts, for on 15th April the British asked Russia to support these guarantees unilaterally, that is getting nothing in return. Russia refused, and instead proposed a military alliance with Britain and France to be followed by a joint guarantee of all the frontiers of Eastern Europe. At the same time, however, Stalin was giving sidelong glances towards Germany. Hitler's speech against Poland on 28th April was encouraging; on 3rd May Stalin replied by dismissing Litvinov, the westerner and the Jew, and appointing as his successor the more parochial, less enterprising Molotov, an obedient party boss.

It took until 23rd August for the cards to be shuffled and dealt, three and a half months which saw the Steel Pact, the mounting Nazi campaign against Poland, the abortive military negotiations in Moscow between Russia and the West. Bonnet at the Quai d'Orsay was the agile ally of Neville Chamberlain in being slightly mesmerised by what they both took seriously as Hitler's anti-Communist mission. Even the Italians, who should have known better, were electrified when they found that Ribbentrop had no time for them because he had hurried to a still hesitant Moscow to sign a pact with Stalin. According to this agreement Russia and Germany undertook to settle their disputes " through friendly exchange of opinion." More to the point, they secretly planned the fifth partition of Poland, drawing their frontier along the east bank of the Vistula, recognising Bessarabia as belonging to Russia, and placing Finland, Estonia and Latvia in her sphere of influence—Lithuania in August 1939 was left to the Germans.

Stalin was surprised by the rapidity of Hitler's success in Poland in September 1939; on 5th September the Germans were already urging him to march into eastern Poland, but it was not until twelve days later that he did so. Now he was beset with doubts. Fairly soon he decided that he would accept the German plan to eliminate Poland without leaving a rump state; but in this case he must revise the August programme. When Ribbentrop paid his second visit to Moscow at the end of September the Russo-Polish frontier was re-drawn along the ethnic line so that the Soviet Armies only liberated their Ukrainian and White Russian ' brothers '; Lithuania, however, came into the Russian sphere of influence. Russian garrisons moved into Tallinn, Riga and Kaunas, and strategic bases— against whom, Ribbentrop might ask himself—were demanded of Finland. When the Finns refused, on 30th November war began between the U.S.S.R. and Finland, the winter war. This again did Russia no good because the Finns successfully stood up for themselves. In spite of all the ugly happenings which seemed to have been accepted since 1933, there was a genuine wave of European indignation against the big bully, Russia, comparable with that against Britain at the time of the Boer War. In March 1940 the Finns surrendered the strategic bases to Russia but they kept a modicum of independence throughout the Second World War and ever after: German soldiers having entered Finland in the winter of 1940-1, the Finns did in fact participate in the attack upon Russia in 1941. Mannerheim, however, launched his own offensive on 10th July, 1941, and no Finnish contingent was sent to join the Germans, as the Italians, Roumanians and Hungarians did.

Until June 1940 Stalin's soldiers lived in peace with the populations of the Baltic states though their governments were on the whole pro-German. The fall of France, however, completely surprised Russia's despot and in a flash he revolutionised his policy: it was as new for Soviet Russia to annex territory to which she had no ethnic claim as for Neville Chamberlain, the year before, to have guaranteed east European frontiers. Quickly Stalin sent Dekanozov to make sure of Lithuania; a Communist coup was engineered in Kaunas bringing annexation by Russia as the German troops marched into Paris on 14th June. In July Vyshinsky did the trick in Latvia and Zhdanov in Estonia; the importance Stalin attached to these operations can be measured by the men he put in charge of them. This was the end, after just over twenty years, of the independent Baltic states, whose small German populations were transferred to Nazi Germany. At the same time Stalin moved in the Balkan peninsula. On 27th June, as German soldiers reached the Pyrenees, the Russian Government presented an ultimatum to Roumania, demanding the immediate cession of Bessarabia and Northern Bukovina. These territories had a considerable Ukrainian population and in any case Moscow had never recognised Roumania's right to Bessarabia. From Bessarabia, again, a German minority was sent off to Germany.

It was for other reasons, and above all on account of her oilfields, that Roumania was to prove politically inflammable in 1940. After the Russian ultimatum in the autumn, Germany and Italy handed over another slice of Roumanian territory to Hungary as to Bulgaria, and then guaranteed the rest with Ploesti—obviously against Russia; from September Germans had arrived in Roumania in considerable numbers including S.S. people who were said to be evacuating the Germans from Bessarabia. This German occupation of Roumania affronted Stalin and piqued Mussolini into his attack upon Greece. In the spring of 1941 the Yugoslavs defied Hitler, and German Armies swept into the Balkan peninsula in April; this, it is always supposed, delayed Hitler's attack upon Russia upon which he had decided on 31st July, 1940, before it was certain that the invasion of Britain would fail. At the Berghof on that day he stated that "Russia must be disposed of, Spring 1941," because "should Russia be smashed, then England's last hope is extinguished." Militarily this was nonsense, but Hitler was true to *Mein Kampf* to the end. "The more quickly we smash Russia the better," Hitler also remarked. "Operation only makes sense if we smash the state heavily in one blow."[1]

1940 was an apocalyptic year. For Hitler it opened with a few frustrations, a phoney war, a recalcitrant Mussolini and

[1] Recorded in Halder's Diary. See D.G.F.P. series D. vol. X. p. 373.

grim and apparently interminable bargaining with Stalin over
Russo-German commercial exchanges. At last on 11th
February the Germans and Russians came to terms, five and
a half months, it is true, before Hitler decided to fight Russia.
It was agreed that Russia was to deliver up to the value of
420 to 430 million marks by 11th February, 1941, and
Germany the same with three months to spare. Hitler was
presumably clear in his own mind that by May 1941 he would
be "disposing" of Russia instead of delivering the goods.
That Stalin should have contributed what he did in grains and
oil to a murderous enemy about to attack him provides one of
the strangest comments on his attitude towards Germany between August 1939 and June 1941.

Now Hitler waited impatiently for the spring when Finland
came to terms with Russia in March. In April the Germans
seized Denmark and Norway, in May they invaded and
occupied Holland and Belgium, annexed Luxembourg and
attacked France, quickly breaching the Maginot Line. May
10th, which brought the Germans into the Netherlands,
brought Winston Churchill into power in Britain as the
successor of Neville Chamberlain, with a National Coalition
Government. From that day on the British knew what they
were fighting for. And the rest of Europe, in so far as it
had not been seduced by Hitler's victories, hung upon the
words which Winston Churchill broadcast, with his slight
lisp, giving back to Europe the soul it had thought to have
sold to Hitler. It was a brilliant summer. The sun shone
relentlessly upon the beaches of Dunkirk from which at the
end of May the British and Allied troops escaped from
Europe until they should return in force in June 1944.

On 10th June Mussolini, afraid of coming too late to
share in the victory, impelled an unprepared and unwilling
Italy into war against France. It was indeed the last moment,
for France surrendered a week later; the Third Republic
was succeeded by the paternalistic halfway régime, the *État
français*, which the Germans allowed Pétain to set up at
Vichy on 1st July. On 18th June, Waterloo Day, another

new tone, this time in French from Charles de Gaulle, was
heard on the B.B.C. Three times he cried that France was
not alone. The fighting in France could not be final because
this was a World War, he said. " *Toutes les fautes, tous les
retards, toutes les souffrances, n'empêchent pas qu'il y a, dans
l'univers, tous les moyens pour écraser un jour nos ennemis.*"

Brave words which emphasised that Britain *was* alone in
her fight against Hitler : she had no allies now but the exiled
governments of the Poles, the Czechs, the Dutch and the
Norwegians : the King of Belgium and the King of Denmark
had stayed at home. The Battle of Britain was fought through
August and September. There were scarcely enough pilots in
the R.A.F. but they held out. On 17th September Hitler
postponed indefinitely Operation Sea-Lion for the invasion
of Britain : it was impossible unless the Luftwaffe was supreme
or the British Navy defeated. Ten days later a Tripartite
Pact between Germany, Italy and Japan was signed in
Berlin : a month after this Mussolini invaded Greece.

During the winter of 1940-1 President Roosevelt of the
United States, who had just been re-elected, worked out with
Winston Churchill methods by which America might help
Britain without making war on Hitler. Roosevelt declared
that America was to become the " arsenal of democracy "
and that to supply Britain with arms was the best way to
defend the United States. In March 1941 the Lend-Lease
Act provided for the supply of war material to Britain
regardless of Britain's immediate ability to pay for it.

Chapter XIII

HITLER'S EUROPE
1941-3

It is time to return to Hitler himself although the pattern of his thought was all too clearly illustrated by the history of Europe from March 1936 to June 1941. Within Germany there was virtually no history after that plebiscite at the end of March 1936 except for the Nazi leaders jockeying for position and the sporadic discontent expressed privately by some retired general or diplomatist. There was only one incident to contradict this statement, but it was a quite extraordinary one. In the night of 10th to 11th May, 1941, Hitler's deputy in the Nazi Party, Rudolf Hess, left Augsburg by air alone and landed by parachute near Glasgow. Hess was a much less well-known Nazi leader than Göring or Goebbels, or even Ribbentrop, or Ley of the Labour Front; his name was less familiar than that of Himmler or the second-in-command of the all-powerful police, Reinhard Heydrich. Most Nazi leaders were either Bavarians or *Auslandsdeutsche*; Hess was an exceptional member of the second category in that he had been born in Egypt. He had been a student in Munich in the 'twenties under Professor Karl Haushofer, the specialist in geopolitics whom he had brought into touch with Hitler when Hitler and Hess were in prison in Landsberg on the Lech in 1924. Of all the party leaders Hess was the only one who could easily be regarded by British people as a " decent sort of chap," and he had made friends with people like the Duke of Hamilton at the Olympic Games held at Berlin in 1936. He may well have believed genuinely in the anti-Communist crusade and he may well have been genuinely rather *exalté*. At all events he believed that he might be able to reconcile in-

fluential opinion in Britain and enrol it in support of
Germany's imminent war against Russia. The evidence suggests that Hitler did not know what Hess intended: Hess
had him informed after he had left, and he was prepared to
be disowned. The fantastic news of the landing of Hess in
Scotland and his identification by Ivone Kirkpatrick of the
Foreign Office, who had known him in Berlin, was the first
piece of obviously bad news for Germany for years: the
fact that the Italians had failed to conquer Greece in the
preceding winter had been overtaken by the German conquest
of that country. Now the B.B.C. cashed in, and Hitler and
Goebbels were obviously angry and at a loss.

Gradually since 1938 the ruthless inhumanity of the
National Socialist régime had emerged more starkly. In
November 1938, on the *Kristallnacht*, as it was called, the
Nazis engineered a pogrom in Germany in which the
remaining Jews were baited, some injured, some killed and
much of their property wrecked. At about the same time, to
the credit of the Berliners who had shown no enthusiasm for
the display of armoured cars that September, Hitler summoned
obedient journalists and explained to them how unfortunate it
was that he had had to speak so much of peace since 1933:
now this must be changed. With the occupation of Prague
and the conquest of Poland Hitler's racial policy could be
carried out on a remorselessly large scale. These two countries
had not been included in the plan for the Nazi domination
of eastern Europe for they had been marked down for
destruction. A large slice of western Poland was annexed to
Germany and germanised; the Poles were expelled from
it to rot in a central area named the General Government
which was to be deliberately neglected. Three million Polish
Jews were shipped off in the same direction more murderously.
The Czechs of Bohemia and Moravia, like the Poles, were
deprived of their universities and schools; they too lived in
terror of expulsion to some waste land.[1] The system of

---

[1] At the secret meeting of 5th Nov. 1937 Hitler had spoken of
expelling two million Czechs. See D.G.F.P. series D. vol. I. no. 19.

concentration camps, which Hitler had planned for years and inaugurated when he became German Chancellor, was methodically extended by Himmler. It had become a preserve of the S.S. since 1934 or earlier. Within these camps any German who did not obey the Nazis was tormented in various ways, often to death; within some of them set up in western Poland, from 1941 onwards, gas chambers were built in which Jews were exterminated in large numbers. Slavs like the Poles and Czechs were saved from extermination partly because their labour was needed for the time being; even some Jews' lives were temporarily saved for this reason. The war again Russia vastly increased the scale of Hitler's war; it also vastly extended the horrors of National Socialism : Russian prisoners could be maltreated, both as Slavs or Mongols, and as Communists. They were regarded as without human rights, and, although not the admitted objects of an extermination campaign, the Nazi régime preferred them to perish (unless they were unusually useful) so that space and food should not be wasted upon them. As the war proceeded and the Germans conquered and occupied Europe, Germany itself depended more and more upon what was in fact slave labour. By 1945 there were about six million forcibly detained foreign workers in Germany.

It may be as well to recapitulate that by the time of Hitler's attack upon Russia Germany had annexed Alsace, Lorraine, Luxembourg, Eupen and Malmédy, the Danzig territory, the Memel-land, Pomorze, Poznania and much of Slovenia. She had occupied Denmark, Norway, Holland, Belgium, Northern France with Paris. Her troops were in Roumania as friends and as enemies in Greece. The régimes in Vichy, Bratislava, Budapest, Zagreb, Helsinki and Sofia were strongly influenced by Germany, as indeed was that in Rome. She ruled as 'sub-states' the General Government of Poland and the Protectorate of Bohemia and Moravia and the undefined military area of Serbia with the Voivodina (before 1918 part of the Hungarian Banat). This peculiar jumble of authorities was partly created as a temporary measure, a preliminary to the greater goal of the conquest of Russia. That once achieved the whole would be surveyed and more tightly organised; the organisation of the future would be after the end of war, the waging of which necessitated mere expedients. Within this empire the laws, regulations and barbarities prevalent in Nazi Germany, including the persecution of the Jews, were enforced: there was no personal liberty, the press and all the arts—or their shadows—were entirely controlled: Himmler's S.S. was everywhere the ultimate police authority using the most atrocious police methods. In the dependent states from Italy to Finland the pressure to follow the German example was great and variously effective. What happened in the new 'independent' Croatia, ruled by the terrorist Pavelić (who had been partly responsible for the murder of King Alexander in 1934) and allotted for the time-being to Italy's sphere of interest, was no better than what happened in Nazi Germany. Indeed the Croat terrorists called Ustaše massacred Serbs, of whom there were many in the now inflated Croatia, more ostentatiously than the Germans massacred Jews. The Germans, who had been brought to Germany from their former homes in the Baltic States and Bessarabia and those arriving from the South Tyrol, wasted in camps until decisions should be made as to their final settlement.

The whole conglomeration was keyed to the war effort. After the Jews the Poles and the Czechs had the lowest rations. One probably lived best in Slovakia where agriculture was on the whole fruitful and there were few cities, only Bratislava being of any size. Slovakia, moreover, profited from the Nazi plan of turning it into Hitler's well-dressed shop-window to display the joys of living under Nazi protection.

Throughout the war Sweden, Switzerland, Spain and Portugal were able to remain neutral: Turkey only declared war on Germany in February 1945. They became hunting-grounds for agents from each side competing for information about the other. Switzerland, the richest of them, was most severely hit. Her army was mobilised to protect her neutrality, there were no more tourists, and the raw materials she depended upon importing, like coal and iron, became increasingly difficult to obtain. Moreover her inland position hampered her trade which normally passed through Genoa or up or down the Rhine through the Netherland ports. As head-quarters of the International Red Cross and the not quite defunct League of Nations, Switzerland had special responsi-bilities, and she was specially accessible to refugees. There were Nazi plans for invading Switzerland, for instance in 1940, should there have been some hitch for the German Armies invading Holland and Belgium. But the Germans prob-ably believed what was true, that the Swiss would have blown up the St. Gotthard tunnel, thus cutting the main railway line by which German coal was carried to Italy; without this Italy was bound to collapse at once. The Swiss Army moreover was seriously prepared to retire to its 'redoubt' in the mountains to make a last stand. Owing to the three great languages written and read by the Swiss, the newspapers of Switzerland played a notable part in the Second World War; of these the most important was the *Neue Zürcher Zeitung.* An accurate report in November 1940 from its London correspondent, Hans Egli, of the bombing of Coventry came to Hitler's knowledge; it conflicted with the account the Luftwaffe had given him. From that time onwards the Führer expected to be informed of the main contents of the *Neue Zürcher Zeitung;* the paper was thus able potentially to influence Hitler, in spite of the fact that beneath the restraint imposed by military censorship it was uncompromisingly opposed to National Socialism. The for-tunes of war could to some extent be gauged by watching the attitude of a country like Switzerland. In spring 1940 the Swiss Government led by the French-Swiss Minister, Pilet-Golaz, seemed prepared to give way to German pressure, particularly with regard to the press. Towards the end of July, however, General Guisan, also a Vaudois, issued a defiant statement. Gradually Guisan's portrait appeared everywhere while Pilet-Golaz was discredited. The French-Swiss tended to belong to bankers' circles which favoured Vichy, or to be Communist workmen, but the German and Italian-speaking Swiss were on the whole genuine opponents of dictatorship, and made a real contribution in many small ways to its final defeat.

On 22nd June, 1941, about a month later than the date originally planned for this Operation Barbarossa, the Germans invaded Russia; it was exactly, to the day, a hundred and twenty-nine years since Napoleon had done so. Stalin, for some reason which has never fully been explained, refused to believe the evidence that this attack was imminent, and at first the Russians seemed to be overwhelmed by surprise and the mobile technique of the by now seasoned German troops. In the West people spoke of Russia being finished by the end of six weeks and indeed by the beginning of August she did not seem far from collapse. The supreme direction of the war was in the hands of a State Defence Committee consisting of Stalin, Molotov, Voroshilov, Berya and Malenkov, but all real power and responsibility remained with Stalin. After ten days of defeat and retreat, on 3rd July Stalin broadcast his speech about scorching the Russian earth. "In occupied regions conditions must be made unbearable for the enemy and all his accomplices. They must be hounded and annihilated at every step, and all their measures frustrated."

Soon the Germans were at the Dnieper, taking a huge number of Russian prisoners. Towards the end of August the Russians were faced with the question of whether, before their retreat from there, to blow up their proudest technical achievement, the great power-station at Dniepropetrovsk. All Europe held its breath. Then on 28th August came the relentless explosion.

The German Army rushed on. In the north on 11th September General von Leeb announced that Leningrad was to be captured quickly, regardless of the cost, and it was cut off and blockaded. On 19th September after a six weeks' battle the Germans entered Kiev to find everything systematically destroyed. They proceeded to conquer nearly all the Ukraine. On 2nd October Hitler issued an Order of the Day to the German troops facing Moscow: "To-day is the beginning of the last great decisive battle of this year " he proclaimed, and the offensive actually began four days later. In November all the Russian Government offices were evacuated to Kuibyshev on the Volga. This caused alarming demoralisation and disorders. Yet the fact that Stalin remained at the Kremlin just when Hitler had issued an order that " the Kremlin was to be blown up to signalise the overthrow of Bolshevism " seemed to save the situation. Stalin was indeed to remain at the Kremlin throughout the war except for such rare occurrences as his appearance at Teheran or Yalta.

Russian casualties were appalling, but in November 1941 it was above all the economic war with Germany which seemed to be lost. From the Russian territory then occupied by Germany had come 65% of the country's pre-war coal production, 68% of its pig iron, 58% of its steel, 60% of its aluminium. Yet the spirit of the Russians seemed invincible; we shall never know whether it was for Communism or for Russia's sake, whose traditional heroes Stalin had by now invoked, that they were prepared to die. The Communist leaders, for all their hostility to ' bourgeois nationalism,' had naturally appealed to national as well as class emotions. " A few parties of our troops " according to the well-known German General, Blumentritt, " from the 258th Infantry Division, actually got into the suburbs of Moscow. But the Russian workers poured out of the factories and fought with their hammers and other tools in defence of their city."

It was not until 1st December that there was a Russian counter-attack under new commanders at Tula. On 8th December Hitler announced that he had suspended all operations for the winter and the German Army was ordered to take up winter quarters near Moscow. Now the Germans, whom Hitler had failed to supply with proper winter equipment, were driven out, and for the first time obliged to retreat. The day before Hitler's announcement the Japanese had attacked American bases at Pearl Harbour in Hawaii in the middle of the Pacific Ocean. Hitler had been urging a move of this kind on the Japanese for months; he and Mussolini welcomed their new ally excitedly and eagerly declared war on America. Thus Hitler had deliberately created an alliance between the British Empire, the U.S.S.R. and the United States. But for the series of staggering blows dealt by the Japanese at the Americans and British in the Far East it would have been clear from now on that Hitler's megalomania would destroy him. Yet for another year he seemed to be completely victorious.

Hitler's attack upon Russia had caused a crystallisation of Central and East European relationships. Since the fall of France, Beneš's Czechoslovak Government in exile formed since March 1939, and Sikorski's Polish Government which had succeeded that of the discredited Colonels, had moved from Paris to London. On his arrival in 1940 Beneš had received only provisional recognition. On 12th July, 1941, a treaty of mutual assistance was concluded between Britain and the U.S.S.R., each undertaking to make no separate peace. This, which by implication blotted out the Munich Agreement, led straight to full British and Russian recognition of the Czechs and a Russo-Czech Agreement signed in London on 18th July. Since the Czechs had burnt with Pan-Slav sympathy for Russia since Munich, this was relatively straightforward. Not so the Russo-Polish question. The German invasion of Russia had brought all inter-war Poland as well as the former Baltic States beneath German domination. Virtually all Poles, except a handful of Polish Communists in Russia, aimed at the restoration of their inter-war frontiers to the east and some gains from Germany to their west. It has been seen that it was a Polish tradition to be intransigent. Sikorski was clear-sighted and moderate; he knew that the smaller nations like the Poles and the Czechs needed to co-operate if they were to enjoy any real independence; he wished, in spite of their mutual dislike, for a Polish-Czech federation. Where he really thought Poland's frontiers should be drawn no one can tell for certain: all Poles, particularly Galicians like Sikorski, felt nostalgic about the problematical city of Lwów because its University, for instance, was much more Polish than Ukrainian. At any rate Sikorski had always to demand more than he wanted in order half-way to satisfy his compatriots. Relations with Soviet Russia were greatly embittered since the autumn of 1939 when the Russians had taken over Eastern Galicia, persecuting the upper classes, who were Polish, and too often maltreating or massacring the Polish troops they captured, particularly the officers.

With the German attack upon Russia Sikorski, who had won his spurs in the battle of Warsaw in 1920, hastened to seek agreement with the Russians. He met the Russian Ambassador, Maisky, at the Foreign Office on 5th July, 1941, and very soon appointed a close personal friend of his, the historian Stanislas Kot of the Polish Peasant Party, to be his Ambassador to Russia. Kot reached Moscow in September with instructions to patch up some kind of friendship with Stalin while carrying out a national rescue operation of the many Poles in detention in the U.S.S.R. An intensely dramatic situation arose at the beginning of December 1941. The Germans were halted at the gates of Moscow when Sikorski, Commander-in-Chief and Prime Minister of the Poles, flew to the besieged city and broadcast to the Russian people, who had lost much, from the Polish people who had lost everything, and had suffered at Russian hands. Two days later on 5th December Sikorski and Kot signed a treaty of friendship with Stalin and Molotov: Stalin agreed to release all Polish soldiers in Russia and allow them to be enrolled in a new Polish Army led by General Anders, himself only recently released from Russian captivity. Sikorski and Kot were very brave men and they did their utmost to lay the ghost of centuries of conflict in Poland's eastern lands which were Russia's western ones. It suited Stalin to make use of their goodwill for a time. Later it suited Stalin and their own more extremist compatriots to discredit them. For the time being the Russo-Polish frontier question was ignored, although Stalin brought up the Polish question when Eden visited him on 16th December 1941.

Meanwhile as early as 16th July, 1941, Hitler, at a secret meeting at his headquarters with Rosenberg, Göring, Lammers, Keitel and Bormann, had discussed what he intended to do with Russia; Bormann recorded what was said by Hitler. The Führer did not wish to make any enemies "prematurely and unnecessarily . . ." "It must be clear to us, however, that we shall never withdraw from these areas." While insisting that it must always be emphasised that the Germans had come as liberators Hitler stated that the Crimea with a large hinterland was to be annexed to the Reich and, the natives having been expelled, was to "be settled by Germans only." "The Führer emphasises that the Volga colony, too, will have to become Reich territory, also the district around Baku; the latter will have to become a German concession (military colony)." The Baltic States, naturally, were to be annexed. "In future there are never to be any but German soldiers west of the Urals." Hitler welcomed the Russian plan for partisan warfare against the Germans: "it enables us to exterminate everyone who opposes us." Thus all Europe east of Germany as far as the Urals was to be annexed and exploited solely for Germany's benefit. Himmler, incidentally, "was to receive no other authority than he had in Germany proper" (where it was complete). It was made clear that there would be as much shooting and re-settling as was found "necessary."[1] The author of *Mein Kampf* had not mellowed: the programme formulated at Landsberg on the Lech in 1924 was being implemented.

Heinrich Himmler, it should here be recapitulated, was the chief of all the German police organs including the Secret State Police or Gestapo. He was also the *Reichsführer* of the black-uniformed S.S. to whom the S.A. had, in so far as they survived, been subordinated since 1934. Himmler also had his own army dressed in military uniform, the

[1] D.G.F.P. series D. vol. XIII. no. 114.

Waffen S.S. which had steadily grown since 1934, although
Hitler had promised the Generals that there should be no
soldiers outside their control. With the outbreak of war
Himmler fused the S.S. security service with the state police
in the *Reichssicherheitshauptamt*. At the same time, precisely
on 7th October, 1939, Hitler appointed him *Reichskommissar
für die Festigung deutschen Volkstums*, thereby putting him
in charge of "re-settling" all the unfortunate people who
had to be uprooted in the name of Hitler's racialist beliefs.
For years Himmler's right-hand had been Reinhard Heydrich
who was cleverer and more cruel by nature. In September
1941 Heydrich was sent to Prague as Deputy *Reichsprotektor*
to terrorise the Czechs and to purge the Protectorate of Jews
or make it, as he said, *judenrein*. What he did in Prague
was only a small part of his activity which included eager
interest in the universal destruction of the Jews. Hitler
appointed Heydrich to be Gestapo chief for Occupied Europe
at about this time, sending him instructions via Göring on
31st July, 1941, to prepare to carry out the "Final Solution."
Originally the Jews had been expelled from wherever they
lived, then concentrated in areas within the Polish General-
Government; both these solutions had been accompanied by
all kinds of robbery, humiliation and other ill-treatment, and
incidental murder. Now that experiments in gassing to death
incurables and mental cases in Germany had been "per-
fected", it had become technically possible to proceed to the
"Final Solution" of wholesale murder. In November 1941
Heydrich informed the High Command of the German Army
that he had been in charge of preparing the "Final Solution"
for years, and since June 1941 in charge also of mass-shootings
of Jews in military areas by his special troops, the *Einsatz-
gruppen*.

It must have been in August 1941 that Heydrich informed
a subordinate of his, an S.S. officer called Adolf Eichmann,
that he, Eichmann, was to co-operate in carrying out the
"Final Solution." The career of this Eichmann is worth a
moment's consideration for the lurid light it throws upon

the period. Eichmann had been born seventeen years later than Hitler and had grown up in Linz in Austria where Hitler went to school: his social background was not dissimilar. Eichmann joined the Austrian Nazi Party in April 1932, going straight into the Austrian S.S. When Austria banned the Nazis he went to Germany, becoming, like many Austrian Nazis, an S.S. guard at the concentration camp of Dachau near Munich in January 1934; he may well have been a witness when the former Bavarian Minister, Kahr, was murdered there on 30th June, 1934. Eichmann was obedient and industrious and took great trouble to acquire information about Jews, their history and their faith. Thus on 1st August, 1938, the centre for deporting Jews in Vienna was put under Eichmann; in the previous spring the *Anschluss*, owing to the high proportion of Jews in the Austrian capital, had augmented the Jewish problem. Eichmann achieved prodigious results in transporting and concentrating Jews, so much so that in October 1939 he went back to Berlin (he had worked there before) as Head of Department IV B 4 (for Jewish affairs) of the *Reichssicherheitshauptamt*. In August 1941 one gets the impression that Eichmann was slightly taken aback at the instructions to kill the people he had hitherto uprooted and crowded into ghettos. But that was all. He and his kind—another was Rudolf Hoess, who was a little later in command of the gassing at Auschwitz—dutifully accepted the orders received from the evil god they worshipped. They were all sworn to secrecy and seem partially to have consoled or fortified themselves by pretending not to know what they were doing.

It is only just to add the story of Kurt Gerstein[1] who deliberately applied to join the S.S. because in 1940 he had heard rumours of the experiments in gassing lunatics; he wished to know the worst and to try to counteract it. He had had a medical training and was soon promoted in January 1942 to a highly responsible position on the scientific side

[1] Introduced as one of the characters in his play *Der Stellvertreter* (The Representative) by Rolf Hochhuth.

of the huge organisation which the S.S. had become. He found out exactly how the Jews were to be gassed and was able sometimes to sabotage the supplies of the gas used. In addition he took fearful risks in order to inform people at home and abroad, particularly leaders of the Churches (he himself was a Protestant). Through a Swedish diplomatist whom he met in a train he conveyed the information to London. In July 1945 he was found hanged in a French prison, whether by fellow-prisoners, or by his own hand, is not known. It took until 1965 for Kurt Gerstein to be fully rehabilitated; there may have been others like him about whom the truth will never be known.

The year 1942 opened with Germany's *Festung Europa*, or European fortress, apparently unscathed; tiny groups of partisans here and there in Yugoslavia were not yet visible. The conquest of what the Germans called the East had given the Nazis new opportunities of exterminating those human beings whom they chose to regard as inferior. On 20th January, 1942, at a conference of representatives of the German Ministries at the Wannsee near Berlin the 'Final Solution' of gassing all the available Jews in the death-camps of Auschwitz, Treblinka, Majdanek and other bases in Poland was corroborated and worked out in administrative detail. With the Jews out of the way, it was clear from the Bormann Minute of 16th July, 1941, that the turn of other "weak" races for more systematic extermination or genocide would come. This monstrous crime, long planned but only now made technically feasible, was an essential factor in Hitler's Europe. It might never be named, thus adding to the terror in the Nazi atmosphere. To be linked with Hitler by nameless crimes was the fate of many more helpless people than Eichmann.

On 27th May, 1942, an attempt was made upon Heydrich's life as he was driving to his office in Prague; he died of his wounds on 4th June. Heydrich's death led to fearful reprisals at Lidice and throughout the Czech area. Its importance was tremendous. A Czech and a Slovak flown in from Britain had struck down perhaps the most powerful man in Germany after Hitler: in a sense the more naïf Himmler had been Heydrich's tool. The attack upon Heydrich came one day after the Twenty-year Alliance signed in London between Britain and Russia (26th May, 1942). Already the British had made real efforts to help the Russians fight and they were to augment these steadily.[1] When Churchill visited Stalin in Moscow in August 1942, however, he was bitterly reproached because he was bound to make clear that the British could not for at least another year muster strength for an invasion of Western Europe. Until D Day came the Russians did not cease to express their suspicions as to the motives of the British.

While Churchill was paying his first visit to Moscow the Germans for the second time appeared to have conquered Russia, and the shape of the battle around Stalingrad, Stalin's city which Hitler was determined to annihilate, was beginning to appear. For months there was something like deadlock. During the autumn of 1942 the Allied landing on the night of 7th-8th November in French North Africa had profound repercussions in Europe. Up to that time the French heart of Europe seemed scarcely to beat, and the smaller countries neighbouring France were paralysed: as yet de Gaulle seemed a freak voice on the London wireless. Yet surprisingly France still had unmilitary weapons. Hitler wanted to be able to tell the world that the French had joined him against Britain. For this reason he allowed an unoccupied, economically unimportant, France to be ruled by Pétain at Vichy with relatively little German interference. Further, in 1940 the French Navy had not been obliged to surrender to the Germans; it was still at Toulon. And beyond that France still had an empire, the main portion of which was North-West Africa. This was cut off from Europe by the British Fleet and had not really taken sides. Hitler's desire to make

[1] Eden, just before he moved from the War Office to the Foreign Office, had visited Stalin as early as mid-December 1941 just after Sikorski's visit. See Avon. *The Reckoning.* 1965.

use of France, her name, her navy and her empire, by not crushing her, collided with the ambitions of both Mussolini and Franco. Gradually the contradictions of Hitler's policy towards France helped to ruin him, if at heavy cost to the French.

Vichy France in theory carried through a "national revolution," authoritarian, anti-masonic, anti-Semitic. It made Pétain into the symbol of its national honour, which, if thus symbolised, seemed not to be lost. But Paris and industrial France were occupied by the Germans, and both parts of France were, like all the territories under Nazi control, exploited economically in Germany's interest. Life became difficult, food, except in country districts, ran short. More and more Frenchmen were sent to work in Germany. For the time being one must wait, and *attentisme* became the average state of mind for some time. At least one had escaped from the war, people said at first, but with less and less conviction. Reynaud and Mandel were condemned to fortress detention while Daladier and Blum and several other leaders of the Third Republic were arrested. Daladier, Blum and Gamelin were at last brought to trial in February 1942 at Riom, when Blum, particularly, put up a splendid defence. Blum's behaviour throughout the war was magnificent. This man, accustomed to every luxury, mocked at as an effete intellectual, never complained over the sordid details of prison life. He never flinched though he was a Jew and his greatly loved son, Robert, was a prisoner in Germany, kept in special detention as a hostage with a son of Stalin's.

Pierre Laval was the villain of the Vichy act. He believed that Hitler's victory was final and that therefore the French must make the best bargain possible with him. Pétain neither agreed with nor liked Laval, and, to the irritation of the Germans, dismissed him in December 1940 : he was even arrested until the Germans came to his rescue. After this Admiral Darlan was the leading Minister at Vichy for some time. He was in command at the time of Germany's attack upon the U.S.S.R. after which both Déat and Doriot volun-

teered for the anti-Bolshevik Legion. In April 1942, however, the Germans insisted upon the restoration of Laval:
they now made him unchallengeable, but he was not all-
powerful since the secretive old Pétain kept a tight, if not
strong, hold on the steering-wheel. The return of Laval
weakened Pétain in that it caused the Americans to withdraw their envoy, Admiral Leahy, who had given the Marshal
helpful support against the Germans, from Vichy.

When the Allied Forces—completely surprising the Germans—descended upon French North Africa in November
1942 the political position was utterly obscure; finally General
Juin brought the armed forces there on to the side of the
Allies. To the disgust of de Gaulle and his Free French
movement, now no longer negligible, the Allies set up a
political government in North Africa with Darlan as High
Commissioner; thus it was difficult to see who had come over
to whom. The Commander-in-Chief was General Giraud,
rival to de Gaulle, a man of the right without much intelligence, but one who had a momentary reputation because he
had romantically escaped from a prison camp in Germany;
in general he was a more conventionally acceptable figure
than his rival.

The new situation strained Hitler's patience further than
he was prepared to allow. On 8th November Vichy asked
for German assistance but, in accordance with Pétain's
guiding principles, refused to declare war on Britain and
the United States. Therefore on 11th November, 1942, the
Germans invaded and occupied Vichy France. They rushed
to Toulon, but, thanks to secret orders from Darlan two years
before and now renewed, "quicker even than the German
mechanised units could speed through Toulon . . . explosion
after explosion sounded the death-knell of the pride of the
French Navy as its last great Fleet sank beneath the waters."[1]

The occupation of the whole of France was, it has been
said, the real end of Vichy. Pétain was, on the whole, still
supported by the German Ambassador, Abetz, who, like Rahn

[1] *Survey of International Affairs 1939-46. Hitler's Europe.* p. 406.

later in Salò,[1] regretted the chances thrown away by the
crudity of Hitler and Ribbentrop. So Pétain continued and
was never unpopular because the French liked his obstinacy
towards the demands of the conquerors. With November
1942 the occupation costs claimed by Hitler were raised from
three hundred to five hundred million francs a day. Shortly
before the occupation of Vichy-France Laval promised that
150,000 volunteer workers should be sent from there to
Germany in return for the release of 50,000 prisoners-of-war.
This led to disturbances, particularly in Lyons. In February
1943 compulsory labour was imposed on certain age-groups
throughout France, although in practice there was much eva-
sion. By the autumn of 1943 it was reckoned that there were
well over a million Frenchmen and Frenchwomen working in
Germany. Exactly as in Italy, Germany's insatiable demands
for labour drove many to join the resistance groups rather than
be sent to Germany.

The history of clandestine resistance movements is particularly difficult to formulate partly because the written evidence
often had to be destroyed immediately, partly because each
small group was bound to try to know as little as possible
about the others at first. In unoccupied France before
November 1942 there were three chief groups, *Combat* which
was mainly Christian-Democrat and was associated with
Georges Bidault, *Libération* with Socialist Trade Union connections, and *Franc Tireur* whose members included Marc
Bloch, a brilliant historian of Alsatian Jewish extraction.
There were also the Communists who went into action
towards the end of 1941. At first the chief activity of resistance groups was to write, print and circulate clandestine
newspapers. In January 1942 a former prefect, Jean Moulin,
was parachuted into France by de Gaulle's Free French and
on 27th November he had a meeting with representatives of
the three big groups and General Delestraint (who was in
charge of the secret army) in Lyons. After this the *Conseil
National de la Résistance* met secretly under Moulin's presi-

[1] See below. p. 208.

dency in Paris in May 1943; in June Moulin was arrested[1]
and Bidault took his place. It should be noted that the
ligne de démarcation between the two Frances was retained by
the Germans because they could not then spare the troops to
occupy in depth to the south of it.

The murder of Darlan on Christmas Eve 1942 removed a
stumbling-block for the organisation of French resistance,
but de Gaulle would not accept the leadership of Giraud who
took Darlan's place. The furious hostility of the two generals
to one another involved Britain and the United States, since
the Americans thought ill of de Gaulle while the British, if
they found him annoying, yet did not wish to disown him.
In the summer of 1943, together with Generals Georges and
Catroux, Giraud and de Gaulle were pushed into forming
the *Comité Français de Libération Nationale* (C.F.L.N.) at
Algiers, and from then on de Gaulle edged out Giraud's
supporters whom he thought little better than Pétainists: for
his part Giraud deplored de Gaulle's collaboration with the
Communists. In fact in August 1943 the U.S.S.R., before
the United States or Britain, recognised the Algiers Committee as representing the French Republic.

While a Second Front of a kind had been opened in North
Africa in November 1942, the Russians and the Germans
were fighting for single houses in the streets of Stalingrad.
Twelve days later came the Russian counter-offensive. By
the end of the year the main German Army had been thrown
back a hundred and twenty miles from Stalingrad. On 1st
February, 1943, von Paulus' Army, which had been encircled
for some time, surrendered to the Russians, and by the end
of that month the Germans were driven out of the Caucasus.
The battle of Stalingrad, and with it the Second World War,
had been lost by Hitler. This was the turning-point though
the greatest sacrifices had yet to be made.

---

[1] Jean Moulin was tortured and killed by the Gestapo. Heroically
he betrayed nothing. On December 19, 1964 what were believed to
be his remains were placed in the Panthéon in Paris as part of the
celebration of France's liberation twenty years after.

Chapter XIV

THE RISE OF TITO AND THE
FALL OF MUSSOLINI

When Mussolini declared war on France on 10th June, 1940, his decision was thoroughly unpopular in Italy; nearly all the Fascist *gerarchi* regretted it. The surrender of the French forestalled the Duce's hopes. In October he attacked Metaxas' Greece, itself a dictatorship, on the flimsiest pretext; the winter was spent in the humiliation of the Italian leadership through its failure, and the humiliation of the ordinary Italian soldiers who felt they had no right to be in Greece. Then came Hitler's spring offensive and the Axis occupation of the Balkan countries in the spring of 1941 and then the German attack upon Russia. Mussolini insisted upon sending ill-equipped Italian contingents as tokens of Axis solidarity to the U.S.S.R.: Stalin rightly chose these and the Hungarian and Roumanian soldiers as the first victims of his counter-offensive in November 1942.

Anti-German feeling in Italy was nourished in 1941 by a number of things, one of which was the question of the South Tyrol. Soon after the Steel Pact of May 1939 Germany and Italy had made an agreement about this, according to which the German-speaking South Tyrolese could in the next few years opt for German citizenship and be settled in Germany. This kind of plan came into Himmler's special task of racial re-settlement and he intended to do the thing thoroughly. The Italians, however, did not want anything so drastic; they only wanted to be rid of the Nazi ring-leaders among the South Tyrolese. Hence they obstructed the working of the agreement, saying with considerable justification that, since there seemed nowhere but a camp to receive the departing South Tyrolese, where was the hurry. In Germany, and particularly among the South Tyrolese themselves, there was support for this attitude since it was loudly assumed that after the war the Duce would give the South Tyrol to Hitler as a token of his gratitude. Hitler, and therefore Ribbentrop too, took their Axis policy and the Brenner frontier seriously for some time yet, and in any case regretted the effect of this kind of talk on Mussolini and Ciano.

Meanwhile, although the Germans tried to deny it, they were not keeping to their promises in deliveries of grain and other goods to Italy, and the Italians blamed the Germans for the strain on their precious wheat-supply for the spaghetti. The trickiest question of all between the Axis partners was Hitler's appetite for Italian workers of whom already in 1941 there were a hundred thousand in Germany. Mussolini was always begging to send Italian soldiers to the Russian front rather than mere workmen to Germany. The fact was that local Nazi Party authorities despised the Italians as racially inferior and no doubt some of the Italians who were sent to Germany were Communists and not always pliable. This led to brutal punishments such as those inflicted upon recalcitrant Polish workers. When things of this kind came to the knowledge of the Italian' Embassy or Consulates in Germany, complaints went to Rome and protests came back : by the end of 1941 the Germans had agreed that Italian workers who behaved badly should be sent to Italy for punishment, though the promise was certainly not always kept. On 5th September, 1941, Mackensen, German Ambassador in Rome, reported how agitated Mussolini had been by a report that the *Kreisleiter* of Recklinghausen (north of Essen in the Ruhr) had punished a German woman by cutting off her hair and smearing her face with asphalt because she had been seduced by an Italian;[1] the *Kreisleiter*, it was stated, would not have punished her so severely if the man had been a Scandinavian or even an enemy Englishman. The Germans tried to make out that this report had been concocted by a mischievous Italian, but even the concoction would

---

[1] D.G.F.P. series D. vol. XIII. no. 281.

scarcely have been possible unless things of this kind were happening.

At least in November 1942 Mussolini had the satisfaction of seeing Hitler virtually break with Pétain, and of sending Italian troops to occupy Corsica. But then came the catastrophe of Stalingrad which hit the Italian contingent in the U.S.S.R. in November too. And the French Empire in North Africa which Mussolini had hoped to plunder was now in the control of the Anglo-American Allies. Further, the Italian authorities in France, as at home in Italy, often protected Jews, often saved them from the terrible journeys that would end in annihilation. This did not endear Italy to Nazi Germany, whose Führer, although he continued to laud Mussolini's person, was fully informed about the dwindling support the latter enjoyed in Italy.

What was happening in the rest of the *Festung Europa* between the German attack upon Russia and the surrender of Paulus? In addition to the Czechs and the Poles, the Dutch and the Norwegians, there was now a Yugoslav Government in exile in London and a Greek one in Cairo. Luxembourg and Belgium were represented in London, too, though the Belgians were confused by their Ministers working from London while King Leopold insisted upon staying in Belgium. The general pattern in Europe was one of non-co-operation with the Germans, gradually developing into more and more highly organised resistance. Norway produced Quisling who became the derided type of collaborator with the Germans; there was Mussert in Holland, Degrelle in Belgium, Nedić in Serbia. The one country that could boast that it offered no Quisling at all was Poland where the nineteenth century had trained several generations in conspiracy. Indeed the Poles with surprising rapidity constructed a secret state complete with its so-called Home Army and couriers coming and going despite all the terrible obstacles between Poland and London. Since the Germans, with the intention of killing the Polish nation as such, closed down their schools, the Poles conducted a clandestine system of education as well as a clandestine press. At the same time the Polish Army in Britain with headquarters in Fife was being trained, and Polish pilots were famous for their wild courage in the R.A.F. The Czechs by contrast were cautious and reliable. Of course they both produced exceptions to these rules.

In spite of the desperate bravery of the Poles it was impossible to organise partisan warfare in a flat open country with no mountains except in the Tatra. The Czechs had killed Heydrich and paid dear for it; in their circumstances there was now no major operation to carry out but to wait. In Yugoslavia, however, that is to say in Serbia, Montenegro, Bosnia, the country was ideal for guerrilla warfare, and many former Yugoslav officers had in the spring of 1941 taken to the mountains with their weapons. The best known of them was Colonel Draža Mihailović who with a mixed following established himself on the plateau of Ravna Gora in Western Serbia on 11th May, 1941. Mihailović was the old style of Serb officer, loyal to the Karageorgević dynasty, disdainful or indifferent towards other Yugoslavs, conservative, Orthodox: many of his followers were Četnici, men formerly armed by King Alexander to intimidate his political opponents. At about the same time the partly Slovene Croat, Josip Broz, moved from the Zagreb of Pavelić to German-occupied Belgrade. We have met him before in Paris organising the transport of volunteers to fight for the Republican Government in Spain late in 1936. In 1937 he had been made Secretary-General of the Communist Party of Yugoslavia which he had proceeded thoroughly to reorganise. From 1941 at the latest he used the name Tito. In September Tito met Mihailović and they agreed to co-operate though they in fact never did—both their aims and their methods were diametrically opposed.

The war in Russia had caused fresh risings in Serbia against the Germans and in Montenegro against the Italians who were the masters there. In Montenegro the Italian Military Governor, General Pirzio Biroli, came to terms with Mihailović's supporters, leaving the mountains to them if they would leave the towns to the Italians. In this way a kind of collaboration was inaugurated between the Italians and the Četnici. The Germans did little until November by which time they had hoped to have beaten Russia to her knees. By then Tito had rallied quite a lot of support. His plan was to fight everywhere one could—seize a village, attack the enemy's communications before he could hit back; then disperse. So much activity attracted volunteers but was hideously expensive, since, when the Germans did arrive, they often destroyed the village, massacring all its inhabitants. Many of Tito's recruits were people who would rather face the risks of partisan warfare than be murdered as part of a reprisal. In November 1941 and on several occasions in the first half of 1942 German troops attacked and drove back Tito's partisans : in the spring of 1942 Pirzio Biroli's troops in collaboration with followers of Mihailović did the same in Montenegro. Tito withdrew to Bosnia, and established himself at Bihać in October. Bosnia was fairly innocent of Axis troops, so much so that at the end of November, scarcely three weeks after the Allied landing in North Africa, he felt it safe enough to summon an Anti-Fascist Council of National Liberation to Bihać itself. Although most of the delegates—not all of them—were Communists, a Six-Point programme was adopted which postponed all radical change until after elections should have been held. The Sixth Point, however, laid down that " The National Liberation Movement fully recognises the national rights of Croatia, Slovenia, Serbia, Macedonia and all other regions. . . . It guarantees that the national rights of all the peoples of Yugoslavia will be preserved." This approach became Tito's great attraction after the terrible massacres of Serbs by Croats under Pavelić and by comparison with Mihailović's interest only in Serbia. Indeed it was becoming known that Mihailović was avoiding military action because he did not wish to endanger more Serb lives. Thus the keenest Yugoslav idealists, Communist or not, tended to join up with Tito's Partisans if they could :

with him the Yugoslav ideal would have a new chance. Since Mihailović had in January 1942 been appointed War Minister in the Royal Yugoslav Government in London, the idealists turned against the Yugoslav monarchy.

Towards the end of 1942 the situation in Yugoslavia created a new bone of contention between Führer and Duce. Mussolini approved of the collaboration of Pirzio Biroli and other Italian officers with Mihailović's Četnici. But Hitler, who now feared an Allied invasion of the Balkans, stormed against all Serbs; he tried to insist that Četnici and Partisans were equally dangerous, for both would help the Allies against the Germans. On 16th December, 1942 at Hitler's instigation the German Commander-in-Chief, General Keitel, signed an order in the following words:

" The enemy employs, in Partisan warfare, Communist-trained fanatics who do not hesitate to commit any atrocity. It is more than ever a question of life and death. This fight has nothing to do with soldierly gallantry or the principles of the Geneva Convention. If the fight against the Partisans in the East (sic), as well as in the Balkans, is not waged with the most brutal means, we shall shortly reach the point where the available forces are insufficient to control this area.

" It is therefore not only justified, but it is the duty of the troops to use all means without restriction, even against women and children, so long as it ensures success. Any consideration for the Partisans is a crime against the German people."

For Hitler the Četnici were Partisans to exactly the same extent as Tito's men. The same difference of attitude between Führer and Duce was created by the troubles of occupied Greece where, by the summer of 1942, starvation was approaching with rocketing prices. Mussolini went to Athens on his way home from a journey to Libya and was so appalled by the conditions reported to him that on 22nd July, 1942, he wrote to Hitler insisting that palliative steps must be taken. To Hitler the sufferings of the Greeks were of no importance, not even as bad publicity for the Axis.

Not only did Hitler and Mussolini differ over the Yugo-slavs and Greeks; for months Mussolini had tried to persuade Hitler to make peace with invincible space in Russia and come to the help of the Italians in the Mediterranean. Hitler was utterly inflexible, while Italian opinion became more and more opposed to the war and to the Germans. In February 1943 Mussolini re-distributed the Italian Ministries. Although his health was bad he took over both the Foreign Ministry and the Ministry of the Interior, with Bastianini, a fairly competent diplomatist, as Under-Secretary at the former. The whole performance was supposed to be a demonstration of strength, but, since Ciano chose to become Ambassador to the Vatican, people felt certain he would embark upon intrigues for peace. Bastianini sympathised with suggestions which were beginning to come from the Hungarians and Roumanians for getting out of the war : in particular he urged upon the Germans that the "New Order" advertised by their propa-ganda must give more recognition to each separate nation. Indeed Bastianini was in this very much of one mind with Laval when the Frenchman said to Hitler in April 1943, *"Vous voulez gagner la guerre pour faire l'Europe; faites donc l'Europe pour gagner la guerre."*

On 5th March, 1943, serious demonstrations began at the big Mirafiori factory of the Fiat works in Turin. On 12th March the workers at the Mirafiori, encouraged by some of the directors, came out on strike; they complained that com-pensation to bombed-out people had been promised but not paid : leaflets were circulated demanding bread, peace and liberty. The authorities seemed afraid and on the following day three hundred lire was paid to all workmen who would "maintain discipline." This was a major event, the first time that Axis Europe had witnessed a formidable labour demon-stration against its rulers. The disturbances died down in Turin, but strikes then broke out at the Caproni, the Pirelli and Breda works in Milan. When early in April Bastianini accompanied Mussolini to visit Hitler at Klessheim near Salzburg, the Italian Under-Secretary in conversation with

Ribbentrop gave these strikes as one reason why Italy could not continue to fight. Mussolini was in wretched health. Of course he failed to persuade Hitler to come to terms with Russia; similarly he failed to get more German help in the Mediterranean, and so on 7th May Tunis fell to the Allies. An Italian Police report at this time said that "The Party has in twenty years lost the confidence and esteem of even its own followers . . . Enormous progress has been made by Communism which is undermining all branches of production."[1]

At this point the German General Staff began to prepare plans for the occupation of Italy if she defected, and the King of Italy began to look round for a successor to Mussolini, receiving Bonomi, a well-known pre-Fascist politician, on 2nd June, Grandi on 4th June and others later. To Grandi he said "The moment will come . . . Leave your King to choose the opportune moment and in the meantime help me to obtain the constitutional means."[2] In the night of 9th to 10th July Allied troops landed in Sicily, meeting no noticeable resistance except from German troops who fought back hard as they retreated. On 19th July Rome was bombed for the first time by the Americans just when Mussolini had gone north in reply to a summons from Hitler: Duce and Führer this time met at Feltre in the Veneto. Mussolini, charged though he was by all his advisers to say that Italy must make peace, allowed Hitler to tell him that German troops under German command would be sent to his rescue and that a new secret weapon was about to bring a triumphant victory for the Axis.

Already on 16th July Mussolini had agreed to a request from the fiercely pro-German Fascist leader, Farinacci, that the Fascist Grand Council should be summoned for the first time since December 1939: the Duce agreed that this should happen before the end of July. The view of the moderate anti-German Fascists like Bottai was that the time had come for the Grand Council to share the Duce's responsi-

[1] F. W. Deakin. *The Brutal Friendship.* p. 323. [2] ibid. p. 341.

bilities. Grandi, Ambassador in London during the Spanish Civil War and the typical bad Fascist for leftist writers in the 'thirties, was now the constitutionalist, drafting a motion for the revival of all the existing organs of government, and the assumption by the King of the command of the Armed Forces : he even discussed his motion with Mussolini on 22nd July. At 5 p.m. on Saturday, 24th July the Fascist Grand Council met : Mussolini and twenty-eight members were present. They discussed Grandi's motion and one from Farinacci and one from Scorza; the two latter rather vaguely demanded a return to the full working of the Fascist constitution under the leadership of the King. There were nineteen votes in Grandi's favour and seven against; the other two motions were not put to the meeting, though Farinacci managed to vote for his. It was all rather obscure and shifty, but it gave the King his pretext. Mussolini, whose duodenal ulcer had been causing him much trouble for the last year or so, seems to have been in considerable pain : he comforted himself with his belief in the King's confidence and in Hitler's magic. He reached home exhausted at three in the morning of Sunday, 25th July. Meanwhile the King had approached Badoglio, and while Grandi and Ciano were half hoping to take over authority Victor Emmanuel on 25th July, before he saw Mussolini, appointed Badoglio as the new Prime Minister. On the Sunday afternoon (still 25th July) he received Mussolini and informed him that Badoglio had succeeded him; he then had Mussolini arrested by *Carabinieri* and removed to their barracks in Trastevere.

" Outside the barrack walls the twenty-one-year-old Fascist movement had soundlessly collapsed like a soap-bubble in the breeze,"[1] and Hitler had done even more than Mussolini to bring about the destruction of this thing that he had admired so fervently since the " March on Rome." It has been seen that he was fairly well informed about its decline, but never did it seem to cross his mind that without the war

[1] I. Kirkpatrick *Mussolini. Study of a Demagogue.* p. 538. 1964.

Mussolini might have ruled over Italy for another ten years. Psychologically the effect of the Duce's fall, inside Italy of course, but throughout Europe too, was tremendous. All talk of the new European Order sounded hollow now.

Other factors were at work. In 1940 the R.A.F. had only barely managed to beat off the Luftwaffe. In the intervening period the worst indiscretion of the B.B.C. had been to claim much greater success for R.A.F. raids on Germany than they had achieved. By 1943, however, they were becoming formidable, and the R.A.F. bombers had a reputation for greater accuracy than the American Air Force. On the night the Fascist Grand Council was sitting the R.A.F. staged the biggest raid they had yet attempted, this time on Hamburg. The Germans, or many of them, could scarcely fail to realise that their nights would be increasingly disturbed from now on.

In May 1943 the Russians began to push back the German Armies. They were fully mobilised now and the reconstructed factories, together with the Allies, were supplying the arms they needed. Now they were beginning to win, not only to make use of their space and the cold. In the middle of July, just before Hitler met Mussolini at Feltre, the Russian summer offensive began; it was the reason Keitel gave the Italian General, Ambrosio, at Feltre for not sending reinforcements to Italy. At about the same time the Russians established a "National Committee of Free Germany" which offered Communist schooling to German prisoners and Communist propaganda on the wireless. It happened that Moscow had found allies in Göring's Air Ministry since early in the Russian war. A certain Harro Schulze-Boysen, the centre of an intellectual circle and with good family connections, was a young Communist who had been horribly beaten up by the S.A. early in 1933 when he was twenty-four. Through his mother-in-law, a Countess Eulenburg who knew Göring, he later got a position in the Air Ministry. He established a secret radio connection with Moscow whither he passed as much information as he could. In August 1942 Schulze-Boysen and his wife and all their group and its connections were arrested by the Gestapo. A court-martial condemned fifty of them to death, but Hitler, who was more than usually enraged, said this was not enough, and the number was increased to at least seventy-eight. The two Schulze-Boysens were executed on 22nd December, 1942, and the executions of their friends continued for some months.

From the other side, that is from the Catholic and Protestant Churches, protests against National Socialism had long been made. Since the initial error of the Concordat agreed by the Catholic Church with Nazi Germany through Papen in 1933, the Catholics had been divided, many approving of Hitler's abuse of Communism. As time passed and the Nazis broke the Concordat more and more flagrantly Catholic criticism had grown. The Protestant Churches had been divided, too, but quite early on a former naval officer turned pastor, Niemöller by name, had attacked National Socialism. Until the Nazis arrested him, in July 1937, he preached at a church in the Berlin suburb of Dahlem; there were usually a number of youngish officers in full military uniform at the services he held.

In the same winter of Stalingrad and the breaking of the Schulze-Boysen conspiracy came the affair of the Scholls. Hans Scholl and his sister, Sophie, were Catholic students at the University of Munich; they had been influenced by the group of Catholics who published the periodical *Hochland*. Hans Scholl was sent to the Russian front for a part of 1942. When he got back to Munich he and his sister and their friends began to write oppositional leaflets, "leaflets of the White Rose" as they called them. Hostility had been engendered by the local *Gauleiter* who had told the girl students that they should be having illegitimate children in order to increase the German master-race in spite of the casualties in Russia. On 18th February, 1943, the Scholls rained leaflets on the University. They were tried by the notorious Nazi judge, Freisler himself, in a so-called People's Court, and they were executed on 22nd February; various of their friends were tried in April and nearly all were executed. It was whispered about in other universities where their leaflets had occasionally penetrated that these things had happened. When terror reigns, however, incidents like these tend to remain isolated. It is thought that the impact of the news from Casablanca in January 1943, that Churchill and Roosevelt had agreed to demand the unconditional surrender of Germany, Italy and Japan, had stiffened the attitude of the average German while probably contributing to the demand for peace in Italy. On the other hand when in the summer of 1943 the Germans learnt of Mussolini's fall, except for small circles of keen anti-Nazis, they were probably more shaken than at any other time before the final collapse in 1945. Thus in the summer of 1943, had the Allies been able to follow up their success in Sicily and the dismissal of the Duce more quickly, there might well have been a chance of winning the war that year. There was, however, a shortage of landing craft, if, as the Americans insisted, preparations for landing in northern France in the spring of 1944 were now to be begun. Churchill greatly regretted the slowing down in Italy which this necessitated. On the other hand his own insistence on backing Victor Emmanuel and Badoglio against Republican feeling in Italy was to play its part in delaying the defeat of Hitler.

With Russia's growing success Stalin did not become less suspicious of his Western Allies. And inevitably the further west the Russian Army moved, the more acute became the question of Poland's eastern frontier. After Sikorski's efforts to come to terms with both Russians and Czechs, in April 1943 there occurred the disaster of the German discovery at Katyn, near Smolensk, of mass graves which might well account for the eight thousand Polish officers missing in Russia whom Ambassador Kot had been unable to trace. The Poles demanded an investigation by the International Red Cross—one could scarcely blame them. Stalin appeared highly indignant and found it easy to implicate the Gestapo; by now the world had learnt to regard Himmler's men as mass murderers. From this time on Stalin prepared to be the patron of a Polish Communist régime which would oppose the Polish Government in London. Since the Czechs took Russia's side Sikorski's efforts to fit a free Poland back into Slavonic Europe were condemned to failure. On 4th July, 1943, he was killed in an air smash near Gibraltar— was it an accident?

Another appalling tragedy in Polish history took place in the spring of 1943. The Germans had crowded some four hundred thousand Jews into the mediæval ghetto of Warsaw and walled them off. They supplied them with enough food to starve, and sent them to be gassed (with the exception of the few taken off to work) as transport allowed. In April 1943 the Jews still in Warsaw decided to sell their lives dearly and they resisted the Germans for some weeks. In the end the Germans killed all but a handful who escaped to join the Polish underground movement. German tactics were to waste as few German lives as possible on this opera- tion which was again kept secret : in the end probably about a thousand Germans were killed in carrying it out. This fight in the drains of the old ghetto of Warsaw was one of the most ghastly incidents brought about in the life of Europe by Adolf Hitler.

Meanwhile Tito's Partisans had cost the Germans some quite serious fighting about which the Russians broadcast news. The Yugoslav Government in London naturally tried to back Mihailović through thick and thin, but it had become notorious that he was doing nothing to fight the Axis and sometimes working in collusion with it. In the spring of 1943 London decided to switch the help it could spare from Mihailović to Tito, and on the night of 28th-29th May two British officers, Captain F. W. Deakin and Captain Bill Stuart, were dropped by parachute at Tito's headquarters, then in Montenegro. They arrived just in time for another German action against Tito which proved as indecisive as the rest, and petered out at about the time of the great Russian offensive of mid-July. Although the Americans at first dis- approved, the British were now committed to helping Tito.

It was a curious situation. The Russians had given publicity
to Tito because it suited them to do so, but they proved
unreliable allies of the Yugoslav Partisans from the beginning,
since Stalin did not like nations to free themselves even when
their liberators were Communists. Tito, on the other hand,
was so good a Communist that he suspected the British of
" imperialistic " motives, although they proved to be his
most serious and reliable allies, ignoring ideology and judging
only by results.

In the rest of Axis-occupied Europe the Dutch performance
stood out. Since Napoleon the Dutch had had no experience
of war or despotism. It has been seen that the great depression hit their over-populated country severely; out of it there
sprouted Musserts, and other Dutch Nazis, and wild young
pseudo-Communists like Marinus van der Lubbe who—so opportunely for Hitler—fired the Reichstag in February 1933.[1]
The German invasion in May 1940 at first stunned the Netherlands. Hitler chose the Austrian, Seyss-Inquart, to be Reich
Commissioner in Holland. He had also had available the oddly
brilliant Dutch Nazi, Rost van Tonningen, who had been
League of Nations financial representative in Vienna in Dollfuss' day, and had, like Seyss-Inquart, helped to betray Austria;
now Rost was made Secretary-General for Finance in Holland.

Already by the beginning of 1941 there were disturbances
in Amsterdam in reply to a Dutch Nazi demonstration. Early
in March eighteen Dutchmen were condemned to death for
alleged espionage and sabotage. In the spring of 1942
Himmler and Heydrich visited Holland, inaugurating a period
of greater severity with the taking of 460 hostages and the
re-internment of officers of the Dutch Armed Forces. As elsewhere the economic position deteriorated swiftly because
Holland was exploited by Germany, and Dutch workers were
taken to work in the Reich. During 1943 tension greatly increased. There was a good deal of sabotage and hostages were
executed. Martial law was proclaimed at the end of April,
and in May the total mobilisation of labour; at this time the

[1] See above p. 97 footnote.

Germans tried to confiscate all wireless sets in order to cut the Dutch off from messages from the Dutch Government in London. Holland, too, was the country of Anne Frank. This was no accident. The Dutch Jews were greatly respected and it is certain that many Dutchmen risked their lives to hide Jewish families precisely as Anne Frank's family was hidden. As it leaked out that the Nazis were exterminating the Jews, indignation in Holland became extreme.

In August 1943 Italy was the centre of everyone's attention in Europe. One despot had fallen: surely the other one could be struck down too. Surely the Italians would make peace and then perhaps Europe could be liberated from war and Nazi occupation. Whether it were the French or the Dutch in the West, or to the East the Magyars, Roumanians or Bulgars who hoped to follow an Italian lead out of the war, the crisis was followed with passionate interest. The mysterious death of King Boris of Bulgaria, after a visit to Hitler's headquarters at the end of August, added to the tension. The forty-five days, however, from Mussolini's fall on 25th July to the publication of the Italian surrender to the Allies, seemed as bedevilled as the years between 1936 and 1939—everything seemed to play into Hitler's hands again. The Italian Government immediately approached the Allies with a view to changing sides, but the Allied Generals were deeply suspicious of the Italians; they did not realise how little the Italians had wanted this war. In order to prevent or postpone a German occupation of Italy Badoglio declared that the war would continue. Italians of all political colours, except for the Fascists who seemed to have disappeared, had dreamt of immediate peace, social reform and political liberty. Instead the King and Badoglio seemed afraid to loosen controls and appointed " non-political " Ministers, soldiers or technical specialists, with a clever diplomatist, Guariglia, at the Italian Foreign Office. People hoped against hope that the Allies would land in Northern Italy and thus cut off and forestall the Germans. Instead they bombed the industrial towns in Northern Italy, Milan particularly; these were the centres of militant anti-Fascism of all kinds. After the early dreams induced by the fall of Mussolini many Italians realised that a hard fight with the Germans, who were wasting no time in strengthening their position in Italy, lay ahead : naturally the Communist and Socialist workmen were often the most genuinely anxious to take their part in the struggle. The King and his Generals were, however, too much afraid of them to respond in any way—they said there was no need to enrol them as volunteers. Thus August seemed lost for Europe, though the Russians were advancing fairly steadily—they were back in the Donetz Basin by now.

September was worse. On 3rd September the British landed in the toe of Italy, not in the north. On 8th September Allied troops risked a landing as far north as Salerno on the coast south-east from Naples. On that day it was announced sooner than Badoglio had expected that Italy had surrendered unconditionally to the Allies on 3rd September : the Italian Navy only left Spezia on 9th September to join the Allies at Malta. By 10th September the Germans had crushed some spontaneous Italian resistance in Rome and seized the capital, while the Allies were still consolidating their positions round Salerno. The climax was reached with the rescue of Mussolini, then in custody at the Gran Sasso in the Apennines, by air by the Germans : his rescuer the S.S. man, Otto Skorzeny, had been ordered to undertake this job—Operation Eiche—by Hitler on 27th July, two days after the Duce's fall : he succeeded in carrying the operation through on 12th September.

Mussolini was, it has been seen, in poor health. After his dismissal he had been hidden from the Germans in various islands until, foolishly, it was decided that the Gran Sasso would be safer. Since 25th July he had displayed self-pity rather than indignation. He asked Skorzeny, as he had asked Badoglio, only to be allowed to retire to his home in the Romagna. Remorselessly, however, he was flown to Munich (where his family had already been taken) via Vienna, and on the next day on to Hitler's grim headquarters at Rastenburg in East Prussia. Hitler was determined to restore the legend of the Axis and he frightened Mussolini into agreeing to become the head of a new Fascist Italy occupied, of course, by the Germans by now. The fact that the King of Italy, never a popular figure, had fled from Rome to Allied territory in the south with Badoglio, gave a certain attraction to a Fascist Republic. Suddenly all the hopes of the occupied countries of Europe were dashed. The liberation of Corsica was some small consolation for the French, but on the whole the European struggle against Hitler became more desperate as he and his apparatus became more ruthless. In Eastern Europe the governments and some of the peoples increasingly dreaded the choice that was being forced upon them between Hitler and Stalin. The myth of the restraining influence of Italy, as at Munich, had to be abandoned, for Hitler now saw to it that Mussolini's Neo-Fascist State was intransigent, without mercy. It was felt too precarious to set up its Government at Rome, which was put under purely German control; early in October the new Republic was established on Lake Garda, at Salò, Maderno, Gardone, with Mussolini himself at the Villa Feltrinelli just north of Gargnano. This was within close reach of the German authorities, the S.S. chief, Karl Wolff, and the new German Ambassador, Rudolf Rahn. The latter was a moderate Nazi who had worked under Abetz in France[1] and similarly dared to believe in the possibilities of conciliation. German military headquarters under Rommel were at Belluno.

Gradually the world got to know that Mussolini had been turned into another Quisling. At first, however, Neo-Fascism sounded more intimidating and more seductive than Fascism had been for some time. It was formulated at a Congress held at Verona in November 1943 when an appeal to the North Italian workers was attempted by the advocacy of workers' control in industry and a degree of nationalisation of

[1] See above p. 190.

the land. Since the publication of the Italian armistice, however, anti-Fascist partisans had been gathering at many centres
in Mussolini's Republic of Salò which would diminish by
stages for the next eighteen months. More remarkable still,
at the end of September the Neapolitans drove the Germans
out of their city in four days of wild fighting, so that when
the Allies arrived the Germans were already retreating : by
1st October Naples was in Allied hands. On 13th October
Badoglio declared war on Germany. By this time in the
Germans' rear, and especially in Piedmont, Italian partisans
were beginning to organise what was to become a remarkable
resistance movement against Hitler and the resurrected
Mussolini.

Events in Italy had important repercussions in Yugoslavia
and Greece. In both countries the Germans hastily disarmed
the Italian garrisons, but Partisans—they had formations in
the Greek mountains by now as well as in Yugoslavia—were
able to seize a certain amount of weapons. Yugoslavia was
more deeply affected, being adjacent to Italy; indeed some
Italian soldiers joined Tito's followers. Further, there was a
race, as it were, between Hitler and Tito down the eastern
Adriatic coast. Just as the Germans now after all annexed
South Tyrol ruling it from Innsbruck, so they also annexed
Istria with Trieste in their *Gau Küstenland* and occupied the
major eastern Adriatic ports south of Trieste. Tito had,
however, seized much useful war material before making way
for them, and he was able to voice a more powerful appeal
to Slovene sentiment with the Germans in Istria. The Slovenes
had been largely cut off from the rest of Yugoslavia by the
Axis occupation in spring 1941. In the portion occupied by
the Germans the Slovene nationality was not recognised—
Slovenes were germanised or else " liquidated " in one way or
another. The Slovene capital, Ljubljana, had been occupied by
the Italians until September 1943; now that, too, fell to the
Germans who placed it under a Slovene General called
Rupnik. Although it would be unjust to label him as just
another Quisling, as a protégé of Hitler he was bound to lose

support, while the more idealistic Slovenes, unless strongly clerical, tended to disappear in the direction of Tito's headquarters.

In November 1943 Tito held another Yugoslav National Council in Bosnia this time at Jajce where his headquarters had been stationed since August. What with the various gains from the Italians and the air support which the British, now led by Brigadier Maclean, had begun to bring him, he was now more definitely established. The Council, following the lead given by Tito in his opening speech, passed a resolution adopting for itself the authority of the Government in exile. "The question of King and monarchy," it was stated, "will be settled by the people by its own will after the liberation of the country." The Government in exile continued to support Mihailović until at last on 1st June, 1944, under British pressure, King Peter was induced to appoint the former Governor of Croatia, a Croat called Ivan Šubašić, as Prime Minister of Yugoslavia: he was accepted as such by Tito.

The last months of 1943 were a period of meetings between the British, Russian and American leaders. At Teheran at the end of November Churchill was obliged to agree to the invasion of France which would reduce Allied activity in Italy: at this time, too, the old Curzon line of 1920, which was ethnically justifiable, was accepted as the future Russo-Polish frontier except by the Poles.[1] Stalin found Communist Poles who were willing to accept his dictation; but the big majority of all classes of the Polish nation supported the Polish Government in London which was by no means, as Stalin claimed, the political equivalent of the former Colonels' régime. It was Stalin, now, who was developing imperialistic aims, and it was logical, though in various ways tragic, that he should gradually claim authority over the under-developed countries where disillusionment with the development Hitler had offered them since 1938 was now all but complete.

Throughout 1943 the international position of Beneš had

[1] Eden had agreed to it when he visited Stalin in December 1941.

been strengthened, largely on account of Russia's military successes. These not only brought to the U.S.S.R. a new, uncritical admiration, an acceptance as the democracy Russia never was, in much of Europe; they also brought reflected glory to the Czechs who took Russia's side against the Poles at the time of the quarrel over the mass-graves at Katyn. Beneš hoped that Czechoslovakia would in the future provide a bridge between the Western Allies and Soviet Russia. He envisaged a largely Socialist Czechoslovak Republic from which the Germans, unless their loyalty could be proved, would be expelled. In December 1943, after the Big Three had had their consultations, Beneš visited Moscow. The Czech Communist leader, Gottwald, who had been in exile there, hoped to debar Beneš from power in the future just as the Polish Communists were preparing to debar the London Poles. Beneš, however, was received by Stalin with apparent warmth. He was even able to interest Stalin and Molotov in a revived Little Entente of the future, persuading them to agree that all Transylvania should go back to Roumania. Molotov insisted that Bessarabia and Northern Bukovina must remain in the U.S.S.R.; it seemed obvious, too, that the Russians would claim formerly Czechoslovak Ruthenia though it does not appear to have been mentioned before 1945.

The year 1944 opened grimly for Europe. In January the Allies landed at Anzio not far from Rome, but they made little progress. Just before this Ciano and four others, who had voted for Grandi's resolution in the previous July, were executed by the pro-Fascist authorities; this seemed to be part of Hitler's indirect revenge on the Italy which he considered had betrayed him. In Southern Italy, where the Allies were in control, the atmosphere was uneasy. Representatives of six political parties, Liberals, Christian Democrats, Socialists, Communists and two others, met at Bari on 28th January and condemned the Monarchy, which Churchill was obstinately determined to support. Indeed Churchill allowed himself to quarrel openly with Count Sforza about this, although Sforza was perhaps the most distinguished survivor of the pre-Fascist politicians and no Communist. To make confusion worse confounded, in March the U.S.S.R. recognised the Royal Government and sent Togliatti back to Italy to follow up this policy. Since the Spanish Civil War Togliatti had returned to Russia where he had played a prominent part in the Comintern until its dissolution in the spring of 1943. He was now a man of fifty-one, an impressive figure in his way which was that of the quiet intellectual. He was, however, an extremely able organiser of labour. No doubt partly at his instigation, Communist policy was to be one of participation in whatever Italian Government was formed. Thus in April Badoglio was obliged to re-shape his Cabinet so as to include the six parties with Croce, Sforza and Togliatti as Ministers : thenceforward it was understood that the King would abdicate in favour of his heir once Rome should be taken from the Germans.

An important event in the spring of 1944 was the German occupation of Hungary. One way or another Hungary had seen less German troops, and thus retained a greater autonomy, than Roumania or Bulgaria during the war. The Roumanian Jews had been seriously persecuted and no political activity of a parliamentary kind had been permitted in Roumania. In Hungary, on the other hand, the Jews had been protected, and small Liberal and Socialist parties had survived : this had been largely thanks to Kállay, appointed Premier by Horthy in March 1942. The Italian armistice had been regarded by Kállay, as it had by Mihai Antonescu, as invalidating the Tripartite Pact, and during the winter 1943-4 the Hungarian Government seemed to have withdrawn from any active participation in the war. In March 1944, however, Hitler considered that the time had come to 'put an end to the Magyar anomaly. So he summoned Horthy to Klessheim and held him there, after abusing him, until the Germans had occupied Hungary. Kállay took refuge in the Turkish Legation and the Hungarian Minister in Berlin, Döme Sztójay, was summoned to Budapest to carry out Hitler's wishes. A S.S. figure called Edmund Veesenmayer who regarded himself as an expert on crises in South-Eastern Europe became German Minister in Budapest, and the inevitable Eichmann arrived to organise his Jewish victims. Between 15th May and 9th July at least 14,000 Jews were transported daily to Auschwitz of whom between 75% and 80% were immediately gassed,[1] but Horthy then intervened to save the rest, the Jews of Budapest.

By this time the Russians had reconquered Bessarabia; thus they were up to the Pruth, and were not very far from the Carpathians. Since the previous September steps had been initiated to evacuate Budapest, just as Berlin had been evacuated since July.

The Greek Partisans were as bitterly divided as those of Yugoslavia between the friends and enemies of Communism. Partly on this account Churchill persuaded Stalin in May, 1944, to agree that, while Roumania and Bulgaria should be regarded as a Russian sphere of influence, Yugoslavia and Greece should comprise a British one.

---

[1] See evidence at trial of Eichmann's subordinates, Krumey and Hundsche, at Frankfurt. December, 1964.

Chapter XV

THE ALLIES IN ROME AND NORMANDY JUNE 1944: THE TWENTIETH OF JULY IN GERMANY

The organisation of French resistance was greatly simplified by the withdrawal of General Giraud in April 1944. De Gaulle and the British were now preparing for co-operation from within France in preparation for the Allied invasion. With the early days of June 1944 came two longed-for events. On 4th June the Allies took Rome and on the night of 5th to 6th June, D-Day, they landed in Normandy; at last an unequivocal Second Front was there in France and successfully followed up. Hitler's fortress was breached, and critically so. On 10th June the Russians attacked in Finland and on 23rd June on the White Russian front.

The immediate results were at first most striking in Italy and in Germany itself. Freed Italy now had its capital and the Republic of Salò was visibly demoralised: the anti-Fascist Partisans in Central and Northern Italy put up a stronger and stronger fight. The capture of Rome put an end to the partnership between Victor Emmanual III and Badoglio. Prince Umberto took over the royal responsibilities and Bonomi became Premier with an all-party team: the conflict between the Monarchy and the Republican Parties was put into cold storage until all Italy should be liberated.

In Germany a number of groups of people to whom it had become clear that Hitler's régime was positively criminal had been growing increasingly restive and had been trying to establish contacts with one another. The police-state in which they lived made this dangerous in itself: in addition the air-war and the consequent destruction of the major German cities made it difficult to meet each other secretly; by the time

one reached someone's home it might have been destroyed or
on the way one might be delayed by air-alarms or ruined
streets. Temperamentally the people involved were bad con-
spirators. This was particularly true of Carl Goerdeler, Mayor
of Leipzig for seven years and Controller of Prices under
Brüning and Papen: he had indeed been thought of as a
possible Chancellor in 1932. Goerdeler was a good-hearted
Conservative of considerable naïveté who, while refusing to
join the Nazi Party, was not alarmed by it until 1937. In
that year he resigned because the Nazis removed a statue of
Mendelssohn from Leipzig; at last Goerdeler understood that
their anti-Semitism was more than a figure of speech. Gradually he worked out plans for replacing the Nazi régime with
himself as *Reichskanzler*. He discussed his plans far and
wide, abroad and at home; indeed it seems probable that the
Gestapo left him free in order that he should compromise
himself and as many other people as possible.

Another prominent figure of the day, German Ambassador
in Rome until the spring of 1938, was Ulrich von Hassell
who had married the daughter of Tirpitz. His diaries are
unusually enlightening for those who want to understand
what he and many others called the "other Germany," beginning with the question which tormented many officials—
was it better to continue in the job and try to exert some
influence inside the Nazi machine or was it impossible to
condone the régime and necessary to cut one's links with it?
Hassell thought Goerdeler very sanguine while Goerdeler con-
fidently named Hassell as his future Foreign Minister.

Both Goerdeler and Hassell were backward-looking and
intensely nationalistic; indeed when dealing with people representing other countries they expected as the basis of
negotiation that Germany should keep Austria and the
Sudeten German territories, and to her east return to the
frontiers of 1914. They would have liked to go back to
William II's Germany with incorruptible officials and scrupu-
lous judges but a marked bias to the right. Younger men,
such as Adam Trott zu Solz, were in favour of social change,

and tried to establish contact with former Socialists. But the younger people, too, were highly nationalistic, telling their foreign friends that they could never compete otherwise with the Nazis for public favour. Increasingly these and others believed that Hitler would have to be assassinated although those belonging to Helmut von Moltke's circle in Kreisau condemned all use of violence. Goerdeler, too, opposed the murder of Hitler.

Thus the opposition in Germany was amorphous and indeterminate. Once or twice an attempt had been made upon Hitler's life before 1944 but without success. By the time of the Allied invasion of France the German opposition became convinced that the Nazi régime must be attacked without further delay by Germans; it was realised that only people in key positions in the Army had the power to attack this highly organised and utterly ruthless police-state. In the Army itself there were a number of officers, notably General Ludwig von Beck,[1] who knew of the criminal activities of the S.S. and genuinely wished to suppress them. Some of the most determined of these people had held positions in German Military Intelligence, the so-called *Abwehr* which was headed by Canaris. The role of Canaris, Franco's friend, has been much disputed. He was certainly not a very liberal man. Like those German officers, who now made a stand as ' officers and gentlemen' and as Christians, he probably felt that Hitler was something indecent which must be struck down : he must have learnt by now that Hitler was the lynch-pin of the Nazi system. The S.S. was naturally suspicious of the activities of the *Abwehr* officers and arrested and liquidated several of them in 1943; early in 1944 Schellenberg, who was Himmler's chief representative in this field, managed to get Canaris dismissed and in effect to inherit his power. The path of the anti-Nazi officers seemed hopelessly blocked. On 1st July 1944, however, a certain Count Stauffenberg was appointed Chief of the General Staff of General Fromm,

[1] He had resigned as Chief of Staff in protest in 1938, a rare gesture in Nazi Germany.

Commander of the Reserve Army. Stauffenberg was still only thirty-seven and had been severely wounded. In his youth he had succumbed to a short attack of Nazi euphoria, but now he was one of those who was certain that Hitler must be struck down. He was a man of brilliant charm, with friends in all classes of society. As chief of Fromm's staff he attended Hitler's secret military conferences and would not be searched when he did so. Stauffenberg, a generation younger than Goerdeler and Hassell, was eager to include Social Democrats in any future German Government; he particularly admired the Socialist, Julius Leber, who on 22nd June 1944, had renewed secret contacts with representatives of the German Communists. The leaders of both Marxist parties were agreed that the German 'masses' were unready for action against Hitler which could only be successfully undertaken, therefore, through the agency of senior Army officers.

This German situation was a strange one for at least two reasons. The 'masses' of the German people were in fact dispersed in the armies abroad while the workers in the factories were mostly terrorised foreigners who would certainly not co-operate with their German oppressors—their national feeling was almost always stronger than their class feeling. The German soldiers and most of the German officers were bewitched by the personal oath they had been obliged to take to Hitler. Until he was struck down by a member of the officers' élite this magic seemed likely to work, although Hitler had broken his promises to the Army in 1934, as soon as he had made them. In return for these promises Blomberg had agreed that Hitler should succeed Hindenburg and receive the personal oath of allegiance from each soldier.

Stauffenberg had intended to meet the Communist leaders after Leber had done so; this was planned for 4th July, but by this time they and Leber had been betrayed and were swiftly arrested by the Gestapo and not long after executed. It may well be that Stauffenberg hoped to save them if he acted quickly. On 11th July he attended a military conference

at the Obersalzberg taking with him a carefully prepared
time-bomb. But he did not use it that day because Himmler
did not attend the conference. Hitler now moved back to
Rastenburg in East Prussia whither Stauffenberg came fully
prepared on 15th July: suddenly Hitler left the room and
did not return. The next conference was on 20th July, 1944.
Stauffenberg and his friends determined to wait for no one
else, but to blow Hitler up that day. At a certain point when
his subject had been dealt with and he had placed his bomb
near Hitler Stauffenberg left the room, having arranged to
fly back to Berlin and join in leading the *coup d'état* there.
As he was driving to his plane he heard and saw the
explosion he had caused and flew to Berlin convinced that
Hitler was killed. In fact, because a different room from the
expected one had been used for the conference, only four
people were killed outright, Hitler being only slightly
wounded. Even so the anti-Nazi military leaders could have
carried out their plans and seized power in Berlin as they
briefly did in Paris. But they bungled the cutting of communications between Berlin and Rastenburg so that Goebbels
in Berlin was able to expose as false their announcement that
Hitler was dead. Stauffenberg and his friends were over-
powered and executed by officers who had hesitated but who
remained loyal to Hitler because he was still alive. So ended
in confusion and disaster the attempt of a military élite to
free Germany from Hitler before she should be conquered
from abroad.

The failure of the attempt on Hitler's life on 20th July
1944 inaugurated the last and most terrible period of Hitler's
rule. For one thing it strengthened his conviction that he
bore a charmed life. For another it enraged him into the
most fearful reprisals. Hassell, Trott and all those known
to have been critical were arrested and Beck forced to shoot
himself, while a price was put upon Goerdeler's head. Those
arrested were tortured in one way or another. They were
subjected to farcical and humiliating trials in People's Courts;
the Nazi prosecutor, Freisler, who had rushed to Munich to

condemn the Scholls in February, 1943, shouted and mocked at them and convicted them—he was the Vyshinsky of Germany. They were executed in a horrible way; Hitler delighted in the details of the cruelties they endured : he had these filmed in order to gloat over them.

Goerdeler was arrested on 19th August. It was all too characteristic that he allowed Kaltenbrunner, Heydrich's successor, to flatter him into the belief that he might yet from his prison cell convert, or at least influence, Hitler by demonstrating in a written account how the cream of Germany had supported, his, Goerdeler's plans. It has been argued that Kaltenbrunner himself wished this to be conveyed to Hitler, or, alternatively, that he was but decoying Goerdeler into more dangerous verbosity. In the end Hitler saw to it that Goerdeler was executed, after five months of waiting, on 2nd February 1945.

It happened that Mussolini was making his last review of Italian soldiers training in Germany in July 1944 and he was due to visit Hitler precisely on 20th July. The whole performance was a little ghostly, for, although the Germans were still fighting hard in Italy, they were now within three weeks of retreating from Florence. To Mussolini there remained only the wry satisfaction of finding that there had been treason in Germany within twelve months of the last Fascist Grand Council in Italy.

Chapter XVI

THE LIBERATION OF FRANCE:
ROUMANIA CHANGES SIDES:
RISINGS IN POLAND AND
SLOVAKIA

Although Churchill had wished to invade the Balkans rather than Northern France, since the German occupation of Vichy-France it was the Churchill-de Gaulle combination which gave cohesion to, and gained support from, the resistance in France. (News came from quite obscure villages that new-born babies were being called Winston where a year or so before it had been Franklin after Roosevelt.) Stiffer resistance brought savage German reprisals in villages where Partisans had been sheltered and this again stiffened resistance. In France as in Italy the Germans sometimes arrested and confiscated whom and what they chose in a place, then brought in Russians enrolled by General Vlassov[1] to loot and get drunk and rape the women. Already by 20th July the *Festung Europa* was crumbling and resistance spreading. In France on 15th August the Allies landed in the south and on 23rd August Paris was liberated.[2]

Twenty years later Charles de Gaulle refused to participate in the D-Day celebrations because he still felt resentment about the Allied landing in Normandy in June 1944; he felt the Free French had been slighted at the time. He entered Paris himself on 26th August and his chief colleagues arrived there on 7th September to set up their administration. President Roosevelt and the Americans were still uneasy about de Gaulle, but Duff Cooper arrived in Paris as British Ambassador on 13th September, and the French returned the compliment in the person of Massigli on 25th September. At about

---

[1] Vlassov was a non-Communist Russian general who worked with the Germans for a time.

[2] The Germans set up Doriot as a French Quisling for one winter.

this time it was suggested at the Conference of Dumbarton Oaks that France should be the fifth permanent member, together with the United States, the United Kingdom, the U.S.S.R. and China, of the Security Council of the United Nations; this was the new body which was to take the place of the League of Nations. On 23rd October de Gaulle was recognised as head of the French Provisional Government by the United States and the U.S.S.R. as well as by Britain which had already backed France as a member of the Allied Control Commission to be set up in Germany. In December 1944 de Gaulle was invited to Moscow where he signed a treaty of alliance with Stalin. Thus in an astonishingly short time France seemed to have become rehabilitated. In February 1945 de Gaulle was not invited to join the Big Three at Yalta. On 4th May, however, at the Conference at San Francisco France was admitted by the sponsoring Powers to their private conversations; it was only five years since the staggering defeat of 1940. There was something about de Gaulle and something about the French which was irresistible. Since 1945 the international status of France, which collapsed, has been much the same as that of Britain, which held out alone: both ceased to be great imperial powers, Britain withdrawing rather more gracefully from her overseas territories. Stalin would not agree to the French being invited to the conference at Potsdam in the summer of 1945, but they were able to assert their views about the German situation thanks to their membership of the Control Commission.

The liberation of France was followed by the British liberation of Brussels and Antwerp on 3rd and 4th September respectively, and the American liberation of Luxembourg on 10th September, 1944. The Allies had occupied Florence on 11th August and were still advancing northwards in Italy in September. The Russians had advanced pretty steadily on several fronts throughout the year. In 1944 Stalin dealt what were called his ten blows. In June Finland was defeated and induced practically to withdraw from the war. In July the Russians swept forward to the Niemen and the Vistula and to the Carpathians; the battle for the Dukla Pass across them began on 8th September and was to last about a month. Again, as in the summer of 1943, the enemies of Hitler believed that he was already beaten. In Poland and Slovakia in August risings against the Germans had been undertaken with several motives—to harass Hitler, not to move too late, to meet the Russians half-way having won at least half one's own battle. In the middle of September, in order to hamper the German retreat, the Dutch Government in London called a railway strike in Holland which was highly successful. In 1940 the Danes had not resisted Hitler because they were disarmed. Hence in Denmark there had been no gross interference by the Germans with the constitution until late in 1942; the king was held still to govern the country. A climax came on 29th September, 1943, when it was known that the Germans intended to deport all the Danish Jews. By now it was understood that this spelt their murder *en masse*, and the Danes were outraged: from this time onwards Danish resistance was indistinguishable from that of the other Nazi-occupied countries. In the middle of September 1944 there was a successful forty-eight hour strike against the German authorities.

It has been seen that in March 1944 the Russian Armies were advancing briskly and had reconquered Bessarabia. By this time Marshal Antonescu had realised that he had backed the wrong horse and he had agreed that young King Michael and the old Peasant Party leader, Maniu, who was strongly anti-Communist, should approach the Western Allies to try to negotiate peace. Owing, it would seem, to Churchill's imminent agreement with Stalin about spheres of interest these Roumanian approaches led nowhere. The King, who had long resented Antonescu's power and disliked his policy, agreed with Maniu, to appoint a pro-Western Government in Bucharest at the end of August, 1944. When Marshal Antonescu, who had seen Hitler on 5th August, came with Mihai Antonescu to report to King Michael on 23rd August, the latter followed the King of Italy's example of July 1943, arresting both Antonescu. The King then announced that Roumania had joined the Allies, declaring war on Germany on 25th August: at the same time he appointed a Cabinet representing the pre-Fascist Parties and the Communists. On 12th September the Roumanian Government was obliged to agree to an armistice with the Russians signed in Moscow. Maniu's new period in power was doomed in advance and Bessarabia finally lost to Roumania.

The Roumanian *coup d'état* cut off oil supplies for Germany and brought Russian troops to the Danube, Bulgaria's northern frontier; this signified the downfall of Germany in the Balkan peninsula. On 5th September the U.S.S.R. declared war on Bulgaria which brought a revolution there and a switch-over with a Bulgarian declaration of war against Hitler: the Bulgarian Army was now on Tito's side instead of trying to fight him. On 12th September King Peter broadcast from London an appeal for Yugoslav unity under Tito. On 20th October, 1944, Russian soldiers and Yugoslav Partisans drove the Germans out of Belgrade. On 14th October Athens had been liberated.

Meanwhile the position of Hungary had become critical. Influential people like the veteran Count Bethlen urged Horthy to come to terms with the U.S.S.R. in spite of the Germans; Stalin, after all, had ostensibly renounced revolutionary aims in Italy and Roumania. At the beginning of October Russian troops crossed the Hungarian frontier and by 10th October they had occupied Debrecen. On 15th October a statement was broadcast from Budapest that Horthy had requested an armistice from the Russians. This was the signal for the Germans to engineer a *coup d'état* bringing the Magyar Nazi, Szálasi, into power for the last lap. On 17th October the Hungarian Commander-in-Chief, General Miklós, went over to the Russians although the Hungarian armistice was not signed until 20th January, 1945, in Moscow. By the middle of March 1945 the Russians had conquered Budapest after a last German attack there.

Meanwhile Churchill had met Roosevelt for a second time

at Quebec from 11th to 16th September, 1944, and Stalin in
Moscow from 9th to 20th October. Both conferences were
two-edged in their results though Churchill felt satisfied about
them. At Quebec the Morgenthau Plan for de-industrialising
Germany after the war was briefly adopted, and certainly
helped to stiffen German resistance before Eden, Hull and
Stimson caused it to be suppressed. At Moscow the future
of Danubian Europe was modified by comparison with the
agreement in May; now in October it was agreed that the
Russians should do what they chose with Hungary and that
they should share influence in Yugoslavia with Britain.

By and large, the autumn of 1944 was tragically dis-
appointing. The Germans suppressed the Slovak rising
while the Russians were fighting them in the Carpathians.
The Polish Home Army had risen against the Germans in
Warsaw on 1st August. For six weeks Stalin refused to allow
American or British planes wishing to drop supplies on
Warsaw to use Soviet bases. At last on 10th September he
relented and the Red Army advanced towards Warsaw, cap-
turing the suburb of Praga on 15th September: some Polish
Communist formations even got into Warsaw itself and fought
side by side with the Home Army for several days. The
position of the latter had, however, become impossible, for
its survivors were faced with starvation. On 3rd October the
Polish General Komorowski (or Bor) capitulated on condition
that he and his army were given full military recognition: the
Germans—improbably—agreed to this.

The Conference in Moscow in October inevitably concerned itself with Poland as well as South-Eastern Europe.
Since September Stalin seemed less hostile to the Poles, but
he could scarcely be expected to abandon the Curzon line as
the Russo-Polish frontier, and because of this, if for no other
reason, there was deadlock between London and Lublin Poles[1]
as to their co-operation in the future.—

---

[1] It was at Lublin in Poland that the Polish Communists had
originally formed the Committee which Stalin intended should supply
Poland's future government.

Although the Germans had expressed some tardy respect for the Polish Home Army by treating with it, they deported the survivors of the civilian population of Warsaw, some fifty to sixty thousand people, to German concentration camps. In that last grim period between 20th July, 1944, and the final German surrender, death from starvation and disease reigned in these terrible places. The Germans carried out savage reprisals for the strikes in Holland and Denmark. As the winter approached the shortage of food and fuel throughout Nazi-controlled Europe—now noticeably shrunk, it is true—was desperate. On 18th October all German males from sixteen to sixty, who had not yet served, were called up to man the *Volkssturm* for the last defence. Since the middle of June flying-bombs had been hurled against Britain. These were Hitler's much-vaunted secret weapon which caused grave casualties but did nothing to alter the course of the war. The Germans directed flying-bombs also at French and Belgian territory after they had lost it. On 17th September, 1944, three airborne Allied Divisions were dropped at Nijmegen and Arnhem in Holland, ahead of the advancing British and Canadian troops. The weather, however, was unpropitious and one of these divisions had to be withdrawn from Arnhem on 15th September after heavy losses. By October, partly thanks to this, there was a greater feeling of stability in Germany[1] and the hope that if one could get through the winter there might be new, more efficacious, "secret weapons," and perhaps more chance of a split between the Western Powers and Russia.

In Italy, too, the story was a sad one. The Italian Partisans had made remarkable progress since the Allies were in Rome. The Committee of National Liberation in the capital worked in clandestine contact with the Committee of National Liberation for Northern Italy based on Milan. The two leading figures in the north were the Radical, Feruccio Parri, who had defied the Fascists in the early days, and the Communist, Luigi Longo, who had played an important part in the

[1] F. W. Deakin—*op. cit.* p. 737.

Spanish Civil War. Increasingly the peasants, as well as the factory workers, helped the Partisans. As the autumn of 1944 advanced the Allied Armies came to a standstill along what was called the Gothic line from Spezia to Rimini. On 13th November General Alexander advised the Italian Resistance fighters to melt away for the winter; the advice seemed tinged with distrust and came near to demoralising the Partisans. To follow this up Mussolini braced himself to go to Milan and make the only public speech he ever made (except when inspecting troops) in the Salò period: this was on 16th December, 1944, and aroused some real applause.

On the same day as Mussolini's speech in Milan, the Germans, now fighting with literally desperate courage, launched their famous counter-attack led by Rundstedt against the Americans in the Ardennes. By the end of January 1945 this had come to a standstill. Nevertheless on 15th February, 1945, the Germans found the strength to attack the Russians in Hungary: by 15th March this effort, too, was played out.

Chapter XVII

THE DISINTEGRATION OF NAZI GERMANY: ALLIED PLANS FOR FUTURE INTERNATIONAL ORGANISATION.

In addition to the facts of the actual fighting, and the facts of life under Nazi rule, or under the new régime of a recently restored French or Belgian Government, or under Tito's Communism, or Stalin's in Russia and the territories now dominated by Russian troops, the last few months of the war in Europe showed at least two new features. On the one hand there was a rush by the Germans to explain to the Western Allies that they had always been on their side and to try to come to terms with them if possible against Russia; on the other the Allies themselves were increasingly concerned with planning the future re-organisation of Europe.

The neatest treachery to Hitler, and to Mussolini—who would himself have liked to have initiated it—was the unconditional surrender of the German Armies in Italy by the S.S. General Karl Wolff, after tricky negotiations with Allen Dulles, the head of the U.S. Office of Strategic Services stationed in Switzerland since 1942. Although the German troops had by now retired beyond the Po and although the Italian theatre of military operations had been made into a secondary one from which resources had been drained away to France, the existence of the factories of Milan and Turin and the docks at Genoa made Northern Italy a focus of economic and political interest. Hitler had characteristically consigned everything to perdition rather than that a single factory should benefit the victors or indeed the survivors. But everyone else had an interest in the preservation of industrial plant in Italy. And should it be preserved, it presented a challenge to those competing for its control. The Communist

Party was well organised in Northern Italy with plans for
workers' control of the factories. Nearly all non-Communists
were interested to prevent Communist domination of North
Italian industry; among others the Catholic Church felt
concerned. This helps to explain the willingness of Archbishop Schuster of Milan to involve himself in negotiations
between the other interested parties. It appears, however, that
late in February or early in March 1945 Wolff managed to
establish contact with agents of Dulles, not through the
Catholic Church, but through a businessman still travelling
between Italy and Switzerland, thanks, it would appear, to a
little protection from the Swiss Intelligence Services—the
Swiss, too, were interested in North Italian industry. This
happened just after Mussolini had dismissed his Minister of
the Interior, Buffarini Guidi, as too much linked with the
Germans; had he kept Buffarini at his post the latter might,
Mr. Deakin thinks, have been able to inform Mussolini of
what was going on between Wolff and Dulles.[1] In the long
run it did not change very much, for the surrender of the
German Armies in Italy only became reality on 2nd May after
the formal instruments of surrender had been signed at Caserta
on 29th April. This was one day after Mussolini's death and
one day before that of Hitler. Within a week all the armed
forces of the Germans and any remnants of those of their
protégés had surrendered to the Allies, and the war in Europe
was over. Mussolini, having approached the Partisans through
the Archbishop, had taken to flight; he was then caught
by Partisan officers two days after the Italian Committee of
National Liberation had given the word for national insurrection. The Northern Italian towns did free themselves, but
the split between their Communist and non-Communist leaders
was then complicated by the arrival of Allied Military Government. The London Poles (in the form of troops led by
Anders), but not the Russians, were represented in Italy, and
gradually the Communists were edged out of control of the
factories.

[1] Deakin *op. cit.* p. 755.

Now that the power of Hitler was broken the short-lived
Nazi régime disappeared from the South Tyrol and Istria.
The port of Trieste, an Italian town with a Slovene hinterland,
was as much the goal of Tito as of liberated Italy or of the
Western Allies who were not afraid to offend Tito as they
feared to anger Stalin. Although some Yugoslav Partisan
formations reached Trieste on 30th April, New Zealand
troops came to the rescue of the representatives of the Italian
Committee of Liberation on 3rd May. In the end, after much
East-West friction and various interim combined plans which
included the establishment of a Free Territory of Trieste under
international control, in 1954 a frontier was drawn which
barely saved the city of Trieste for Italy; its hinterland right
up to the houses of Trieste went to Yugoslavia.

Perhaps the biggest Russian offensive of 1944 was that
launched on 22nd June which, it has been seen, brought
Russian troops to the Vistula by the beginning of August; it
brought them also up to the frontiers of East Prussia. From
this time onwards until the German capitulation in May 1945
the predicament of Germany and of Germans east of the Elbe
was a terrible one. Until 1943 East Prussia, Silesia and the
Protectorate of Bohemia and Moravia had seemed safe, protected areas, particularly to people brought up to despise the
Russians. With the increase of British and American air-
raids on the Rhineland, the Ruhr territory and Berlin, people
had been evacuated to eastern Germany and to the *Sudetengau*.
In the East, then, the population was inflated by evacuees in
1944, and from June onwards the congestion increased because
German officials, German settlers and finally the German
Armies, were in retreat to the different areas of eastern
Germany on their way back from Russia and Poland. But
the Germans were completely unprepared for defeat. East of
the Elbe people tended to be less sceptical towards Goebbels'
propaganda and they had no neutral neighbour like Switzerland to nourish scepticism. Apart from the fact that Hitler
and Goebbels said that defeat was impossible, their *Gauleiter*
in the East were unwilling to make any preparations for

disaster for the two reasons that they were afraid of punishment and afraid of losing face. The result was confusion. It
was typical that the population of the Memel-land was
ordered to evacuate there on 4th August, 1944. A fortnight
later this order was reversed and the Memel-landers came
back until they were again ordered to leave on 7th October.
Since the Russians attacked the city of Memel on 9th October,
it was by now too late for many people to get away. In the
last winter of the war, much of which was particularly cold,
Germans of all kinds east of the Elbe were trying to get to
the west, some being soldiers who were willing to surrender
in the west but not to the Russians. The calling up of the
Volkssturm, which from a military point of view was worth-
less, often removed the last males from the family, while
their Russian or Polish servant disappeared in an easterly
direction.

The vicissitudes of the city of Breslau, the capital of
Prussian Silesia, were typical. Hanke, the local Nazi authority,
ordered a partial evacuation on 20th January, 1945, so that
the inhabitants of Breslau, now swollen by an extra hundred
thousand, only began to move out on that day. By then the
roads were so crowded and the weather so cold that many
turned back to Breslau. By the time the Russians encircled
the city on 16th February, a third of its population had
returned. Breslau was then cut off, only surrendering on 6th
May, one day before the general capitulation. About a week
later news was brought by the Poles, who early in February
had become the occupying and administering authority, that
the University of Lwów (now in the Russian Ukraine),
together with a considerable part of the Polish population of
the latter city, were being moved into Breslau, now renamed
in Polish, Wroclaw. Another tragedy occurred in the middle
of February 1945 at Dresden in Saxony. The air-war had
proved highly controversial; on the whole it had been shown
to be ineffectual psychologically but worthwhile when concentrated upon communications and key industrial points. At
Dresden in February 1945 there was nothing important of

this kind to be aimed at then, but a tremendous confluence of refugees of all kinds, that is to say of homeless people in the cold spell. In addition Dresden was one of the architectural gems of Europe, a rococo rhapsody. On the night of 13th-14th February the R.A.F. (followed by the United States Air Force at midday on 14th February) sullied its good name by a fearful raid on Dresden which cost many lives and great suffering, and destroyed the loveliest buildings there; it cannot be shown to have shortened the war.

In Dresden at the time of the raid there were many refugees trying to reach the Protectorate of Bohemia and Moravia which still seemed to Germans relatively sheltered from onslaughts from the East. President Beneš, however, set off from London on his final return to his country in the middle of March. He travelled first to Moscow and from there to Slovakia on 3rd April, the Germans having at last been driven out; there he established his government at Košice for six weeks. It was in the Protectorate of Bohemia and Moravia that the Germans held out longest of all, led by the intransigent Nazi General, Schoerner. In Prague, which had been subjected to the Nazis for over six years, Czech demonstrations broke out on 4th May, and on the 5th May, Czech patriots seized the broadcasting station. The German General in the city capitulated on 8th May to the Russians who began to arrive on 9th May. But Schoerner flew off to surrender to the Americans while some of the troops he had commanded continued to fight wildly. There were some appalling S.S. savageries in Prague; the ill-equipped Czechs fought back desperately and broadcast appeals for the Allies (the Americans were at Pilsen) to come to their rescue. When at last Marshal Koniev and the Russian troops arrived in full force on 11th May the traditional bitterness between Czechs and Germans had been nurtured afresh by this post-armistice ordeal of the Czechs. On 16th May President Beneš entered Prague and set about the establishment of the Second Czechoslovak Republic. It had been publicly stated by him since 1943 that it would be a national state and it was understood that this would mean the expulsion from it of the Sudeten Germans who had cost the Czechs so dear; exceptions would be made only for those who had proved their fidelity to the Czechoslovak State.

The original cause of the human misery of the period, Adolf Hitler, who had spent much of the time since his attack upon Russia at his headquarters in Rastenburg in East Prussia, had been obliged to retreat to Berlin on 20th November, 1944. He only left it again for a few weeks in December and January to supervise the Ardennes offensive from the Taunus. Since 20th July, 1944, although he had interpreted his survival as demonstrating the favour of providence, his health, and with it his judgment and sanity, had deteriorated, and in the autumn he was often ill in bed. During the last few months of his life he issued to commanders who could no longer resist orders forbidding surrender; once the need for surrender became overwhelming Hitler outdid Stalin in his decrees for the scorching of the earth of Germany. Of Hitler's close collaborators only Goebbels showed himself as much in love with destruction as his Führer, killing at the last his whole family before he killed himself. Otherwise there was only Martin Bormann who proved completely faithful. He was a characteristic Nazi with brutal, narrow views. Since Hess had flown to Scotland in 1941 Bormann had taken over the organisation of the Nazi Party, and he had attached himself as closely as he could to Hitler's person. It was thus Bormann who recorded Hitler's statements during the last period,[1] with the object, in spite of—indeed because of—the defeat which even Hitler and Bormann must have recognised by now, of bequeathing, if nothing else, a Nazi legend to posterity. Not without some encouragement from Bormann and some justification offered by them, Hitler now regarded all the other Nazi leaders as having betrayed him. Among the Generals all but Keitel and Jodl were condemned as defeatists, and he looked rather to an Admiral, Dönitz. Of Ribbentrop, little was heard

[1] See *The Testament of Hitler*—Cassell 1961.

towards the end except that he began to use his contacts in
Stockholm to initiate some kind of negotiation. On 26th
March Mussolini's Ambassador in Berlin, Anfuso, who was
no fool, returned from there to Salò and spoke of Ribbentrop's intrigues. He described Berlin as "a mad world of
flames." . . . Real power was in the hands of the *Gauleiter*
in what Anfuso called "the principalities"—"they were the
Mansfelds of the Thirty Years War. Each Nazi leader would
seek his own separate peace."[1] In his confused way Himmler
struggled to remain faithful to Hitler. Yet with all his secret
wires he cannot but have been aware, not only of the infidelity
of his young colleague, Schellenberg, but also of the queue
of other Nazi leaders who were trying to win acceptance by
the British and Americans as allies against the Russians. One
of the most obvious was Heydrich's successor, the Austrian,
Ernst Kaltenbrunner, whose role in handling Goerdeler had
been so ambiguous. Wolff's approach to Dulles had indeed
been made with Himmler's connivance. For "his (Himmler's) interpretation, too, was coloured by the conception of a
rift in the enemy coalition but also by the need in extreme
circumstances, as supreme head of the S.S. to treat as a quasi-
independent authority and to seize the opportunity now
created by the shift in the balance of power within Germany
since the July Plot in his favour, and at the expense of the
Army. It might be the role in history of the *Reichsführer*
S.S. to seize the initiative before the fatal crash, save the
remnants of the Reich from extinction in a last-minute compromise with the enemy, and place the S.S. Divisions at the
disposal of the Allies in an anti-Soviet capacity."[2] Himmler
tried a similar manœuvre through Count Bernadotte of the
Swedish Red Cross whom he met at Lübeck on 22nd April,
1945.

On that very day Hitler held a meeting of such leading
officers as were available at his bunker in Berlin; now at last
he admitted defeat, clothing the admission in a frenzied rage

[1] F. Anfuso. *Da Palazzo Venezia al Lago di Garda* 1957. p. 466.
[2] Deakin *op. cit.* p. 761.

of reproach against all who had deserted him; later even he touched on the possibility of negotiation which Göring could handle better than he could, it seems that he said.[1] Göring had been Hitler's Crown Prince for years, and, soon after the flight of Hess to Scotland in June 1941 he had been officially decreed to be Hitler's successor. He had, however, fallen from favour, both with the public and with the Führer, since the Luftwaffe had failed to defend Germany against enemy air attacks. Now it appears that Bormann carried through a successful intrigue which caused Göring (who was in Bavaria) to be finally dethroned and disgraced. When Roosevelt died on 12th April Hitler had hailed the event as the miracle which would save his cause since it threatened the unstable cohesion of his enemies. Nonetheless all German feelers to the Western Powers were met to the end with the demand for unconditional surrender to Soviet Russia as well.

On 25th April, 1945, the Russians surrounded Berlin: this was five days after Hitler's fifty-sixth birthday. On 29th April Hitler married the unfortunate but devoted photographer's assistant, Eva Braun, who had joined him in his bunker on 15th April. Having nominated a new government and enjoined rigorous fidelity to his anti-Semitic legislation—no mention now of the Final Solution which had broken down since Himmler[2] had anomalously sought accommodation with the Western Allies and the gas chambers were in Russian hands —Hitler and his wife committed suicide on 30th April. According to his injunctions their bodies were immediately burnt. This was two days after some Communist Partisans had shot Mussolini with his mistress near Mezzagra on Lake Como: the other remaining Fascist leaders who were caught were shot on the same day. Of the Nazi eminences only Bormann disappeared completely; it has never been certain

[1] H. Trevor-Roper. *The Last Days of Hitler.* p. 135.
[2] In the last year of the war Himmler increasingly accepted huge payments as against Jewish lives. The most notorious case was that of the Hungarian Jews who were allowed to go to Switzerland in return for their industrial property.

whether he was killed in the fighting in Berlin or not. The rest
fell into Allied hands, though Himmler upon capture, and
Göring after his death-sentence at Nürnberg, committed suicide.
Admiral Dönitz obeyed Hitler's command to succeed him, not as
Führer—as such Hitler was presumably irreplaceable—but as
President of Germany. The rest of Hitler's nominations prob-
ably never reached Dönitz; in any case, since Hitler had
named Goebbels, who was dead, to be Chancellor, they were
out of date. In fact Dönitz appointed the undaunted Count
Schwerin von Krosigk, who had been German Minister of
Finance since the Cabinet of the Barons in 1932, as his
Foreign Minister. Together they ruled in a remote corner of
Schleswig for about a fortnight. In so far as they could, they
took trouble to counteract Hitler's instructions to destroy
installations. A good deal had effectively been done for some
months to prevent these instructions from being carried out
by a still young architect, Albert Speer, who had succeeded
Todt in February 1942 as Hitler's Minister of Munitions. He,
too, became a prisoner of the Allies: thanks to Russian
insistence, Speer, Hess and the Nazi Youth leader, Baldur
von Schirach, are still in 1965 in prison in Berlin.

The last scene in the war in Europe was dominated by the
war with Japan. The Americans were apprehensive about the
time it might require to conquer the Japanese: the chiefs of
staff planned to win the war in Asia by November 1946.
This anxiety, as well as that regarding future international
organisation, helped to make Roosevelt and his advisers and
successor so much afraid of losing Stalin's friendship. Their
fear, to Churchill's consternation, led to the deliberate making
way to the Russians throughout Eastern and Central Europe.
On 21st April Eisenhower positively assured the Russians
that he would not send his troops across the Elbe and Mulde
rivers: some American detachments which had established
bridgeheads across the Elbe were brought back. Actually the
American and Russian Armies met on 25th April at Torgau
on the Elbe just north-east of Leipzig. On 1st May Eisenhower submitted to the Russians that his line should extend

to Lübeck in the north and southwards through Carlsbad, Pilsen, Linz. Thus the Americans could well have reached Prague at the time the Czechs began to broadcast their appeals for help and before the Russians; they could probably have reached Berlin at much the same time as the Soviet troops. That the Americans held back for, as they claimed, strategic reasons, and held the British back, gave the Russians the advantage in the cold war that was to come, bringing the isolation of Berlin and Vienna in Russian-occupied territory.

Early on 7th May Jodl on behalf of Dönitz signed the unconditional surrender of Germany at Eisenhower's headquarters at Rheims. Although Russian as well as French representatives took part, Stalin insisted on a second German capitulation on 9th May at Zhukov's headquarters in Berlin, when Keitel, Friedeburg and Stumpf represented Germany. The Western Powers celebrated their victory in Europe on 8th May without the Russians. Thus German manœuvres did perhaps help to divide the British and Americans from the Russians, though too late to help Hitler or Germany.

By July 1945 there were distinct signs of war-weariness in Japan, and at Potsdam an American declaration supported by Britain called upon the Japanese to surrender to the overwhelming force soon to be arrayed against them. They were thus given warning of the atomic bomb, which was successfully experimented with on 16th July, and which Truman and Churchill decided to use if there was no Japanese surrender. This was done at Hiroshima on 6th August by the Americans and three days later, without the British being informed, at Nagasaki. It brought the end of Japanese resistance. Thus the Russian declaration of war on Japan on 8th August was completely superfluous; indeed it seemed rather in the nature of a taunt—the Western Allies had given away Europe east of the Elbe for this unnecessary gesture which cost the Russians nothing.

A very large part of the energies of the British, and then

the Americans, during the Second World War were consumed in preparing for its liquidation: there was an almost obsessive anxiety to avoid what were felt to have been the mistakes of 1919. On the one hand the Germans must be taught their lesson this time; on the other more preparation must be made for economic reconstruction through international co-operation, much more so in view of the colossal amount of destruction. The League of Nations must be succeeded by a more successful international venture from which neither the U.S. nor the U.S.S.R. would be tempted to back out.

From the outbreak of war in 1939 the United States, although neutral, had felt concerned with future peace terms. The first positive Anglo-American steps were taken, still before the Americans were at war, as the result of the meeting of Churchill with Roosevelt in August 1941. On 14th August they published a joint declaration henceforth known as the Atlantic Charter; its eight points included the expression of respect for the right of all peoples to choose their own form of government. (It was never quite clear to what extent unconditional surrender would disqualify the vanquished nor what would happen if a people chose an unfree form of government.) Free access to raw materials, much fuller international economic co-operation and the abandonment of the use of force were also advocated.

The earliest piece of reconstruction to be planned was the United Nations Relief and Rehabilitation Administration (U.N.R.R.A.). An office directed by Sir Frederick Leith Ross of the British Treasury produced a " Suggested Outline of Post-War Relief " in February 1942. This led to a definitive agreement with the Americans on U.N.R.R.A. in November 1943. That autumn at the Conference at Moscow the Americans persuaded the Russians to become involved in future international co-operation through the " Four Power Declaration on General Security." The future treatment of Germany began to be discussed and Eden proposed a European Advisory Commission: the latter first met formally on 14th January,

1944, to draw up the terms of the enemy's surrender and to decide on the policy to be applied thereafter. At Moscow in October 1943 a Declaration on German Atrocities was made, in the hope of curbing them by threatening very severe punishment at the end of the war.

In July 1944 an international and monetary conference was held at Bretton Woods in the United States under the Chairmanship of the Secretary of the American Treasury, Henry Morgenthau. The conference was indeed dominated by the Americans, and Keynes, who brilliantly represented Britain, had to give way to their more conservative attitude. The outcome was the suggestion of an International Monetary Fund to secure the stability of currencies, and an International Bank for Reconstruction and Development intended as " a source from which nations could borrow funds for long-range capital improvements." In the following month an international conference at Dumbarton Oaks explored the terrain for the establishment of a bigger and better League of Nations. The clash, between America and Britain on the one hand, and Russia on the other, was made manifest. The U.S.S.R., afraid of isolation, by claiming a Great Power veto in the envisaged Security Council vetoed the possibility of international control of the Great Powers themselves. By demanding at Dumbarton Oaks separate representation for each of its sixteen republics, it sought to avoid the effects of isolation. It is perhaps worth remembering that the Conference of Dumbarton Oaks synchronised with very bitter feelings between West and East over the Polish insurrection.

By February 1945, when Stalin invited Roosevelt and Churchill to Yalta in the Crimea, post-war problems had acquired something like immediacy; Hitler's last offensive in the Ardennes had now failed. The questions of the future of Germany and of Poland and of the frontier between them naturally attracted most attention; in a sense the frontier was the most urgent problem, made more acute by the declaration on 5th February that the Polish Communist authorities had taken over the administration of the country east of, and up to, the line of the Oder and the western Neisse rivers; the British pressed for the eastern Neisse, but in vain.[1] It had been generally agreed that in the Europe of the future there should be no German minorities such as those which in the 'thirties had acted as what Franco had called a Fifth Column on behalf of Hitler. On the contrary the example of the transfer of the Greeks from Anatolia in the early 'twenties was to be followed. At Yalta on 7th February, 1945, Stalin said this presented no problem for the new Poland since the Germans had all run away; it was true, as has been indicated above, that large numbers of Germans had taken to flight.

Briefly the results of the Yalta Conference were, then, that the Polish-German *de facto* frontier was drawn along the Oder and the western Neisse, that the Polish Government was to include London as well as Lublin Poles and that the British, at first fearing the withdrawal of the American troops after two years,[2] persuaded the Russians to agree that the French should join in the occupation of Germany. It had already been agreed that, while in principle East Prussia was to go to Poland, Königsberg with its hinterland would be Russian. At Quebec for a brief moment in September 1944 Churchill, it has been seen, had agreed to Morgenthau's plan for de-industrialising Germany. Now, better briefed by the Foreign Office, he had become intensely aware of the need to reconstruct German industry and find food for the refugees from Eastern Europe, many of whom crowded into the zone soon to be occupied by the British. The Germans expelled now or later from Czechoslovakia mostly went to the south-west less industrialised zone which was to be occupied by the Americans, or to Austria. Now it was Stalin, Lenin's successor, who demanded stiff reparations from Germany in the spirit of Poincaré—he wanted the figure of twenty milliard dollars to be fixed in advance, half of which should go to Russia.

On 25th April, 1945, the day the Russians encircled Berlin,

---

[1] This emerged from some Polish evidence in 1965.
[2] Actually Roosevelt withdrew this threat while still at Yalta.

the day the partisans rose in the North Italian cities and the Russian and American Armies met at Torgau, an International Conference opened at San Francisco to "prepare a charter for a general international organisation for the maintenance of international peace and security." This charter of the United Nations was worked out and then approved in plenary session on 25th June. The U.S.S.R. had agreed at Yalta only to demand separate representation for the Ukraine and White Russia, but she still seemed afraid of the United Nations becoming what the League of Nations before 1934 and then in 1939 had seemed to her, an anti-Russian alliance. At San Francisco many of the small Powers appeared and had their say for the first time since the war had begun, in spite of the privileges which the U.S.S.R. had earmarked for the great.

By the end of the Conference of San Francisco the Russians were in a very much more powerful position than at the beginning. For they were well on the way to establishing 'people's democracies' controlled by them in the whole of Eastern Europe. The Big Three now met at Potsdam from 17th July to 2nd August to continue the Yalta discussions in terms of their victory in Europe. They were now in occupation of their respective zones of Germany, the extent of which had been announced on 5th June; although the French had been drawn into the occupation of Germany as of Austria, the Russians would not invite them to Potsdam. In recording the Potsdam Conference it is necessary to note that the United States were this time represented by President Truman. As for the British, owing to the breakdown of the Coalition Government on 23rd May and the defeat of Churchill and the Conservatives in the General Election in July, their representation changed half-way through the Conference when Attlee and Bevin appeared in the place of Churchill and Eden. These changes, too, contributed strength to Stalin's position. On the whole he got what he demanded, partly because of the *fait accompli* of his military control of eastern Europe which included eastern Germany. The British and Americans agreed to the Oder-Neisse frontier between Poland and Germany only provisionally; the final delimitation of the western frontier of Poland was to await the Peace Treaty that has never been made. It was stated that the expulsion of Germans from Poland, Czechoslovakia and Hungary was to be orderly and humane; from now on a mainly successful effort was made to transform this immense operation, this fearful comment on Hitler's programme, into an international undertaking, and it was approximately completed by the end of 1946.

With regard to reparations Stalin was obliged to abandon the idea of twenty milliard dollars, but nevertheless just about fifty per cent of what Germany forfeited in gold, foreign assets and industrial stocks and equipment went to Russia. The assertion was made that Germany should be treated as a single economic unit; this formula proved as meaningless as that of unconditional surrender—for some conditions seem always to attach to surrender. Most other decisions were postponed, including that about the relations of the Western Powers to Stalin's protégés, the semi-Communist States of Eastern Europe. Stalin did at Potsdam agree to French membership of the Reparations Commission (Control Council). The rest was left for Conferences of the Foreign Ministers of the U.S., U.S.S.R., Britain and France, to work out: early in 1947 they arrived at peace treaties with Italy, and even with Roumania, Hungary and Bulgaria which in this way came to be recognised. The fiction that the four Foreign Ministers could agree to a German Peace Treaty was abandoned at about the same time. It should perhaps be added that, whereas Stalin had forced a Communist Government on King Michael of Roumania in March 1945, and Bulgaria, like Yugoslavia, more or less chose to have a Communist régime, Hungary like Czechoslovakia was far from being a Communist preserve before 1948.

The history of Austria since 1938 deserves special notice. possibly the majority of its inhabitants had welcomed the *Anschluss* which they felt to have been overdue for twenty years. Four things soon changed the attitude of the Austrian population : they had counted on Austrian regional autonomy, they had thought that Hitler meant peace, and, like everyone else, they had failed to believe that he carried out his savage threats to the last detail : lastly though many Austrians, like many Bavarians, were anti-Clerical, as Catholics they resented Hitler's persecution of the Catholic Church. Many anti-Semites were disturbed when they became aware, as many did, of how the Nazis really dealt with Jews. Although Vienna was relatively sheltered from the war until the spring of 1945, the old Socialist leaders and some Clerical and Peasant ones began to prepare action in favour of Austrian independence long before this;[1] the Italian alliance had done nothing to endear Hitler to them. When at last the Russians conquered Vienna on 13th April, 1945, they agreed to set up an Austrian Government led by the old moderate Socialist politician, Karl Renner, who had been a leading advocate of the *Anschluss* in 1918. When elections were held in November 1945, while the Communists did poorly, Renner's party polled 'well and the Western Allies recognised Renner's Government. Although Austria, like Germany, had been divided into four occupational zones with Vienna, like Berlin, divided between the four Powers inside the Russian zone, unlike Germany, Austria had a Government which expressed public sentiment and knew what it wanted. Renner ended his political career as first President of the second Austrian Republic : it was just about fifteen years since he had failed to become President of the first Republic in 1930. Although one can see the results of Adolf Hitler's career wherever one looks in Europe to-day, few are more bizarre than the national consciousness he provoked among his own Austrian Germans who before 1938 had nothing but a little nostalgia for the Habsburgs and possessed various regional traditions, Tyrolese or Styrian : they were then scarcely more of a nation than the Bavarians or the Saxons.

---

[1] At the Allied Conference at Moscow in October 1943 it was agreed to restore Austrian independence.

Chapter XVIII

LITERATURE AND THE ARTS:
SCIENTIFIC DEVELOPMENT:
LIFE IN GENERAL

The third decade of the twentieth century was an extraordinary one in literature and the arts. Suddenly the old, essentially aristocratic character of European society had come to an end; there was an unprecedented break with tradition. In the last few years before the war, movements like Futurism in Italy had been born; they looked to the future, to machines and industry, the industrial masses and an acceleration of movement. Indeed they seemed to foretell explosive events such as war or rapid industrial development, or both, or both together. With the Russian Revolution and the collapse of the Central Empires, there came a tremendous feeling of release from restraint; the Italian Futurists, the German Expressionists, an international group formed in Zürich during the war called the Dadaists, took the centre of the stage; not quite independently of the perfection of photograhpy, the break with art as representation had come. Under the leadership of a French Dadaist, André Breton, in 1924 this revolution reached a climax when Breton published his book *La Révolution Surréaliste*.

Before 1914 Marcel Proust had been writing; in a sense he was highly representative of the Impressionists. Paradoxically, although Proust had outlived his age when he died in 1922, in the new world which rejected his attitude, his influence was profound, for instance on Virginia Woolf. Before 1914 there had been the Cubists and the Fauves and Modigliani (an Italian Jew) in Paris, the young Braque, and the young Picasso who was a Spaniard. There had been Marc and Klee (who was half-Swiss) in Germany, and above all the Russian,

243

Kandinsky, who joined them in the *Blaue Reiter* group in Munich. It is interesting that it was in 1919 that Klee wrote in his *Confession "Kunst gibt nicht das sichtbare wieder, sondern macht sichtbar"*—art does not reflect the visible, rather it gives vision.

In Eastern Europe the Croat sculptor, Meštrović, was eminent, an artist intensely aware of his Byzantine heritage but evidently related to the German Expressionists. It was Habsburg Austria, however, which produced Freud, Hofmannsthal, Karl Kraus, Rilke, Kafka and Musil. Although among these there was no contributor to the plastic arts or music, all six of them were to exert a powerful influence on literature; more particularly Freud and Kafka were to do so. Most of all the doctor from Vienna's famous school of medicine, Sigmund Freud, affected every aspect of art, indeed of life: his teaching was received by many as if it were revealed religion. It is worth noting that he did not become internationally famous until the end of the war when he was already sixty-two. Curiously enough Freud and Kafka were German-speaking Jews from Bohemia and Moravia; Rilke was Bohemian too. The Czech, Karel Čapek, also made important contributions at this stage to literature and drama.

It was above all Berlin which became the intellectual and æsthetic centre of Europe in the twenties. Vienna, no longer an imperial capital, was beginning to look provincial, while Berlin was on the road from Paris to Moscow. It was typcial of the time that the great musician, Arnold Schönberg, an Austrian Jew and creator of the twelve note system, succeeded Busoni at the Musical Academy of Berlin in 1925. The Austrian Jewish producer, Max Reinhardt, had by now settled in Berlin, which had become Europe's capital for theatre as for cinema. One of the leading new playwrights who was much produced in Germany was Georg Kaiser; he was concerned with one of the new cares of the new artist, the masses, though he did not love them, as his rival Toller did.

It was now, after the war, that the cinema became an important medium. And it was revolutionary Russia, as yet unstifled by Stalin, which created the great new films. Eisenstein and Pudovkin were the makers of *Battleship Potemkin*—Eisenstein was only twenty-four when he made this—of *Storm Over Asia* and *The Mother*, which were promptly shown in Berlin. In Berlin Erwin Piscator, the leftist producer at the Berlin *Volkshühne* from 1924 to 1927, also experimented with a play, *Rasputin*, in which for the first time theatre and cinema were combined. The Germans themselves made some highly expressive films, such as *Dr. Caligari* and *Metropolis*: some of their greatest cinema was devoted to the pacifist presentation of the evils of the last war by Remarque. In 1926 sound films began to succeed silent onces, revolutionising the techniques used by film producers.

Munich offered some competition with Berlin. For one thing Thomas Mann, who had just expressed the uncertainty of the age in his novel, *The Magic Mountain*, lived in Munich with his obstreperous family indulging in all the experiments then in vogue. It was in Munich that the medical student from Augsburg, Bertolt Brecht, collaborating with Kurt Weill, produced the *Drei Groschen Oper* in 1928 when Brecht was thirty. There was no doubt, nevertheless, that Berlin outshone Munich.

Walter Gropius had launched the new functional architecture, technically founded upon reinforced concrete, just before the war. His *Bauhaus*, which enlisted Kandinsky and Klee to work for it, was based now at Dessau, now at Weimar, in the shadow of Berlin. North Germany and Holland were the earliest scenes of the new building. The French-Swiss, Le Corbusier, based on France, became a second and greater source of this kind of inspiration with the publication of his book *Vers une architecture* in 1923. Neither he nor Gropius nor Brecht were Jews, nor was Käthe Kollwitz, an East Prussian, whose drawings of poverty had as great an influence as anything else in the period. The fact remained that Berlin, the capital of the new liberal Republic, was the centre of an outburst of predominantly Jewish brilliance which included the drawings of George Grosz and the architecture of Erich Mendelssohn. Feuchtwanger's novel, *Jud Süss*, was the sensation of 1925. The leading journalists in Berlin, as in Vienna, had long been Jewish, and this was a great age of written journalism gradually reinforced by broadcasting. The Jewish firm of Ullstein had considerable control of the press and of publishing; of course people said the Jews boosted one another. Richard Strauss was not a Jew although Hofmannsthal, his librettist, was. In 1927 the musician, Hindemith, came to Berlin and worked there. The French musician, Darius Milhaud, together with his exact contemporary, Arthur Honegger, composed remarkable work in Paris, but still in the 'twenties Berlin and its Jews overshadowed the French and the non-Jews.

Before 1914 the German aristocracy, and the middle class which followed its example, had spoken deprecatingly of *Juden und Literaten* as rather inferior people. Now they felt themselves crowded out of the picture by these same *Juden und Literaten*, and all around them after 1924 they saw examples of the new architecture, new buildings bought by local authorities, novelty which they found disquieting. And of course the innovators did go to extremes, deducing from Freud that all repression was dangerous : this led to the condemnation of any kind of educational discipline. Further, a Jewish critic like Tucholski was desperately destructive as well as brilliant.

Apart from Lenin and Trotsky and those splendid films, Russia had produced Maxim Gorki who felt that he had explored the experience of poverty perhaps for the first time since Balzac. It had also produced some remarkable musicians among whom Stravinsky was the composer of the age, creating the explosively modern *Rite of Spring*, a ballet performed in Paris in the spring of 1913. The Russian ballet, for which he wrote much of his best work, achieved its zenith just before and after the First World War under Diaghilev, with Nijinsky as its greatest dancer. Diaghilev left Russia after the revolution and made his ballet company into a focus of international art, based upon Paris and London. For its magnificent décor he used the work, not only of the Russians Bakst and Benois, but also of Picasso and Derain: the very uprooting of his company made it more cosmopolitan so that it knocked down the walls of Bloomsbury's ivory tower when in 1925 Maynard Keynes married the Russian dancer, Lydia Lopokova.

Italy in the 'twenties was in as much turmoil as Germany, though its turmoil is always more individualistic, conforming less to a recognisable pattern and mixing politics with the arts in licentious fashion. Fascism was at first associated with the futurist, Marinetti, and with D'Annunzio who chose to mix nationalism with their protests. It engaged the philosopher and friend of Croce, Gentile, to reform the schools in 1923. In the 'twenties the Sicilian playwright Pirandello, absorbed with problems of personal identity, was at the height of his fame. In 1927 the novelist, Riccardo Bacchelli, produced what is often considered his best novel, *Il Diavolo al Portelungo*; in 1929 the young Moravia, then only twenty-two, published *Gl' Indifferenti*. By this time political journalism had been stifled, and outstanding figures in intellectual life, such as the historian Gaetano Salvemini, had gone into exile. The poets, Ungaretti and Montale, recreated the old anguish of Italian poets, precisely the sense of banishment now felt inside Italy: actually Ungaretti spent many years in France and was closely associated with Paul Válery. The home of Benedetto Croce, it has been seen, remained as a liberal oasis in Fascist Italy, a shrine to which pilgrims journeyed.

It should be emphasised that the strangest characteristic of the European consciousness in the 'twenties, even early in the 'twenties, was a romantic optimism, a starry-eyed belief that paradise was round the corner; this was a powerful influence among the young whose attitude contrasted sharply with the debunking approach of the young since 1945. The lesson drawn from the Freudianism in the air was that guilt was a false accusation and that if poverty were abolished vice would disappear.

With Stalin's decisions of 1928 Soviet Russia became

isolated as well as choked. With the economic shocks of 1929 elsewhere in Europe there was a widespread reaction against the pacifist, internationalist, anti-traditional approach, particularly in Germany. One reverted to the harder tones in Stefan George, now very old but still occasionally to be seen at the *Romanisches Kaffee* in Berlin. Ernst Jünger and a cult of metallic strength came into vogue. A nationalistic mysticism was obscurely expressed in a bad but highly successful book called *Das Dritte Reich* by Moeller van den Bruck. People went back to Spengler's *Decline of the West* which had first appeared in 1917; the tremendous influence of Freud and Marx was shaken. In Germany and Austria as in Hungary and Poland and even Roumania, wherever people were a little afraid of the new post-war art, they began more openly to resent its many Jewish creators. The pessimism of Benda's *Trahison des Clercs*, published in 1927, was quoted to show that *Juden und Literaten* were no good.

In the 'thirties, first Hitler in power in Germany, then the Spanish Civil War, shaped the history of literature and the arts. On 10th May, 1933, Goebbels and the Nazi Storm Troopers organised the 'spontaneous' book-burning when, opposite the Opera House in Berlin, but also all over Germany, the works of Marx, Freud and any other Jewish writers such as the Zweigs were thrown into the flames: with them went books by Voltaire, Thomas Mann, Romain Rolland, H. G. Wells. One outstanding musician, Richard Strauss, came to terms with the Nazis, becoming the leader of the Reich Chamber of Music. And one outstanding philosopher, Martin Heidegger, chosen to be Rector of the University of Freiburg in Breisgau, a week or so after the burning of the books proclaimed his allegiance to Adolf Hitler. Heidegger was the exponent of the new existentialism before Sartre, bringing out his *Sein und Zeit* in and after 1927. His behaviour in 1933 appalled some of his disciples at home and abroad.

The Nazis' capture of Germany wiped out the licentious brilliance of life in Berlin before then. Not only the Jews but also Gropius, Brecht, Piscator and Thomas Mann (whose wife was Jewish), went into exile; they enriched American and Scandinavian life. Peripherally, Britain gained by the emigration of an anti-Nazi like Kokoschka, and by that of many scholars and scientists. The main result, however, was that Paris was restored as Europe's intellectual and æsthetic capital. Not that Paris had been idle from this point of view. In addition to the Surréalistes, Mauriac, Claudel, Gide, Valéry, Cocteau had been at work, one of Gide's masterpieces, *Les Faux Monnayeurs*, appearing in 1925. Further, it had been in 1922 in Paris, in an American book-shop it was true, that James Joyce found a publisher for *Ulysses* in Sylvia Beach. Joyce, like other Irish writers, had turned his back on Ireland, but he went, not like Wilde or Shaw to London, but to Europe, to Paris, to Zürich, to Trieste. And *Ulysses* had European repercussions although its chief influence was seen in English and American literature in familiarising the technique of the "stream of consciousness."

After 1933 Paris became Europe's unchallenged head-quarters for theatre and film, with Auguste Renoir's sons, Pierre and Jean, on the stage. The younger, Jean, really became famous as a film producer, but Pierre Renoir was the actor who, with Louis Jouvet as theatrical producer, helped create Jean Giraudoux' heroes such as "Siegfried." Perhaps the most brilliant film producer of this time was René Clair with *"Sous les toits de Paris"* and *"Le Million."* Charles Chaplin was one of the tragi-comic masters of the day, but Clair had more finesse. Cocteau's film, *Orphée*, reached beyond nature and was great enough to do so.

The Spanish Civil War was the emotional watershed of the 'thirties, certainly for the British and the American intellec-tuals. It was noteworthy, if one had reason to regard Hitler as the main menace to peace and to civilisation, that they seemed less completely shattered by Hitler's *Machtergreifung* in 1933 or by the outbreak of international war in 1939: they were more aware of the Spanish than of the Austrian or the Czechoslovak crisis. This was probably true of the

French intellectuals, too, and necessarily so of the Italians since they were so deeply involved on both sides. George Orwell, Ernest Hemingway, André Malraux were among the volunteers : anti-Nazi German writers were represented by Ludwig Renn. One can, after all, understand that Czechoslovakia was little but a clumsy name, one of many new states far away and land-locked in Central Europe. If it had been known that the Czechs were Bohemians it might have been different : as it was the attitude of the intellectuals was not unlike that of Neville Chamberlain towards Prague. Jan Masaryk, the Czechoslovak Minister in London for a long time, had many friends there, but they were his personal friends rather than those of his country, and only a tiny minority of people admired the baroque of Prague in those days. If people knew any Czechs they tended to see them through Austrian or Hungarian spectacles : in no case did they know their language, seldom realising its close relationship to Russian.

Spain was quite another thing. English-speaking travellers, as they often do, had tired of visiting Italy. Spain seemed more exotic, more remote, more disturbing : it was also cheaper. In the 'thirties to travel in Spain became the thing to do and bull-fights were the thing to talk about. Jutting out into the ocean, Spain was more accessible to westerners in peace or in war than Czechoslovakia : for the French it was next door and one did not feel as guilty about the Spaniards. In any case in July 1936, when the Civil War began in Spain, only Central European specialists were aware that Austria and Czechoslovakia were in grave danger.

The English-speaking intellectuals who concerned themselves with Spain were almost all on the side of the Spanish Government, except for a few Roman Catholics. In fact the experience was of first-rate importance in the case of George Orwell but Malraux had produced his masterpiece *La Condition Humaine* about the Civil War in China three years before. That John Cornford and Julian Bell, who was Leslie Stephen's grandson and Virginia Woolf's nephew, should be killed in Spain was tragic, not stimulating. The writer who was made by the Spanish Civil War was a Central European Jew called Arthur Koestler, who had been a Communist at first but whose illusions were destroyed. As for the other arts, it has already been seen how the Andalusian, Picasso, reacted to the German attack on Guernica and how he involved the world through his experience and its expression. No one surpassed Picasso as a painter in these years. The Spanish or rather Basque writer and philosopher, Miguel Unamuno, who was Rector of the University of Salamanca, made a dramatic gesture in favour of intellectual freedom in Nationalist Spain in October 1936. After this he was inevitably in disgrace, and on 31st December, 1936, he died, being already seventy-two.

The 'thirties, which had begun with the great depression had seen the destruction of all Soviet Russia's original leaders but Stalin. While this happened one was also obliged to contemplate the horrors of Hitlerism in Central Europe and then the Spanish prologue and then war itself, comprising an uncreative period of despair. On the Continent of Europe there was nothing like the outburst in all directions of the 'twenties. In France Gide, Mauriac, Montherlant, Giraudoux continued to write their novels and their plays. Nothing came out of Nazi Germany beyond Goebbels' polemics, and Italy was silent. Only in German-speaking Switzerland, at the heart of Europe yet theoretically neutral, during the war years Max Frisch, and then Friedrich Dürrenmatt, began to show their worth.

The period between the wars which proclaimed itself the age of the Common Man, of the masses, did not find a great European historian to work in these terms. It is true that Karl Marx profoundly affected historical thinking outside Russia too, and that the history of society received greater attention. In France, George Lefèbvre interpreted the French Revolution and Napoleon in Marxist terms as far as this was possible, while Marc Bloch, later a Jewish martyr of the French Resistance, widened history to mean everything which concerned human beings. A Polish Jew, who became British,

Lewis Namier, showed politics—at least in eighteenth century London—to be essentially a matter of personal relationships. Economics became more widely established as an academic discipline, the influence of Keynes reducing the reputation of Marx, but itself being counteracted by dictatorial obscurantism.

There were extraordinary developments in mathematics, physics, chemistry and medicine, all of which led to extraordinary technical achievements. Max Planck's Quantum Theory and Einstein's formulations about relativity had come at the beginning of the century together with Freud's publications about dreams. Chemical experiments with nitrogen prepared the way for a great development of fertilisers on the one hand and explosives on the other.

In 1932 in the Cavendish laboratory at Cambridge under the direction of Rutherford who had already split the atom, Cockcroft first developed nuclear power. In 1933 the Joliot-Curies in Paris (she was Polish) made amazing discoveries in artificial radioactivity. Radar was invented in Britain at about the same time. This was a major event which made possible the survival of Britain during Hitler's war.

In medicine the conception of vitamins was formulated early in the period. In 1922 insulin was discovered. In 1928 came Alexander Fleming's discovery of penicillin; other anti-biotics preceded and followed this, although they did not come into general use until a good deal later. Experimentation with the sulphonamides went back to experiments made by scientists working for the great chemical concern in Germany, the *I.G. Farbenindustrie*. With Hitler in power Germany lost her best scientists as well as her best artists. There had been great activity in the laboratories of Göttingen in the 'twenties, work on atomic energy, but the atomic bombs dropped in 1945 had been worked out in the United States, the Germans only achieving the V. weapons: over radar, too, they had dropped behind.

The period was in love with psychology. Freud had formulated his views since 1900, but it was only at the end of the First World War that the educated public of Europe became aware of them. They then led to the study of psycho-analysis and on through the Swiss, C. G. Jung, to the study of the myth as part of society's subconscious mind. Freud's emphasis on sexual explanations and his insistence upon the significance of dreams seemed to link science with the arts and to reinterpret life.

Another study which was considerably developed in this period was that of anthropology. One big stimulus came from Sir James Frazer in Cambridge. His book *The Golden Bough*, was published between 1890 and 1920 and thus bore fruit in the inter-war period. Combined with the new attitude towards the popular masses, greater interest thus developed in primitive societies whose habits also had their Freudian interpretation. The Polish-born Malinowski was another pioneer of anthropological studies also in Cambridge; this influence, too, spread to the Continent.

One figure of the age who should not be forgotten was the art-dealer and critic, Bernhard Berenson. He was a Lithuanian Jew educated in the United States who then made his home in Tuscany just outside Florence during all these years. His influence ran counter to the spirit of the epoch; perhaps this was why, like Proust, it stimulated Berenson's visitors. His house, *I Tatti*, was a minor court which, like Croce's, did no homage to Mussolini. And it instilled real scholarship in the history of art and profound appreciation precisely of representation in the past. It was partly thanks to Berenson's influence that Geoffrey Scott wrote *The Architecture of Humanism*, a book which heralded to-day's admiration for the mannerists and baroque. Berenson was passionately concerned with politics, too. He liked to be consulted about pictures by princes and potentates not only for reasons of prestige but because these people interested him. English was the first language of *I Tatti*, but Italian, German, French and Russian were spoken there too, perhaps in that order.

During the inter-war period in the highly developed countries the motor car changed from being a luxury to being commonplace. Flying, from being rare and peculiar, became a normal method of travel. Television appeared in time for the Olympic Games at Berlin in 1936 to be televised but it remained exceptional. The techniques of the day helped the journalist and hindered the ambassador whose importance diminished with the growth of communications.

It should perhaps be observed that although the inter-war period enfranchised women and provided them with educational opportunity in most of Europe, and although an élite of women entered the professions, very few obtained great distinction—it has seemed worthwhile to mention only Käthe Kollwitz, Geneviève Tabouis, Irène Joliot-Curie, and Virginia Woolf in the present context. The great technical development of the period was essentially the work of men. In politics Rosa Luxemburg and *La Pasionaria*, two women on the extreme left, were the only ones to have been really prominent.

Chapter XIX

CONCLUSION

It has been observed that half inter-war Europe was what was later to be called under-developed, or pre-economic " take-off." The major portion of the under-developed part was in Eastern Europe, roughly east of the Elbe—or perhaps more accurately of the Oder—with the important exception of Upper Silesia. But Spain, Portugal, Southern Italy, and Eire also came into this category. All these backward territories challenged the leaders of Europe to carry them along, too, as the rest of Europe progressed. Individual Western investors in Yugoslavia, Roumania, Poland, aroused ' anti-colonialist' resentments without developing the internal markets of the countries concerned. After the turning-point of 1936 Hitler saw his advantage in developing these areas and Spain in his own interest, but in the end the insolent brutality of his methods awoke greater resentments than before. He desired and brought about a war against Communist Russia which revealed him as the willing master of foreign slaves rather than the economic saviour. Indeed Stalin with the help of Britain and America was able to steal his thunder. When the U.S.S.R., thanks to the ruthless process of Stalinist industrialisation, began to be victorious, the evil side of Stalin's Government was forgotten and world opinion was not unwilling for Communist Russia to try its hand at developing Eastern Europe. Like the clang of destiny the Iron Curtain fell along the old traditional line of the river Elbe, and the industrialisation of Eastern Europe has been carried through by Communist Governments. Much-loved peasant leaders, such as Maniu, Maček and Jovanović were harshly pushed aside, tasting Communist persecution now.

Twenty years after the German capitulation no definitive peace settlement is in sight; this is partly because the initial *de facto* partition of Germany between Russia and the Western Powers after the victory divided the partitioning Powers themselves. For twenty years, however, Hitler's war has had certain clear results. Definite solutions have been offered to the economic problems of the inter-war period. The menace of the old trade cycle with its depressions has been met east of the Elbe by Communism, west of it by a Keynesian policy of expanding credits rather than deflation. The various forms of economic help supplied by the Americans as Marshall Aid made possible a relatively rapid recovery in Western Europe, particularly in Western Germany, in spite of the far greater destruction brought about by the Second World War compared with that of 1914-18. The ghost of the Great Slump of the early 'thirties is still so powerful that full employment at the cost of creeping inflation is demanded, and generally obtained, by the trade unions of the whole area. Only Spain, Portugal, Eire and still to a considerable extent Southern Italy, lag behind, while the other western countries absorb a certain amount of their labour.

The *de facto* frontiers of Europe since 1945 have been much the same as those drawn in Western Europe in 1919, or they have followed the trends of 1919 rather further in Eastern Europe. The Ukrainians are now all united within the Soviet Union at the expense of former Poland, Czechoslovakia and Roumania. Except for Finland and Congress Poland the U.S.S.R. has more than regained the European Russia of the Tzars. Poland is nationally homogeneous, geographically more western than between 1919 and 1939 and politically dependent upon Russia. Transylvania is Roumanian again and Austria independent. Yugoslavia has gained territory from Italy, and continues to contain Macedonia if not all Macedonians.

It has been seen that the Germans were deposed in 1919 from their ruling role as self-styled *Herrenvolk* and then lived in the Weimar Republic, the Republic of Austria or as minorities—newly named so—scattered across the underdeveloped countries of Eastern Europe which they continued to despise. Since 1945 or 1946 they have been concentrated in Germany west of the Oder and Western Neisse, and in Austria, but chiefly in what has become the Federal Republic of Germany west of the Elbe. Indeed an operation that was feared as about to overcrowd Western Germany disastrously provided the skilled labour for a fresh wave of successful, highly technical industrialisation which has greatly enriched the Federal Republic.

For better or for worse Adolf Hitler, who planned an extended Empire with a German ruling caste, was the fundamental cause of this concentration of the Germans within a far smaller territory than they regarded as German. It was Hitler who made the agreement with Mussolini in 1939 for the German-speaking population of the Italian South Tyrol to be moved north of the Brenner; at first these people were to be allowed to opt, but Himmler planned to force them to re-settle. Owing to the war the operation was only half carried through and many of the South Tyrolese who had emigrated returned. Indeed the Italians claim, when friction occurs to-day, that this is the only German-speaking minority which has been allowed to remain outside Germany's frontiers since 1945.[1] It was Hitler who, in 1939 and 1940, agreed with Stalin to "bring home" the Germans of Bessarabia and the Baltic States. In other words he was utterly indifferent to human attachment to an environment except for propaganda purposes. When it came to the "inferior" Slavonic Czechs, Poles or Russians, they were to be as mercilessly transported to suit his racialist imperialism as the Jews were to be directly murdered. Inevitably these peoples have hit back in some way, the Jews only by kidnapping Eichmann in South America and hanging him after a meticulous trial for his crimes during the war.

The value of the Allied trials of the major Nazi Criminals was lessened by the fact that they were carried through by the victors: they could be written off by the Nazi-minded as

[1] There is in a fact a German minority of about the same size in Hungary.

revenge. The trials of former Nazis by the Germans themselves have aroused less controversy. It must be emphasised
that a large part of our knowledge of the history of the Nazis
is based upon the evidence brought forward at these trials,
under Allied authority or German. A notable section of
German opinion has welcomed these and all other opportunities to face the exact truth about the Nazi period as far
as it is ascertainable. Yet the German unwillingness to admit
defeat or guilt, still less to pay the price, is still strong. This
leads to an exaggerated deference to the pressure groups
formed by the diminishing number of discontented East
Germans in the Federal Republic. Consequently it is an
axiom in official circles at Bonn that the reality of the Oder-
Neisse frontier with Poland must never be admitted because
it must be retained to the end as a bargaining counter.
Another German axiom is that Europe will never be at peace
more than superficially so long as Germany west of the Oder-
Neisse frontier is divided between the Federal Republic, the
Soviet Zone or German Democratic Republic and the city of
Berlin still subjected to Four Power occupation. On the whole
non-German opinion favours the union of these three on
condition that the Germany which emerges does recognise
the Oder-Neisse line as its definitive frontier with Poland.
If it did so Poland would be less dependent on Russia.

If Hitler had won it is impossible to do more than guess at
the cruel extravagance of racial intolerance which would have
prevailed. On the other hand his defeat and the discrediting
of racialistic barriers has undoubtedly accelerated the liberation of Asia and Africa from European domination. The
Italians lost their African Empire thanks to Mussolini's
alliance with Hitler. The impoverishment of Britain and
France and Belgium and Holland, owing to their struggle
against Nazi Germany, made a minor contribution to the
process of " de-colonisation," and Portugal's neutrality during
the war perhaps helps to explain the unique survival of her
authority in Africa—Spain's is negligible. The Charter of the
United Nations, and the Trusteeship system created by it,

have also contributed to this dominating feature of the post-war world, with its negative yet important results for Europe.

It has often been said that the two chief victors at the end of the Second World War were Communism and Catholicism. The Catholic Church had gained in power and prestige by coming to terms with the Fascist State in 1929. When the Fascist State fell and the Italian Monarchy was discredited, the Papacy emerged as the strongest authority in Italy: its privileges were accepted by the new Italian Republic in 1947. The relations of the Vatican with Hitler were at first equivocal. In 1933 Papen helped to negotiate a Concordat between Germany and the Pope, who, together with the Catholic hierarchy, sympathised with Nazi hostility to Communism. Hitler, however, broke this agreement more and more shamelessly, and his racialism was rank heresy in Catholic eyes. The Vatican, moreover, had approved of Doll-fuss' corporative state in Austria and of his heir, Schuschnigg. By March 1937 Pope Pius XI, in his message *Mit Brennender Sorge* to the Catholic Clergy of Germany, condemned National Socialism in no uncertain terms. During the war Pope Pius XII was exceedingly cautious; it has been claimed that papal protests in public might have impeded the carrying out of Hitler's "Final Solution" of the Jewish question. The Vatican, however, considered that this would have led to reprisals against the German Catholics. In spite of papal caution an increasing number of Catholics committed themselves to resisting the Nazis; often Catholics and Communists shared the terrible experience of the Nazi concentration camps, just as they often shared the experience of Partisan warfare against the Nazis. When Hitler fell and National Socialism was exposed for what it was, the Catholic cause, like the Communist one, gained supporters. Non-Communist resistance to Hitler in Western Europe had preached European union, and the new Christian-Democrat Parties which the Resistance nurtured shared their European programme in association with the Vatican. The old anti-clericalisms were said to be dead, those who felt anti-clerical in France or Italy now usually voting Communist : this contributed to a big Communist vote in both these countries, particularly in Italy. Since 1945 a newer and larger membership has impelled the Catholic Church to become less Italian, less authoritarian, less narrow and more international in its organisation and thus less European. Here again the end of the Second World War accelerated the deposition of Europe from its old position of dominance.

MAPS

ETHNIC TABLE

FURTHER READING

INDEX

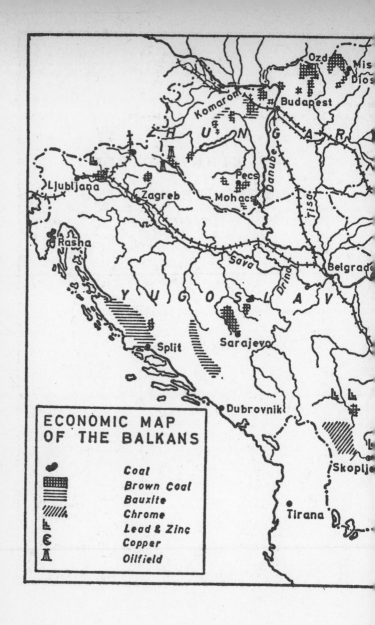

ECONOMIC MAP
OF THE BALKANS

Coal
Brown Coal
Bauxite
Chrome
Lead & Zinc
Copper
Oilfield

JOHN HARVEY

EUROPEAN TREATY ADJUSTMENTS 1919

DENMARK

NETHERLANDS

Baltic Sea

Elbe

Berlin

G E R M A N Y

P R U S S I A

ALSACE

SWITZERLAND

AUSTRIA

ITALY

Rome

Adriatic Sea

ESTONIA
1918

LATVIA
1918

LITHUANIA
1918

WHITE
RUSSIA
1921

R U S S I A

POLAND

Warsaw 1918

GALACIA

RUTHENIA

BESSARABIA

CZECHOSLOVAKIA

HUNGARY

AUSTRIA-HUNGARY

RUMANIA

BANAT

YUGO-SLAVIA

BOSNIA

SERBIA
1918

Danube

BULGARIA

JOHN HARVEY

☰ Ceded by Germany	▶ Rhineland zone of Allied occupation.
‖‖ Ceded by Austria-Hungary	▦ Plebiscite areas ceded or retained through popular vote assignment by the League of Nations or decision of the Allied Council of Ambassadors 1920-1922
▬ Ceded by Bulgaria	
▨ Ceded by Russia	
...... Boundaries in 1914	▨ German areas demilitarized
---- Boundaries in 1926	

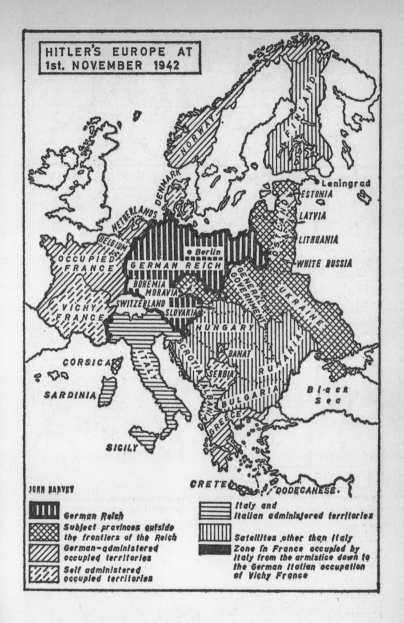

HITLER'S EUROPE AT
1st. NOVEMBER 1942

NORWAY

FINLAND

Leningrad

DENMARK

ESTONIA

LATVIA

LITHUANIA

NETHERLANDS

WHITE RUSSIA

BELGIUM

• Berlin

OCCUPIED
FRANCE

GERMAN REICH

OSTLAND

GENERAL GOVERNMENT

BOHEMIA

UKRAINE

MORAVIA

SWITZERLAND

VICHY
FRANCE

SLOVAKIA

HUNGARY

CORSICA

ITALY

CROATIA

BANAT

RUMANIA

SERBIA

SARDINIA

ALBANIA

BULGARIA

Black
Sea

GREECE

SICILY

JOHN HARVEY

CRETE

DODECANESE.

German Reich

Subject provinces outside
the frontiers of the Reich

German-administered
occupied territories

Self administered
occupied territories

Italy and
Italian administered territories

Satellites other than Italy

Zone in France occupied by
Italy from the armistice down to
the German Italian occupation
of Vichy France

EUROPE IN 1945

JOHN HARVEY

ETHNIC TABLE

(The figures can only be very rough estimates as they obviously varied during the 20 years between 1919 and 1939. Most of the figures used derive from census tables of about 1930)

TOTAL POPULATIONS		MINORITIES	
CZECHOSLOVAKIA	14,700,000	*Germans*	3,250,000
Czechs: just over	6,500,000	Magyars	700,000
Slovaks: just under	3,000,000	Ruthenes	400,000
		Poles (Teschen)	70,000
ESTONIA	1,700,000	*Germans*	17,000
		Russians	170,000
FINLAND	3,600,000	Swedes	300,000
HUNGARY	8,700,000	*Germans*	500,000
ITALY	42,000,000	*Germans*	250,000
		Slovenes and Croats	500,000
LATVIA (under)	2,000,000	*Germans*	65,000
LITHUANIA	2,500,000	*Germans* (chiefly in Memel-land)	100,000
POLAND	32,000,000	*Germans*	800,000
		Ukrainians and White Russians	6,000,000
		Jews (mostly unassimilated)	3,000,000
ROUMANIA	18,800,000	*Germans*	750,000
		Magyars	1,500,000
		Jews (mostly unassimilated)	700,000
		Ukrainians	600,000
		Russians	400,000
		Bulgars	360,000

SWITZERLAND	4,000,000
German-speaking	2,900,000
French-speaking	831,000
Italian-speaking	242,000
Romantsch-speaking	27,000

YUGOSLAVIA	14,000,000	*Germans*	500,000
Serbs	5,500,000	Macedonians	600,000
Croats	4,500,000	Magyars	500,000
Slovenes	(over) 1,000,000	Albanians	500,000
		Moslems or Turks	700,000

FURTHER READING

GENERAL

Surveys of International Affairs—Published by Royal Institute of
International Affairs since 1920
Documents on British Foreign Policy
AVON—*Facing the Dictators* (1962)
AVON—*The Reckoning* (1965)
CARR, E. H.—*The Twenty Years' Crisis* (1939)
CHURCHILL, W. S.—*The History of the Second World War* (1948-54)
JOLL, J.—*Intellectuals in Politics* (1960)
KOESTLER, A.—*The Invisible Writing* (1954)
NAMIER, L. B.—*Diplomatic Prelude* (1948)
Europe in Decay 1936-40 (1950)
NOLTE, E.—*Three Faces of Fascism* (1965)
WALTERS, F. P.—*History of the League of Nations* (1952)
WHEELER-BENNETT, J. W.—*The Wreck of Reparations* (1933)
WISKEMANN, ELIZABETH—*Undeclared War* (1939)

FRANCE

BLOCH, MARC—*L'Etrange Défaite* (1946)
BONNEFOUS, E. & G.—*Histoire Politique de la Troisième République*
—(5 vols. 1956-62)
BROGAN, DENIS—*The Development of Modern France 1870-1939*
(1940)
COBBAN, ALFRED—*History of Modern France 1871-1962* (1965)
DE GAULLE, C.—*Mémoires de Guerre 1954-59*. Trans. as *Memoirs*
GIDE, ANDRE—*Retour de l'U.R.S.S.* (1936)
HERRIOT, E.—*Aristide Briand*
SOULIÉ, M.—*Vie Politique d'E. Herriot* (1962)
TABOUIS, G.—*Vingt Ans de " Suspense" diplomatique* (1958)
THOMSON, DAVID—*Democracy in France* (1964)
WEBER E.—*Action Française* (1962)
WERTH, A.—*The Twilight of France* (1962)
Documents Diplomatiques français 1932-39 (from 1964 onwards)

269

Documents on German Foreign Policy

D'ABERNON—*Ambassador of Peace* (3 vols. 1929-30)

ANGRESS, W.—*Stillborn Revolution: The Communist Bid for Power in Germany 1921-23* (1964)

BRACHER, K. D.—*Die Auflösung der Weimarer Republik* (1955)
   ,,   AND OTHERS—*Die Nationalsozialistische Machtergreifung* (1960)

BULLOCK, A.—*Hitler* (1964)

CARSTEN, F. L.—*Reichswehr und Politik 1918-33* (1964)

EYCK, E.—*Geschichte der Weimarer Republik* (2 vols. 1954-56. English translation 1962-3)

HASSELL, ULRICH VON—*Vom andern Deutschland* (1946) trans.

HITLER—*Mein Kampf* (1933; after that year it was cut)
   Hitler's Table Talk (1953)
   The Testament of Hitler (1961)

JETZINGER, F.—*Hitler's Youth* (1958)

KLUKE, P.—*Der Fall Potempa*, article in *Vierteljahrshefte für Zeitgeschichte* (1957)[1]

KOGON, E.—*Der. S. S. Staat* (1946)

MAU & KRAUSNICK—*German History 1933-45* (first published in German 1956)

RAUSCHNING, H.—*Die Revolution des Nihilismus* (1936)
   Hitler Speaks (1939)

REITLINGER, G.—*The Final Solution* (1953)
   S.S.; Alibi of a Nation (1956)

RITTER, GERHARD—*Carl Goerdeler* (1955)

TOBIAS, F.—*The Reichstag Fire* (1963)

TURNER, H. A.—*Stresemann and the Politics of the Weimar Republic* (1963)

TREVOR-ROPER, H.—*The Last Days of Hitler* (1957)

WHEATLEY, R.—*Operation Sea-Lion* (1958)

WHEELER-BENNETT, J.—*The Nemesis of Power*—new edition due.

---

[1]NOTE: *The Institut für Zeitgeschichte* in Munich was originally founded in order to expose the history of National Socialism. Its periodical, *Vierteljahrshefte für Zeitgeschichte*, and the books it has published, have maintained a high standard.

GERMANY AND RUSSIA

DALLIN, A.—*German Rule in Russia 1941-45* (1957)
FREUND, G.—*Unholy Alliance* (1957)
KOCHAN, L.—*Russia and the Weimar Republic* (1954)

RUSSIA

CARR, E. H.—*A History of the Bolshevik Revolution 1917-23*
  The Interregnum 1923-4
  Socialism in One Country
DEUTSCHER, I.—*Trotsky* (3 vols. 1954-63)
  Stalin (1949)
SUMNER, B. H.—*A Survey of Russian History*
WERTH, A.—*Russia at War* (1965)

ITALY

Documenti Diplomatici Italiani

BATTAGLIA, R.—*Storia della Resistenza Italiana* (1953)[1]
BINCHY, D. A.—*Church and State in Fascist Italy* (1941)
CIANO, G.—*Diario 1937-8* (1948) and English translations
  Diario 1939-43 (1946)
  (The translations of Ciano are sometimes misleading)
DELZELL, C.—*The Enemies of Mussolini* (1961)
FERMI, L.—*Mussolini* (1961)
KIRKPATRICK, IVONE—*Mussolini* (1964)
MACK SMITH, DENIS—*Italy* (1959)
MUSSOLINI—*My Autobiography* (1928)
  The Political and Social Doctrine of Fascism (1933)
    Memoirs 1942-43 (1949)
WEBSTER, R.—*Christian Democracy in Italy* (1961)

[1]NOTE: *The Istituto Storico della Resistenza Italiana* in Milan has
  published various studies on this subject.

ITALY AND GERMANY

DEAKIN, F. W.—*The Brutal Friendship* (1962)
WISKEMANN, ELIZABETH—*The Rome-Berlin Axis*

SPAIN

BRENAN, G.—*The Spanish Labyrinth* (1943)
THOMAS, HUGH—*The Spanish Civil War* (1961)

GERMANY, AUSTRIA AND CZECHOSLOVAKIA

BENES, E.—*Memoirs* (1954)
BROOK-SHEPHERD, G.—*Dollfuss* (1961)
ČELOVSKY, B.—*Das Münchner Abkommen* (1958)
GEHL, J.—*Austria, Germany and the Anschluss* (1963)
SETON-WATSON, R. W.—*A History of the Czechs and Slovaks* (1943)
WHEELER-BENNETT, J.—*Munich* (1948)
WISKEMANN, ELIZABETH—*Czechs and Germans* (1938)

POLAND, HUNGARY AND THE BALKANS

BARKER, ELISABETH—*Macedonia* (1950)
CLISSOLD, S.—*Whirlwind (Rise of Tito)* (1949)
KOT, S.—*Conversation with the Kremlin* (1963)
MACARTNEY, C. A.—*Hungary and her Successors* (1937)
    October 15th—A History of Modern Hungary (1961)
    Independent Eastern Europe (1962)
    with PALMER, A. W.—*Independent Eastern Europe* (1962)
MACLEAN, F.—*Eastern Approaches* (1949)
MORROW, I.—*The German-Polish Borderlands* (1936)
REDDAWAY, W. F. (ED.)—*The Cambridge History of Poland* (1951)
SETON-WATSON, HUGH—*Eastern Europe between the Wars* (1945)
    The East European Revolution (1950)

INDEX

Aaland Islands, 49

Abetz, Otto, 159, 189, 208

Abyssinia, Italian attack on, 109, 111; (or Ethiopia), 135

Action française, 14, 53, 55; suppressed, 109

Adriatic Sea, or coast, the, 25, 26, 209

Albania, 62, 63, 64; seized by Italy April 1939, 155

Alexander, King of Yugoslavia, 23; declares own dictatorship, 64; visits Bulgaria, 122; murdered, 164

Alfonso, King of Spain, 131, 132

Algiers Committee, the, 191

Alsace, 32, 176; clericalism in, 55

Ambassadors, Council or Conference of, 25, 49, 50, 79

Anatolia, 49, 123, 239

Anders, General, 182, 228

Anfuso, P., 233

Anglo-German Naval Treaty, June 1935, 109, 111

Anglo-Polish Alliance 1939, 157, 165

Anschluss, The, (union of Austria with Germany), 100, 116-17, 139, 144, 158, 168

Antonescu, Marshal, 222

Antonescu, Mihai, 212, 222

Ardennes offensive, 232

Arnhem, 225

Atlantic Charter, 237

Atomic power, 252

Auschwitz, 185, 186, 213

Auslandsdeutsche, 34, 66, 87, 99, 174

Austria, 17, 18, 19, 62, 65-6, 72,

88, 99-102, 256; Austro-German Customs Union Project, 88, 118; Austro-German Agreement of July 1936, 115, 143; Annexed by Hitler, 116-17; Austria since 1938, 241-2

Austria-Hungary, 10, 16, 18, 21, 24

Azaña, Manuel, 132, 140

Badoglio, Marshal, 111, 112, 203, 206, 207, 208, 209, 214; succeeds Mussolini, 200

Bakst, Leo, 247

Baldwin, Stanley, 93, 135, 137

Balfour, A. J., 18; Balfour Note, the, 45

Balkan Entente, the, 122

Baltic Barons, 34; Baltic Entente, 126; Baltic States (see also Estonia, Latvia, Lithuania), 28, 34, 66, 122, 126, 170, 183, 257

Bank for International Settlements, at Basle (=B.I.S.), 71-2

Barbarossa, Operation, 179

Barcelona, 130, 132

Barthou, Louis, 54, 105; death of, 106, 152

Bastianini, G., 198

Bauer, Otto, 65, 66

Bauhaus, the, 245

Bavaria, 38, 40, 41, 66

B.B.C., The, 173, 175, 201

Bech, J., Prime Minister of Luxembourg, 125

Beck, Joseph, 81, 152, 155

Beck, General Ludwig, 216, 218

Belgians, Belgium, 14, 15, 45, 62, 68, 124, 258; frontiers

273

Fontana Press

Fontana Press is the imprint under which Fontana paper-backs of special interest to students are published. Below are some recent titles.

- ☐ A History of the Soviet Union *Geoffrey Hosking* £4.95
- ☐ The Conservative Party from Peel to Thatcher
     Robert Blake £3.95
- ☐ Ethics and the Limits of Philosophy
     Bernard Williams £3.95
- ☐ Musicology *Joseph Kerman* £3.95
- ☐ Durkheim *Anthony Giddens* £2.95
- ☐ Piaget *Margaret Boden* £2.95
- ☐ Popper *Bryan Magee* £2.95
- ☐ The Realities Behind Diplomacy *Paul Kennedy* £5.95
- ☐ Ireland Since the Famine *F. S. L. Lyons* £5.95
- ☐ Subject Women *Ann Oakley* £3.95
- ☐ The Perceptual World of the Child *Tom Bower* £2.95
- ☐ Europe Divided *J. H. Elliott* £3.95
- ☐ Europe: Privilege and Protest *Olwen Hufton* £3.95
- ☐ Renaissance Europe *J. R. Hale* £3.95
- ☐ Roman Britain *Malcolm Todd* £3.95

You can buy Fontana Press books at your local bookshop or newsagent. Or you can order them from Fontana Paperbacks, Cash Sales Department, Box 29, Douglas, Isle of Man. Please send a cheque, postal or money order (not currency) worth the purchase price plus 15p per book (maximum postal charge is £3.00 for orders within the UK).

NAME (Block letters) _____

ADDRESS _____

_____

_____